SEE THE WORLD BY TRAIN

To my father, Jean-Marie Bonaventure.

JEAN-BAPTISTE BONAVENTURE

See The World by Train

80 UNFORGETTABLE RAILWAY ADVENTURES ACROSS THE GLOBE

TRANSLATED BY CLAIRE COX

greenfinch

FOREWORD

Let's play a little game. Clear your mind, take a deep breath and read this list of names out loud: Trans-Siberian Railway, Orient Express, Darjeeling Himalayan Railway, Polar Bear Express, Ebony Train, Desert Train, Train to the Clouds, End of the World Train... This is the magic spell for conjuring up the imaginary powers possessed by each of these names and summoning up their passengers. A samovar dispensing piping-hot water into a glass as the snowy wastes of Siberia flash past the train windows. The clinking of champagne flutes echoing off the marquetry in a carriage full of passengers dressed up to the nines. A tiny choo-choo train climbing up steep slopes carpeted with lush Himalayan vegetation. The bogs and boreal forests of the Canadian muskeg, colourful Beninese market stalls pitched right beside the railroad tracks, the lost libraries of the holy town of Chinguetti, the Saharan monoliths of Ben Amera and Ben Aïsha, cloud-filled Argentine passes and the rugged splendour of Tierra del Fuego.

Humans have often given trains poetic names. These romantic epithets or affectionate nicknames may in some cases have become the official term, but they don't always describe exactly the same thing. Sometimes they may refer to a route, sometimes to what's known as the 'rolling stock', and occasionally somewhere between the two. Above all else, they define a travel experience that is sufficiently special to warrant its own name. They are no longer just a starting point and a destination, a simple means of getting from A to B. Therein lies the fundamental power of the train – to provide its passengers with an adventure in itself. An adventure that is rewarding and uplifting, dazzling and captivating. A horizontal, overland journey that takes you back to nature and brings you into contact with fellow human beings.

All of these journeys and opportunities have been made possible by laying tracks in some of the most astonishing places in the world – as we shall discover in this book. Don't forget that we can only describe one reality for each of these rail trips; it will be just one version, albeit immersive, realistic and quirky, of what you may experience when you venture onto one of these trains. It goes without saying that no two train journeys are ever the same, nor will anyone else's experience necessarily be the same as yours. You can only enjoy it for what it is and tell the tale, transforming one person's reality into other people's fiction. The reverse is also true when others board the train in their turn and make memories of their own.

Contents

P.8

Europe

P.112

Africa

P.150

Russia & the Middle East

P.188

Asia

P.262

North America

P.312

South America

P.346

Oceania

P.362

Index

Europe

25 TRAIN JOURNEYS
21 countries
Spectacular trains in the birthplace of the railway
FROM STOCKHOLM TO BAR

① **Stockholm → Narvik**
🇸🇪 *ARCTIC CIRCLE TRAIN*
p. 10

② **Fort William → Mallaig**
🇬🇧 *JACOBITE STEAM TRAIN*
p. 14

③ **Edinburgh → Isle of Bute**
🇬🇧 *ROYAL SCOTSMAN*
p. 18

④ **London → Edinburgh**
🇬🇧 *FLYING SCOTSMAN*
p. 22

⑤ **Belfast → Derry**
🇬🇧 *BELFAST-DERRY-LONDONDERRY COASTAL TRAIN*
p. 26

⑥ **Paris → Istanbul**
🇫🇷 *VENICE SIMPLON-ORIENT-EXPRESS*
p. 30

⑦ **Dole → Saint-Claude**
🇫🇷 *DOLE-SAINT-CLAUDE*
p. 34

⑧ **Clermont-Ferrand → Nîmes**
🇫🇷 *LE CÉVENOL*
p. 38

⑨ **Neussargues → Béziers**
🇫🇷 *NEUSSARGUES-BÉZIERS*
p. 42

⑩ **Miramas → L'Estaque**
🇫🇷 *CÔTE BLEUE*
p. 46

⑪ **Bastia → Ajaccio**
🇫🇷 *U TRINICHELLU*
p. 50

⑫ **Ponte-Leccia → L'Île-Rousse → Calvi**
🇫🇷 *U TRINICHELLU*
p. 54

⑬ **Venice → Istanbul**
🇮🇹 *GOLDEN EAGLE DANUBE EXPRESS*
p. 58

⑭ **Monterosso al Mare → Riomaggiore**
🇮🇹 *CINQUE TERRE EXPRESS*
p. 62

⑮ **Rome → Palermo**
🇮🇹 *INTERCITY NOTTE*
p. 68

⑯ **Catania → Riposto**
🇮🇹 *FERROVIA CIRCUMETNEA*
p. 72

⑰ **Arbatax → Gairo**
🇮🇹 *TRENINO VERDE*
p. 76

⑱ **Zermatt → Saint Moritz**
🇨🇭 *GLACIER EXPRESS*
p. 80

⑲ **Chur → Tirano**
🇨🇭 *BERNINA EXPRESS*
p. 84

⑳ **Alpnachstad → Pilatus-Kulm**
🇨🇭 *PILATUSBAHN*
p. 88

㉑ **San Sebastián → Santiago de Compostela**
🇪🇸 *TRANSCANTÁBRICO CLÁSICO*
p. 92

㉒ **Lleida → La Pobla de Segur**
🇪🇸 *TREN DELS LLACS*
p. 96

㉓ **Porto → Pocinho**
🇵🇹 *LINHA DO DOURO*
p. 100

㉔ **Kalavryta → Diakopto**
🇬🇷 *ODONTOTOS RACK RAILWAY*
p. 104

㉕ **Belgrade → Bar**
🇷🇸 *BELGRADE-BAR RAILWAY*
p. 108

Stockholm → Narvik

Heading for the back of beyond

on board the
ARCTIC CIRCLE TRAIN

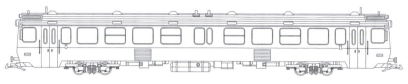

A train fit for the Arctic Circle.

The far north of the European continent is a frozen mass that is hard to access and almost entirely devoid of inhabitants; no wonder it has steadfastly repelled human advances. Over the centuries, many have tried to conquer this vast region, only to find themselves lacking. Yet man's determination, ingenuity, greed and nose for the bountiful resources concealed in this part of the world know no bounds. The laborious task of building railway lines up to and beyond the line of the Arctic Circle was driven by the quest for these abundant riches, rather than a desire to see the Northern Lights.

Opposite page: Rombaken fjord, near Narvik, in Norway.

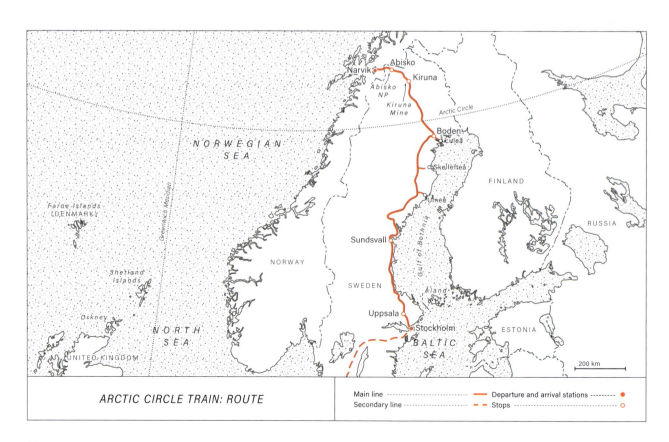

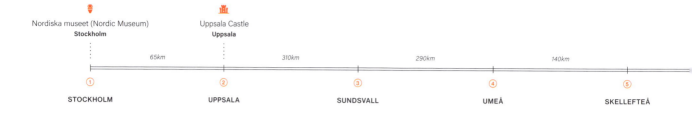

| ① STOCKHOLM | ② UPPSALA | ③ SUNDSVALL | ④ UMEÅ | ⑤ SKELLEFTEÅ |

Nordiska museet (Nordic Museum) — Stockholm
Uppsala Castle — Uppsala

65km · 310km · 290km · 140km

CONSTRUCTED
1890–1920

JOURNEY LENGTH
18 hours 45 mins

DISTANCE
1,410km

COUNTRIES VISITED
Sweden
Norway

- *Stockholm, starting point for this journey.*

- *Herd of reindeer, symbol of the Sámi people.*

JOURNEY TO THE HOME OF THE SÁMI

The region we know as Lapland, which covers parts of Norway, Sweden, Finland and Russia, owes its name to the Swedish term for the indigenous people of this area: the Sámi. While this term may still be used in the geographical sense, it is no longer used to describe the area's first inhabitants. The word 'Lapp', despite its complex and ancient roots, has nothing in common with these nomadic people, most of whom now tend to be settled in one place. Over the years they have endured forced assimilation policies and often violent attempts to plunder their heritage. We felt honour-bound to explain this important point – it is their territory we are visiting over the next two pages, after all.

This journey starts in the magnificent city of Stockholm, where you will have no trouble spending a couple of days. The Swedish capital is a modern, yet tradition-rich city, elegant and easy to get around. It extends across a number of small island districts, each with its own unique personality. With its cobbled streets and old buildings, the old town, Gamla Stan, is a paradise for devotees of all things historical. If you'd rather have a more contemporary vibe, try Södermalm, just down the road, where you'll find any number of vintage shops, bars, galleries and alternative venues. Culture vultures, on the other hand, should definitely head for the island of Djurgården, known for its museums. This is where you'll find the mind-blowing Vasa museum, featuring a warship that sank in the 17th century and was salvaged in one piece in the 20th century, the Nordiska Museet, dedicated to Nordic people and their culture, and of course the Abba Museum, which needs no further introduction.

EN ROUTE FOR THE FAR NORTH

Let's begin by entering Stockholm's attractive central station to board our train. While not exactly the height of luxury, the train is well designed nevertheless, with standard seats, six-berth couchettes (some of which are gender-specific) and private two-berth compartments. It also has showers, a buffet car offering decent hot and cold meals and tables where you can dine in comfort. Our first stop, just 40 minutes after leaving Stockholm, is Uppsala. This charming university city is a favourite not only among Swedish students, but their international counterparts too. It is home to the oldest university faculty in Scandinavia, established in 1477, a 16th-century castle and a 15th-century Gothic cathedral. Uppsala is a beautiful city, peaceful haven and the epitome of Swedish style – well worth a detour if you're keen to explore this country's cultural heartland. If you're not that way inclined, the remainder of the 16-hour journey to the far north awaits.

- *Uppsala and its renowned university.*

STOCKHOLM → NARVIK

INSIDE THE ARCTIC CIRCLE

Through the train windows we can now see vistas of forests marching on as far as the eye can see. They emerge from the snow-covered ground as if impervious to the cold, standing tall as if drawn to the non-existent sun. Despite continuing virtually unchanged over hundreds of kilometres, interspersed only by a scattering of towns such as Sundsvall, Umeå and Boden, this is a view you can never tire of. With verdant forests and snow-white expanses, it is comforting in its very constancy.

When we wake up the next morning, the snow and the trees are still there, although the vegetation is perhaps a little sparser, hugging the ground more closely, while the snow has increased its grip on the landscape. This is the start of the white wilderness, where cold holds solitary sway. When we arrive at Kiruna, 145km north of the Arctic Circle, the cold becomes more and more defining. Not for nothing is our mode of transport called the Arctic Circle Train. With some 18,000 inhabitants, this mining town was founded following the discovery of a seam of iron ore, which is still being mined even now. Night falls early at this latitude. Whether you're staying in the town or just passing through, you should make a point of visiting the pretty little houses with their painted wooden façades as early in the day as possible. The same applies to the mine itself, where you can wander through huge rock caverns, and of course the spectacular Ice Hotel and the Sámi Cultural Centre, Nutti Sámi Siida, both of which are to be found in the nearby village of Jukkasjärvi.

• *Church in Kiruna, a Swedish mining town.*

• *Kiruna Ice Hotel, a veritable ice palace.*

• *Abiskojåkka, a river in Lapland.*

THE NORTH END OF NOWHERE

The next morning, we rejoin the Arctic Circle Train to continue our northwards trajectory, heading for Abisko with its national park covering some 77km². This is a timeless spot, at the north end of nowhere, an ideal place to seek out the Northern Lights – surely on every world traveller's bucket list? There are so many ways of ticking off this trophy experience, with something suited to every taste and budget, whether from the windows of a chalet, on foot, on skis, from a quad bike, or simply stretched out in the snow, warmly clad in appropriate thermal gear to withstand the cold. Then onwards again through a landscape of unparalleled hostility, where even the vast frozen lakes brood menacingly alongside the tracks, before we finally cross the border and arrive at our destination: Narvik. Welcome to the edge of the white wilderness.

• *Lake Torneträsk, Abisko.*

📣 THE OFOTBANEN, THE FIRST RAILWAY BEYOND THE ARCTIC CIRCLE

The railway runs between Kiruna and Narvik on what is known as the Ofoten Line (Ofotbanen in Norwegian). Opened in 1903, it is regarded as the first railway line to be built beyond the Arctic Circle. It continues to carry the abundant iron ore from the Nordland region to this day. It has also been used for tourism in the past few decades but is the only Norwegian line to be connected to the Swedish rail network rather than its own national network.

13

EUROPE

Fort William → Mallaig
Steaming through the Highlands

on board the
JACOBITE STEAM TRAIN

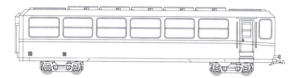

Said to have inspired J K Rowling's Hogwarts Express.

This venerable steam train traverses a stately stone viaduct, leaving long trails of white smoke in its wake. These will disperse in a matter of minutes, evaporating into the untold vastness of the Highlands, the austere reaches of which extend as far as the eye can see. This may be a well-known film scene, but it has its roots in reality, in the form of the Jacobite Steam Train.

Opposite page: Sheep grazing on the slopes of Ben Nevis.

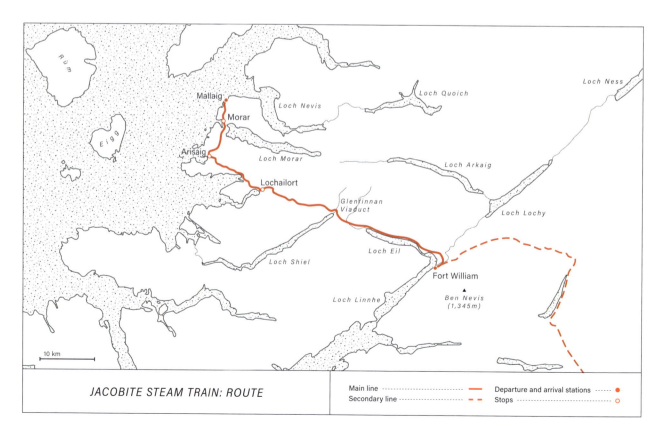

JACOBITE STEAM TRAIN: ROUTE

EUROPE

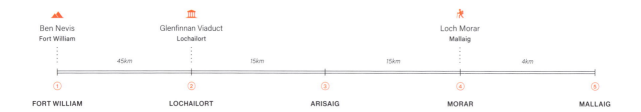

①	②	③	④	⑤
FORT WILLIAM	LOCHAILORT	ARISAIG	MORAR	MALLAIG

OPERATING SINCE
1984

JOURNEY LENGTH
2 hours

DISTANCE
135km

COUNTRIES VISITED
United Kingdom (Scotland)

A TRAIN INSPIRED BY REBELLION

If old steam engines are more your bag than luxury trains with on-board spa facilities, you can explore the West Highland Line on a much more modest train than the Royal Scotsman. The Jacobite Steam Train is hauled by a different steam locomotive most days and operates on one of the most impressive sections of this line. For several months of the year, it serves the 135-km stretch between the town of Fort William and the port of Mallaig. As the largest town in the region, Fort William is a must-see venue for anyone interested in Scottish culture. Mallaig, a much smaller place, feels like the last bastion of humanity before the end of the world. A lovely place for a stroll and to appreciate the vastness of our beautiful Planet Earth.

- *The Jacobite Steam Train, full steam ahead in the 21st century.*

LENGTH OF THE GLENFINNAN VIADUCT
380m (21 arches)

📢 **BACK TO THE AGE OF STEAM**

The steam locomotives used for the Jacobite Steam Train are not heritage vehicles but the original locos, brought back into service. These charmingly old-fashioned vehicles were decommissioned from the West Highland Line in 1967, only to be returned to service in 1984 on the short Jacobite Steam Train route to encourage tourists to visit the area.

- *Loch Eil, near Fort William.*

A SLOWER PACE OF LIFE

Regarded as one of the world's most spectacular rail routes, the line served by the Jacobite Steam Train has the virtue of being accessible to all, whether you happen to have special magical powers (like J K Rowling's wizards) or are endowed with a healthy financial budget (like the passengers travelling on the Royal Scotsman). The minute you step on board, your eye cannot help but be drawn to the magnificent sight of Ben Nevis, at 1,345m the highest mountain in the UK, a fabulous hike if you're that way inclined. After skirting tranquil Loch Eil, the train veers off slightly to cross the world-famous Glenfinnan Viaduct, as does the Royal Scotsman. It continues its journey through towering hills, dominating the track with their majesty.

LOCHS LAPPING BENEATH THE RAILS

On both sides of the track there are lochs, some of modest proportions, others on a much larger scale. Some even seem to lap beneath the rails of this train from a bygone age. Others, more remote, can only be fully appreciated by those who take the trouble to disembark and use Shank's pony to get up close and personal. From time to time, a building materializes in the green open spaces, maybe the ruins of an old castle or a tiny, abandoned church. Such a magical journey over such a short distance – you never want it to end… In the absence of a time-turner, passengers on the Jacobite Steam Train have no option but to stop off at every one of the picturesque villages studded along the route: Lochailort, Arisaig, Morar. Just saying their names out loud seems to prolong time itself. It would be a travesty to deny yourself the pleasure of a visit.

- *Arisaig, on the shores of Loch nan Ceall.*

16

- *Ben Nevis, the highest mountain in the UK at 1,345m, a hiker's paradise.*

Edinburgh → Isle of Bute

A right royal welcome to the Highlands

on board the
ROYAL SCOTSMAN

The train has 72 luxury cabins and 6 grand suites.

Black, rocky outcrops pierce the green backdrop of valley after valley. The sound of bagpipes filters through the broken window of a semi-ruined castle as a shadow passes the window frame. A distinctive round head crests the mist-shrouded surface of an enormous loch... Could this be the legendary monster? Travelling through the Highlands on the Royal Scotsman is a journey that meets every expectation.

Opposite page: The Royal Scotsman crossing the Glenfinnan Viaduct.

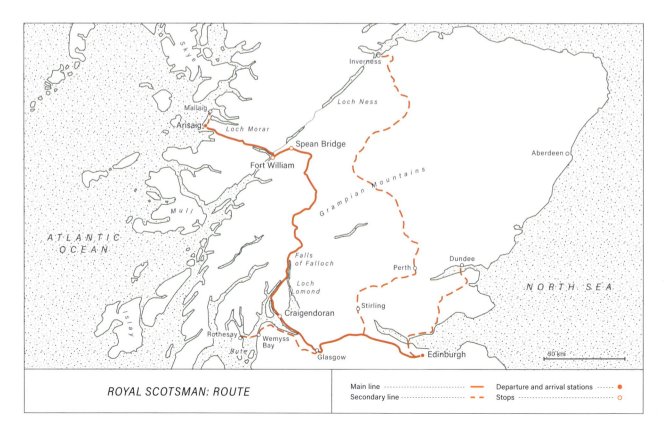

ROYAL SCOTSMAN: ROUTE

Main line — Departure and arrival stations ●
Secondary line — Stops ○

EUROPE

① EDINBURGH — 80km — ② GLASGOW — 50km — ③ CRAIGENDORAN (The Falls of Falloch, Craigendoran) — 151km — ④ SPEAN BRIDGE

OPERATING SINCE
2005

JOURNEY LENGTH
4 days, 3 nights

DISTANCE
745km

COUNTRIES VISITED
United Kingdom (Scotland)

LENGTH OF THE GLENFINNAN VIADUCT
380m

LENGTH OF THE WEST HIGHLAND LINE
331.1km

• *Edinburgh, Scotland's capital city.*

LEAVING EDINBURGH WITH A HEAVY HEART

After enjoying the majestic splendour of Edinburgh, with its unforgettable castle, whisky distilleries and Aberdeen Angus Beef burgers, it's time to board another train, this time one that goes by the name of the Royal Scotsman, A Belmond Train, Scotland. A little pompous to be sure, but it promises an experience on a whole other level. Part of the Belmond Group, which specializes in luxury hotels, trains and cruises, the Royal Scotsman offers the most affluent passengers the opportunity to explore Scotland on a variety of tours in a sophisticated top-end environment. We opted for the tour entitled Western Scenic Wonders, which links Edinburgh and Arisaig, a small village nestled on the shores of Loch nan Ceall, then continues on to the Isle of Bute before returning to Edinburgh. The journey takes four days and three nights.

• *Delightful cottages in Edinburgh.*

• *Edwardian-style cabins.*

A JOURNEY THROUGH THE MISTS OF TIME

The Royal Scotsman's tour de force is that it is able to transport its passengers to another place before it even leaves the platform. The immediate impact is visual, not least down to the stunning Edwardian decor to be found in most carriages on this unique train. From its four single cabins, fifteen doubles and three triples, to the two dining cars, Raven and Swift, not forgetting the observation car and spa, every square inch of the Royal Scotsman plays a part in achieving the overall ambience of sumptuous tranquillity.

A BOX OF ON-BOARD DELIGHTS

All along the train, each cabin's large windows ensure that you never lose sight of the fabulous views. Liveried staff do their utmost to satisfy their passengers' every whim in the relaxation and dining areas. After all, when you can recline in generous fabric-covered armchairs surrounded by marquetry, what else is there to do but enjoy the moment and unwind? Then, of course, there's the delicious cuisine served on board and the resident musicians playing traditional Scottish music. Some routes and tours cater for enthusiasts of golf, fishing, clay pigeon shooting or photography, enabling them to indulge in their favourite pastime in the Scottish Highlands.

EDINBURGH → ISLE OF BUTE

WHEN SPLENDOUR BECOMES THE NORM

After departing Edinburgh to the sound of the bagpipes, the Royal Scotsman heads for Craigendoran, where it joins the West Highland Line. The train windows gradually reveal the vast grandeur of Loch Lomond opening up before your eyes, quickly followed by the Falls of Falloch. Dinner is served as you approach the village of Spean Bridge. Fort William and Arisaig are on the itinerary for the next day, with the opportunity to stride out on the famous Morar sands and catch a glimpse of the Isle of Skye. The high point of the trip has to be the Royal Scotsman's passage over the world-renowned Glenfinnan Viaduct, which owes its global celebrity to the Harry Potter series of films. A whole box of delights to imprint on your memory as you partake of afternoon tea at the Inverlochy Castle Hotel, then enjoy your second night on board this queen of the railways, as it steams on towards the village of Bridge of Orchy.

• *Loch Lomond, to the south of the Highlands.*

• *Loch Morar, fifth largest of Scotland's lochs.*

📣 THE ROYAL SEAL OF APPROVAL

In 1863, William Scarlett, third Baron Abinger, built Inverlochy Castle Hotel according to the strict rules of Scottish baronial architecture. Queen Victoria stayed in this luxury establishment some 10 years later, declaring this to be the most wonderful and romantic place she had ever visited.

PICTURESQUE SCENE ON THE ISLE OF BUTE

On the third day of its journey, the train once again wends its way through the Highlands until it reaches Wemyss Bay. Here, passengers transfer to a ferry for the crossing to the Isle of Bute, a place of such intense beauty it inspired a well-known painting by artist William Andrews Nesfield. And then it's time to relish one last outstanding dinner on board as we head for Kilmarnock. The following morning, the train embarks on the final leg of its journey back to Edinburgh, where this breathtaking luxury tour will come to an end. Just a few more, only too brief but welcome, hours to savour the last splendours of the Scottish countryside from the observation car.

• *Boats moored on the shores of the Isle of Bute.*

21

London → Edinburgh
Taking wing towards Scotland

on board the
FLYING SCOTSMAN

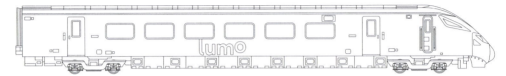

The present-day Flying Scotsman is capable of speeds in excess of 200km/h.

In service since the second half of the 19th century, the Flying Scotsman is one of the most iconic trains in the world. Once synonymous with the great age of rail adventures, it has now become part of a modern and efficient train service connecting the might of England with its rebel counterpart, Scotland. And yet it remains a symbol unique to the United Kingdom as a whole.

Opposite page: Edinburgh, the Scottish capital, has a charm all of its own.

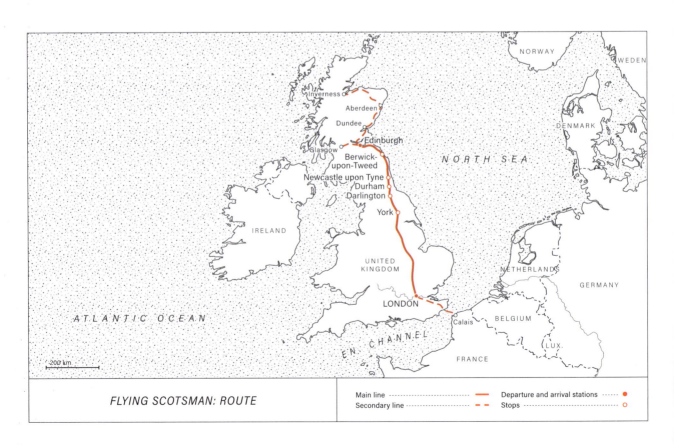

FLYING SCOTSMAN: ROUTE

OPERATING SINCE
1862

JOURNEY LENGTH
4 hours 20 mins

DISTANCE
632km

COUNTRIES VISITED
United Kingdom (England, Scotland)

LENGTH OF DIGSWELL VIADUCT
475m

LENGTH OF DURHAM VIADUCT
240m

🔊 FLYING LOCOMOTIVES

The A3 and A4 locomotives are undoubtedly the most iconic in the history of the Flying Scotsman. The former was christened the 'Flying Scotsman' in recognition of the passenger service it provided over a great many years. The second of these, the A4 class locomotive known as Mallard, is famous for holding the world steam locomotive speed record, 125mph (miles per hour), which works out at just over 200km/h. Set in 1938, this technological feat was achieved on a section of the same line linking London and Edinburgh still served by the Flying Scotsman to this day. Between Peterborough and Grantham, eagle-eyed passengers might even spot a small sign commemorating this record on the right-hand side of the tracks.

ALL ABOARD FOR SCOTLAND!

We begin our journey to Scotland at London's King's Cross station, hundreds of kilometres south of the country famed for its warriors clad in multicoloured tartan. Famous home of the fictional Platform 9¾, where J K Rowling's trainee wizards and witches embarked for Hogwarts School of Witchcraft and Wizardry, this is also the starting point for the Flying Scotsman.

- London's King's Cross station is home to Platform 9¾, departure point for the Hogwarts Express.

THE HISTORIC FLYING SCOTSMAN

The Flying Scotsman train service has been running between London and Edinburgh since 1862, although until 1924 it operated under the name of the Special Scotch Express. The UK's most famous passenger rail service, it used to take around ten hours to travel between the two capital cities, compared to the 4 hours, 20 minutes it takes nowadays via the Azuma trains that have been in operation since 2019. Much faster than the legendary steam locomotives of yesteryear, these newer trains propel the Flying Scotsman at 125mph, or around 200km/h.

Modern in appearance, these trains are set out in double rows, each with two seats, in Second Class, and two rows, one with two seats and one with just one seat, in First Class. In the latter, you can even have a range of food brought to your seat so you can eat while watching the countryside flash by. After passing close by Alexandra Palace, where the BBC used to broadcast its first regular televised news bulletins back in the 1930s, the Flying Scotsman speeds through a stretch of typically British woodland and farmland before slowing down to cross the Digswell Viaduct.

- The Flying Scotsman operates at 200km/h.

- In Newcastle upon Tyne, the Tyne Bridge (1925) vies with the Millennium Bridge (2001) for the best bridge trophy.

FOLLOWING IN THE SHADOW OF THE RAILWAY PIONEERS

Just over 300km from London, the Flying Scotsman makes its most auspicious stop in the city of York, renowned for its exceptional cultural and architectural heritage. This city was the capital of a number of kingdoms and provides travellers with the opportunity to immerse themselves in a place that is forever England. Narrow cobbled streets, towering Gothic cathedrals, its Viking past and castles built by William the Conqueror. An unmissable stopover on your way to the Highlands, in other words.

The Flying Scotsman then continues northwards, stopping at Darlington, Durham – look out for the magnificent view of the city from the viaduct – and Newcastle, legendary home to the Geordies. Each of these is well worth a detour if you have time, but if you can't wait to head off into the Highland mists, by all means stay on board. At Berwick-upon-Tweed, the train finally crosses the Royal Border Bridge. Designed by Robert Stephenson, son of George Stephenson, and officially opened by Queen Victoria in 1850, this bridge is 659m long, allowing passengers ample time to admire the view of the surrounding landscape. Then, just a few miles north of Berwick, the train crosses the border between England and Scotland, winding its way along a short but no less stunning coastal route, before finally leaving the sea to head for our final stop: Edinburgh.

• *York, a city with a rich architectural heritage.*

EUROPE

Belfast → Derry
Along the shores of Ulster

on board the
BELFAST-DERRY-LONDONDERRY COASTAL TRAIN

Revisiting the site of Bloody Sunday – by train.

The line between Belfast and Derry-Londonderry was constructed in several phases in the mid-19th century and is still regarded as one of the most glorious rail routes in Europe. Its coastal section beside the North Atlantic Ocean is an ever-changing delight, on a par with the beauty of Ulster.

Opposite page: Derry-Londonderry, a city with divided loyalties (Protestant/Catholic).

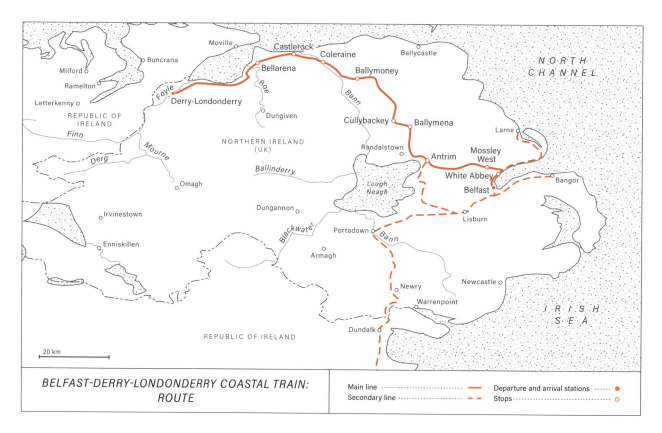

BELFAST-DERRY-LONDONDERRY COASTAL TRAIN: ROUTE

EUROPE

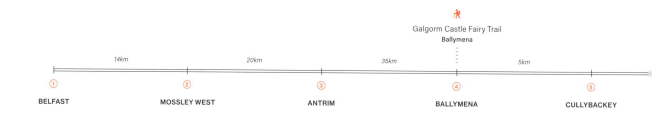

① BELFAST — 14km — ② MOSSLEY WEST — 20km — ③ ANTRIM — 35km — ④ BALLYMENA (Galgorm Castle Fairy Trail) — 5km — ⑤ CULLYBACKEY

CONSTRUCTED
1848–1855

JOURNEY LENGTH
2 hours 2 mins

DISTANCE
153km

COUNTRIES VISITED
United Kingdom (Northern Ireland)

LENGTH OF BANN BRIDGE
240m

LENGTH OF PEACE BRIDGE
235m

BENEATH APOCALYPTIC SKIES

After a substantial Ulster Fry, that Northern Irish breakfast comprising fried eggs, sausages, bacon, black pudding, potato farls, baked beans, porridge and soda bread, we make for Lanyon Place. This Belfast station looks and feels very much like an airport, contrasting not only with the Edwardian buildings of the Northern Irish capital but also with their contemporary counterparts. On the partially covered platform, an overcast, grey sky lends a rather end-of-the-world atmosphere to this tranquil scene, where office workers and families are serenely waiting for their trains. Yet here, nobody seems the slightest bit concerned about the doom-laden ambience all around.

We've barely taken our seats when this brand-new train sets off, Belfast's streets stretching out all around. We leave behind the thousands of painted murals adorning every street corner, along with the city's landmark structures, two gigantic yellow cranes known locally as Samson and Goliath, as we reach the outskirts of the city. The landscape gradually turns green, with a mix of fields and clusters of woodland. The lush vegetation reminds us that this country is no stranger to downpours, any more than it is to witnessing the blood of its countrymen. Truth be told, blood was still being shed on these lands as recently as the 20th century.

▪ Departing Belfast, capital of Northern Ireland.

▪ The Bann flows into the sea at Coleraine.

THE MELANCHOLIC CHARM OF THE MOORS

This vast and verdant agricultural plain is broken only by tiny pockets of civilization dotted here and there. To fully appreciate the glory of their names, you need to hear them in the local accent: Ballymena, Cullybackey, Ballymoney and, last but not least, Coleraine, where the scenery suddenly changes. Located at the mouth of the River Bann, which flows into the North Atlantic, this little seaside resort is a compact version of Ulster in miniature. Like a postcard to the austere beauty of the area, where church spires are reflected in glinting waters and the surrounding moorland displays the melancholic charm of its endless expanses. Even someone just passing through can grasp how hard it must have been for the Irish to leave their home soil and set sail for America in the 19th century. Famine and the prospect of death meant they had no choice. The same thought resounds in our heads as the train carries on to Derry-Londonderry, Northern Ireland's second most populous city. Don't ask which is the official name – no one ever seems to know.

▪ Giant's Causeway, a spectacular volcanic formation, accessible from Coleraine.

BELFAST → DERRY

WHERE THE SEA AND THE SKY ARE AT WAR

Beyond Castlerock, the line enters its most stunning section, Northern Ireland's Causeway Coast, and runs cheek-by-jowl with the sea, just a few metres away in some cases. For miles and miles it skirts alongside silver beaches backed by dark and forbidding rocky cliffs. Overhead, thick white clouds attempt to cover the sea, which refuses to cooperate, ebbing and flowing constantly on the shoreline. This is a veritable battle of the Titans, where the powerful forces on show are as old as time itself and winning is a futile objective. Some see this as relentlessness, others as tenacity. On the other side of the train, to the left, small villages composed of whitewashed cottages remind us of the price humans have to pay for daring to live in this hostile version of paradise on Earth. Paintwork cracks under the force of the elements, while the buildings themselves are sheltered between the rocks in an attempt to stave off the wind. No doubt also in a bid to protect these fragile man-made structures, their homes, farms and boats, from squalls of rage issued by the gods of yore. And all the while, horses and cattle graze peacefully on the lush grass – their thick coats offering them at least some protection.

• *Mussenden Temple, near Castlerock.*

• *Coastal path to Castlerock beach.*

🔊 A LONG SUNDAY OF SUFFERING

On Sunday, 30 January 1972, during a peaceful march by organizations defending the civil rights of the Northern Irish people, the British army shot 28 unarmed civilians in the Bogside area. Thirteen men, including a number of teenagers, were killed instantly by the soldiers' bullets. Worse still, it later came to light that many were shot in the back. This became known as the Bloody Sunday massacre and this dramatic turn in the struggle for Irish independence went on to inspire countless songs, poems, films and all sorts of other artistic endeavours.

• *The port of Portrush on the North Atlantic coast.*

LAND OF MEMORIES

As our train passes Bellarena, there's a subtle change in the scenery. On the seaward side, the sandbanks become longer, deeper and better suited to a bracing walk in rain gear. It may not be raining right now, but you can rest assured it won't hold off for long. Looking landwards, the low hills are now a few miles distant, leaving the stage clear for vast fields in a sumptuous shade of dark green. Taking centre stage, isolated fields glow with the hues of golden wheat, before giving way to small lakes that are little more than marshland. Further afield, a thick mist clings to the hills, shrouding them in mystery.

Eventually, we move inland from the coast to arrive in Derry-Londonderry, entering along the River Foyle, which bisects the city. To the east is the Protestant area, Waterside, while the Catholic area, Bogside, and the historic walled city centre lie to the west. Peace may have returned at long last, but conflicts and memories linger on. The city's name may not be immediately familiar to a worldwide audience, but the name of the massacre that took place here has gone down in history: Bloody Sunday. Keep this memory in your mind as you walk around the city, its beauty sadly enhanced by violence.

29

Paris → Istanbul
Following in the tracks of a legend

on board the
VENICE SIMPLON-ORIENT-EXPRESS

The heir to the Orient Express.

Self-proclaimed successor to the legendary Orient Express, the Venice Simplon-Orient-Express (or VSOE) did not merely adopt the name of its illustrious predecessor. Its timeless elegance, meticulous service and its reputation for offering the very latest in modern comforts combine to make this an utterly outstanding palace on rails. This may be as much to do with the luxury experience as the exorbitant prices it charges.

Opposite page: Carriages from the original Orient Express, forerunner of the Venice Simplon-Orient-Express.

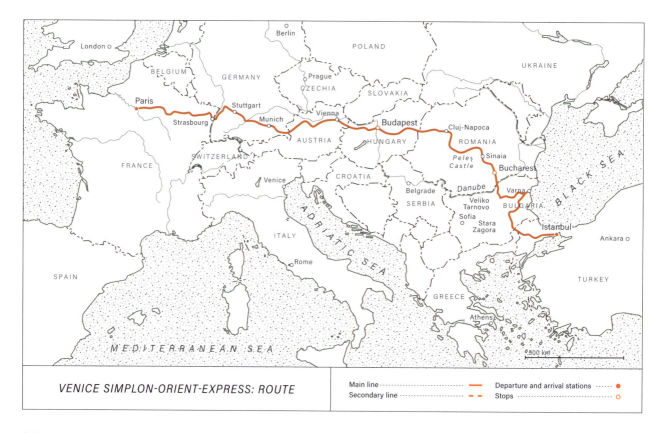

VENICE SIMPLON-ORIENT-EXPRESS: ROUTE

EUROPE

| 470km | 160km | 230km | 510km |

① PARIS — ② STRASBOURG — ③ STUTTGART — ④ MUNICH — ⑤ VIENNA

OPERATING SINCE
1982

JOURNEY LENGTH
6 days,
5 nights

DISTANCE
3,820km

COUNTRIES VISITED
France
Germany
Austria
Slovakia
Hungary
Romania
Bulgaria
Turkey

- *VSOE, a train with the charms of yesteryear.*

A JOURNEY INTO THE VERY HEART OF HISTORY

It's a fact that no other train in history is quite as famous as the Orient Express. The opulence of its fixtures and fittings, the stellar service on offer and the prestigious clients on board contributed to a magical image that will forever be associated with the notion of travel by train. Not only has it been an inexhaustible source of inspiration for writers and film-makers, it also motivated American entrepreneur James Sherwood to revive this legendary train in 1982. The result is a magnificent ensemble that rivals its predecessor's splendour, thanks in no small measure to the company purchasing carriages from a variety of luxury trains. Let's board this train today for our journey from Paris to Istanbul.

VICTORY OF BEAUTY OVER TIME

This journey even starts in the most elegant style, departing as it does from the Gare de l'Est in the 10th arrondissement of Paris. Built in the reign of Napoleon III, this station makes an imposing focal point for the entire district with its columns, its huge picture window and the sheer scale of its magnificent masonry structure. Yet unlike the tens of thousands of passengers who pass through it on a daily basis, we aren't going to travel on one of the RER express lines or Metro trains that serve this station. Our train has nothing in common with commuter trains. Oh no, ours is a splendid rake of 17 blue and gold carriages, merely waiting for their privileged passengers to arrive.

Once on board, we are immediately welcomed by the train's staff, who lead us down the corridors to our quarters for the next few days and nights. All around us we see marquetry, lacquered wood, beautifully restored period furniture and velvet upholstery in warm hues. Each step we take feels like a victory of beauty over time and progressing inside the train turns into a fabulous game of turning back the clock. Yet there are barely enough superlatives to describe what we see when we open the door to our suite. You might be fortunate enough to be in the Istanbul suite, with its subtle references to the style and geometry of Islamic art. Or perhaps the Venice suite with its glass lamps and Venetian furniture with a nod to the Renaissance and Baroque periods. Or even the Budapest suite, which captures the essence of both sides of the River Danube. No matter; they are all quite breathtaking.

- *Marquetry, period furniture... An extraordinarily luxurious train.*

32

PARIS → ISTANBUL

UNDER THE BUDAPEST SUN

We've barely had time to settle into our splendid surroundings and throw on some evening attire, when dinner is served. The Venice Simplon-Orient-Express has already left Paris, but we didn't even notice. Our journey is much less about the geography and more about a trip back in time. But now we need to take our pick of the three restaurants on board: the Côte d'Azur, the Oriental and the Étoile du Nord. Three gastronomic universes in their own right, where each dish, served by liveried waiters on tables with immaculate white tablecloths, is prepared on the train by chefs worthy of

• *Budapest, capital of Hungary.*

the highest culinary accolades. As the meal draws to a close, there's time for one last glance out of the windows, where the landscape is changing by the mile. Perhaps just one final chaser before retiring to our fabulous sleeping quarters?

At sunrise, there's a knock on the door: a steward delivering our continental breakfast. As the croissants disappear one-by-one from our plates, Austria gives way to Hungary, and then to its capital, our first stop – but not before we've enjoyed a three-course lunch. We take a break from the train here, staying overnight in a hotel, and enjoying a cocktail reception overlooking the river. The next day, our dedicated train guides take us on a whistlestop tour of the many delights of Budapest, not least its parliament building, a stunning piece of architecture. And then we're back on board our travelling palace.

📢 CARRIAGES FROM A BYGONE ERA

Iconic symbol of the resurgence of luxury trains, the Venice Simplon-Orient-Express came about when its owners bought up vintage carriages with a history all of their own. As you stroll along the train, you'll be stepping in the hallowed footsteps of the Train Bleu, the Étoile-du-Nord, the Pyrenees Côte d'Argent Express and the Oiseau Bleu. It brings a whole new meaning to the concept of journeying through time...

IT'S A KIND OF MAGIC...

This time when we waken in our opulent surroundings, it's to another breakfast and a new stopover. After brunch, we alight from the Venice Simplon-Orient-Express to spend a couple of hours exploring the Romanian town of Sinaia and Peleș Castle. Perched high in the mountains, this architectural gem played host to the first Orient Express visitors back in 1883. Unfortunately, history doesn't tell us whether they, like us, were able to don comfortable clothes and walking shoes to negotiate the steep ascent to the castle. Luckily for us, we were able to do a quick change into our glad rags on rejoining the train to head for Bucharest and one of its finest hotels.

Hard to believe it's already our fifth day on board. And yet the Venice Simplon-Orient-Express hasn't lost of any of its magic. Those gargantuan breakfasts and fine-dining lunches just get better and better. As for the train, it wends its way along the Danube, crossing the border into Bulgaria before coming to a halt in the seaside resort of Varna, where we sip aperitifs against an exceptional backdrop. Back on board, we savour our final dinner on the move as we cross the ancient Upper Thracian plain. This is a meal like no other: they've definitely saved the best for last. By this time, we've got to know all the other passengers, clinking our glasses as we promise to keep in touch. Who knows, maybe we'll meet again somewhere, perhaps on board another

train? Promises made under the influence of a glass or two, with fine food under our belt, admittedly, but who cares?! When we wake up, we'll be in Istanbul – the most beautiful city in the world, or so we tell ourselves. Just one tip, if I may: take a trip on the Bosphorus on a passenger ferry known as a vapur, seagulls in your wake. You won't regret it.

• *Istanbul, journey's end after six dreamlike days.*

33

Dole → Saint-Claude
Travel to new heights with the Ligne des Hirondelles

on board the
DOLE-SAINT-CLAUDE

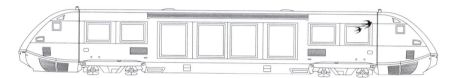

Communing with the birds since the day it was built.

Legend has it that when this line was under construction, the labourers, or navvies, were so high up that they could talk to the swallows ('hirondelles' in French) soaring above the Jura mountains. Hence the charming name adopted by the locals for this 123-km long railway line as they kept an eye on progress from their windows.

Opposite page: The Arbois wine region.

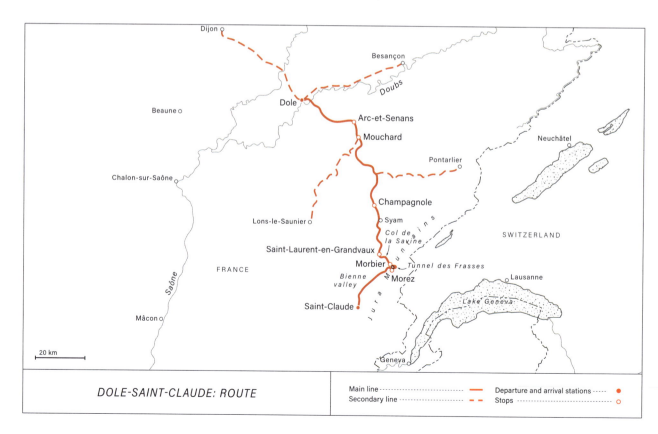

DOLE-SAINT-CLAUDE: ROUTE

Main line ———
Secondary line - - -
Departure and arrival stations ●
Stops ○

EUROPE

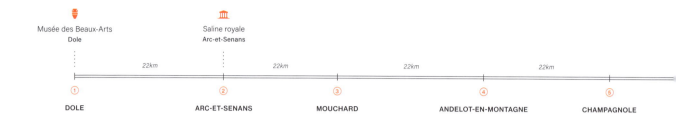

①	②	③	④	⑤
DOLE	ARC-ET-SENANS	MOUCHARD	ANDELOT-EN-MONTAGNE	CHAMPAGNOLE

Musée des Beaux-Arts — Dole
Saline royale — Arc-et-Senans

22km · 22km · 22km · 22km

CONSTRUCTED
1862–1912

JOURNEY LENGTH
2 hours 30 mins

DISTANCE
123km

COUNTRIES VISITED
France

LENGTH OF
MOREZ VIADUCT
203m

LENGTH OF THE
TUNNEL DES FRASSES
1,000m

NUMBER OF TUNNELS
36

- *Collégiale Notre-Dame, the town's main church, dating back to the 16th century.*

DOLE, VENICE OF THE JURA

Fort Lauderdale in the United States, Recife in Brazil, Ganvie in Benin, Suzhou in China, and Martigues in Provence… there is no shortage of places claiming to be the next 'little Venice' on our planet. The French department of Jura is no exception to this rule. Its 'little Venice' goes under the name of Dole. Built on the banks of two rivers, the Doubs and the Clauge, this town of some 23,600 inhabitants is also a stopping point on the Rhône-Rhine canal and the Canal des Tanneurs. With such a wealth of waterways and an outstanding architectural heritage, no wonder the town was awarded the prestigious 'Villes et Pays d'art et d'histoire' title back in 1992 for towns and regions with significant historical or cultural significance. So don't forget to take a trip on the water before you board the regional train to explore the Ligne des Hirondelles.

FIRST STOP: THE SALINE ROYALE AT ARC-ET-SENANS AND THE VINEYARDS OF ARBOIS

After leaving Dole station, our regional express train (TER) immediately diverts off the main Dijon-Besançon line and heads towards the Forest of Chaux, a vast and verdant tract renowned for having one of the largest collections of deciduous trees in the country. With every passing kilometre, this natural beauty eventually subsides as our train nears the Saline Royale at Arc-et-Senans. Designed by architect Claude Nicolas Ledoux during the reign of Louis XV, this former saltworks isn't merely a UNESCO World Heritage site and original masterpiece combining harmony and elegance; it's also a must-see destination in its own right. The perfect circle formed by its gardens, the magnificently restored building and the cutting-edge cultural programme blew us away the minute we set foot on site.

Having feasted our eyes on this architectural treasure, we continue our journey to Mouchard, where the line starts to climb as it enters the heart of the Jura mountains. The swallows are still way above us, but they are definitely getting closer. In springtime, romantics on board swear they can virtually hear the rustle of their wings – if it weren't for the constant clickety-clack of the train. The mountains remain a dominant presence for the rest of the journey.

Both modest and immense at the same time, they only offer a brief respite with a glimpse of the extensive vineyards at Arbois, home to the wines so fondly remembered in the famous song by Belgian singer Jacques Brel. Salt, then wine – whatever next? Metal, as it happens. This time in the forges found in the village of Syam, notable for its grand Palladian villa dating back to the early 19th century.

- *Saline Royale, Arc-et-Senans.*

- *The vineyards of Arbois, near Château-Chalon.*

36

DOLE → SAINT-CLAUDE

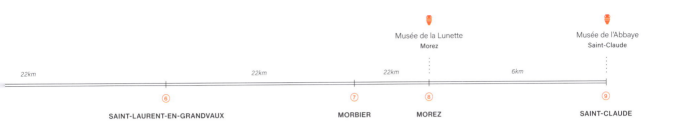

- Morez Viaduct, constructed in 1912.

SUMMIT OF COL DE LA SAVINE AND ONWARDS TO MOREZ

Despite the delights of our journey so far, the real high point of the Ligne des Hirondelles is yet to come, shortly after passing Morbier. Now we're winding our way through majestic trees – their leaves practically caressing the train as we pass by. Gradually we gain height, travelling from tunnel to viaduct and vice versa. Then, all at once, almost without us realising, we reach the highest point on the line, the Col de la Savine, 984m above sea level. As we cross the Crottes Viaduct, greenery suddenly gives way to the Bienne valley, disappearing into the distance. At this stage of our trip, the track follows such a sinuous route that we are able to appreciate the various engineering structures on the line itself, those we have already passed and those that are yet to come, not least the Tunnel des Frasses. One kilometre long, this was designed in the shape of a horseshoe – the only one of its kind in France. It enables the train to descend (or ascend if travelling in the opposite direction) 26 metres in the space of a few minutes. You may not be aware that the little town of Morez is the epicentre of the spectacle-making industry, but it is perhaps better known for the viaduct that bears its name, most spectacular of all the viaducts along this line. Indeed, this particular specimen incorporates open spandrels. Not only is this an excellent word for Scrabble, it also describes the voids left in the area above the arches of a bridge to lighten the load on the arch. In the case of the Morez Viaduct, however, these cavities also act as flight paths for the swallows, enabling them to fly below the train at this point on the route.

🔊 THE HIGH PRICE OF COMMUNING WITH THE BIRDS

The Ligne des Hirondelles was constructed between 1862 and 1912 as a means of encouraging industry to the Jura mountains. However, the particularly rugged topography of the region led to astronomical costs. Some sections cost up to one million gold francs per kilometre, a figure which would equate to 4 or 5 million euros per kilometre in today's money.

- Saint-Claude, a small town with fewer than 9,000 inhabitants.

FINISHING WITH A FLOURISH: SAINT-CLAUDE

Just 30 minutes of our journey remain before we arrive at Saint-Claude. But fans of superlative stonework can rest assured that the show isn't over, not by a long chalk. Half of the engineering treasures on the Ligne des Hirondelles are yet to come – 36 tunnels and 18 viaducts, to be precise. Silent witness, if one were needed, of man's determination to cross mountains. They convey us to the world capital of the wooden pipe industry, the terminus for our journey through the Jura.

37

Clermont-Ferrand → Nîmes
Plunging through the Allier gorges

on board the
CÉVENOL

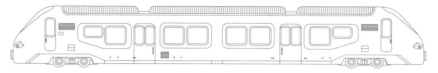

A passenger train with panoramic views to die for.

Sometimes, major rail projects can become delightful tourist attractions in their own right. This is precisely what has happened with the Cévennes line; after starting out as one of the most ambitious rail routes in the history of the French railways, it gradually turned into a regional train line and is now primarily used by tourists. Nevertheless, it is still one of the most stunning journeys in France.

Opposite page: Mountainous terrain in the Allier department.

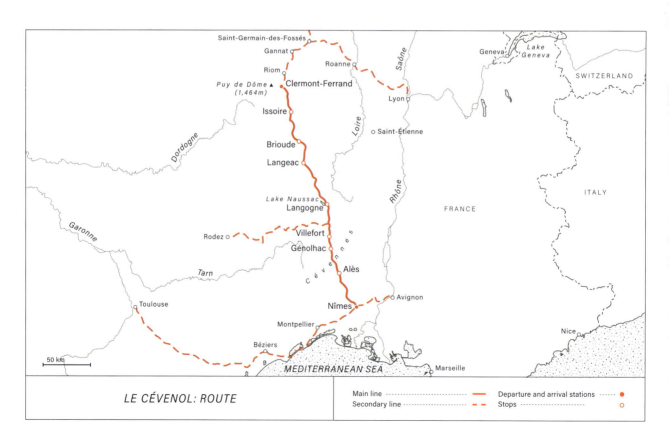

LE CÉVENOL: ROUTE

①	②	③	④	⑤
CLERMONT-FERRAND	ISSOIRE	BRIOUDE	LANGEAC	LANGOGNE

CONSTRUCTED
1840–1870 then 1955

JOURNEY LENGTH
3 hours 56 mins

DISTANCE
304km

COUNTRIES VISITED
France

NUMBER OF BRIDGES, TUNNELS AND VIADUCTS
171

LENGTH OF CHAPEAUROUX VIADUCT
433m

LENGTH OF CHAMBORIGAUD VIADUCT
409m

- *Place des Gras, in Clermont-Ferrand.*

A LEGEND IN FRANCE'S TYRE CAPITAL

This journey begins in Clermont-Ferrand in the Massif Central. Historic capital of Auvergne, this city's main claim to fame lies in its role as the headquarters of the Michelin tyre company. It nestles at the foot of the Puy de Dôme, one of the best-known volcanoes in mainland France. Inexplicably overlooked when the high-speed train line between Paris and Marseille was built, the nation's tyre capital is still well worth a detour by any tourist in search of the 'real' France. Check out the city's cathedral, built entirely in black lava stone, or the Temple of Mercury dating back to the 2nd century. Or you could stroll through the medieval district and sample the gastronomic delights on offer. You could even make it your mission to scale one of the nearby volcanoes. When you've had your fill, you can finally board the Cévenol in anticipation of one of the most spectacular rail journeys in France: the route between Clermont-Ferrand and Nîmes.

- *View of Clermont-Ferrand Cathedral.*

- *Limestone landscape in the Cévennes.*

- *The hilltop village of Chanteuges.*

A BREATHTAKING TRIP THROUGH THE ALLIER GORGES

The Cévenol's itinerary is nothing short of extraordinary. It was designed in the 19th century as part of the first rail line linking Paris and Marseille, but the Cévennes line, as it's also known, also passes through the departments of Allier, Puy-de-Dôme, Haute-Loire, Ardèche, Lozère and Gard. The stunning terrain in these regions would certainly have posed obstacles for any construction project. No fewer than 6,000 labourers and engineers were employed in overcoming the difficulties posed by the landscape, requiring them to come up with ever more ingenious solutions year after year. Thanks to their combined brains and brawn, the end result includes some 171 bridges, tunnels and viaducts, along with over 200,000m^2 of retaining walls. The valley and gorges of the River Allier are the most impressive of these natural obstacles. After rejoining the course of the river near Martres-de-Veyre, the line wends its way in a typically French casual manner to the village of Brioude, where a festival of railway films is held on an annual basis, then onwards to Langeac, an important logistics hub in a bygone railway era. The extraordinary journey proper begins a little further south, beyond the breathtakingly beautiful hilltop village of Chanteuges. As the valley narrows to form a gorge, the train starts to follow the contours of the land as it eases its way from one bank of the river to the other, flirting with one before coyly heading back to the opposite side.

SOARING AT 1,023M ABOVE SEA LEVEL

The line continues to run directly alongside basalt cliffs, vast green expanses and freshwater beaches. This region was a favourite among tourists who fled here during the pandemic of 2020, yet it remains surprisingly peaceful and unspoiled. The very scale of the landscape is such that it simply shrugs off any human attempts to tame it with hiking trails and campsites. Of course, the Cévenol is all about people and getting from A to B; it presses on regardless through dozens of tunnels and gravity-defying viaducts. En route, it stops at the station of Prades-Saint-Julien, starting point for many glorious walks where you can enjoy the wonders of nature, listed Romanesque chapels and imposing basalt columns.

After a short stop to experience a snapshot of forever France, the train resumes its slow ascent, passing over one of the most impressive structures along the route: the semi-circular Chapeauroux Viaduct, some 433m long. From here, it carries on to Langogne where it reaches the highest point on the journey, La Bastide-Saint-Laurent-les-Bains station at an altitude of 1,023m. No problem for the train as it nonchalantly sets off again and begins its descent of the Cévennes. A change of strategy is required here. The train no longer follows the river; instead it criss-crosses the water, making use of a series of viaducts, each more magnificent than the one before: Chassezac, Villefort, La Malautière and of course Chamborigaud, with its 409 metres of curved masonry walls.

▪ *Saint-Gervais-Saint-Protais, in Langogne.*

▪ *The curved Chamborigaud Viaduct.*

ANOTHER PARIS-MARSEILLE LINE

For many years, the Cévenol was regarded as an alternative to the more recent high-speed line between Paris and Marseille. France's state-owned railway company, SNCF, eventually decided that this line, with barely 100,000 passengers a year, wasn't worth their while, only for it to be rescued by a local initiative. Trains never die if they occupy a corner of their passengers' hearts.

MINING TERRITORY

Eventually, the line enters the steep-sided Gardon valley, forging ahead through a number of small tunnels. This is mining territory, where numerous local railway lines were built to access the mines, mostly concentrated around the city of Alès. Regarded as the gateway to the Cévennes, this city isn't merely the starting point for exploring the nearby national park. Alès has a fascinating historical and mining backstory of its own; well worth a visit to the mining museum with its restored model mine (Mine Témoin). When you emerge from the bowels of the earth, it's time to get back on board and head for the great plains surrounding the city of Nîmes, with its awe-inspiring Roman amphitheatre, the Maison Carrée temple, the Tour Magne and beautiful gardens. This is where our journey comes to an end, but there's certainly a great deal of this area left to explore.

▪ *Roman amphitheatre in Nîmes, evidence of the city's ancient history.*

EUROPE

Neussargues → Béziers
Railway heaven and hell on the Ligne des Causses

on board the
NEUSSARGUES-BÉZIERS

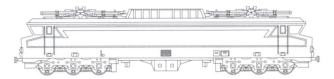

This train follows the most spectacular railway line in France.

Originally built in the 19th century to link the South of France with Paris, these days the sole purpose of the Ligne des Causses seems to be admiring the stupendous views of the Cantal, Lozère and Aubrac regions. This relic of the golden age of rail reminds us that there was a time when trains ventured into the mountains rather than remaining resolutely on the plains.

Opposite page: Castelbouc, a tiny hilltop village in Lozère.

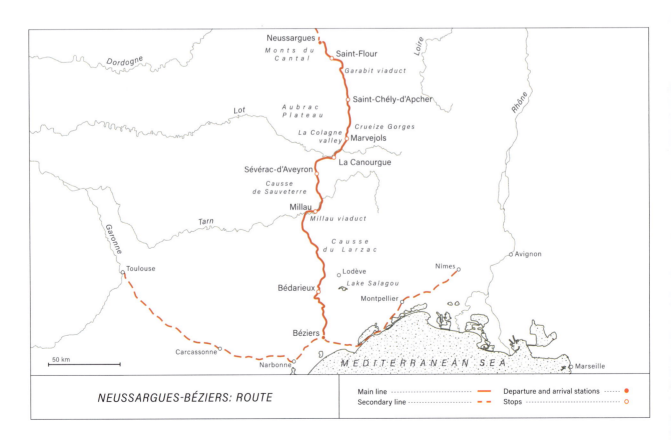

NEUSSARGUES-BÉZIERS: ROUTE

EUROPE

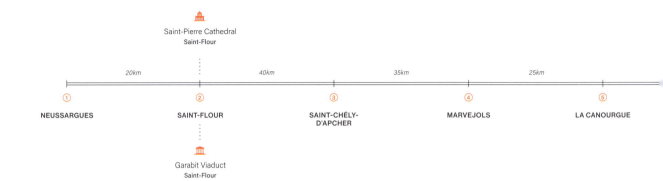

CONSTRUCTION BEGAN IN
1858

JOURNEY LENGTH
4 hours 56 mins

DISTANCE
277km

COUNTRIES VISITED
France

LENGTH OF GARABIT VIADUCT
565m

VAL-D'ACORMIE, ALTITUDE
1,087m

• *Cantal, renowned for its cheese.*

WINDING DOWN TO THE MEDITERRANEAN

The beauty of the Cantal department and the staggering collection of churches in Neussargues-en-Pinatelle weren't enough to prevent this rural village, with a population of under 2,000, from isolation. Now that it is no longer the important rail hub that it was until the end of the 1990s, the station here is only used by local residents. Perched high up at an altitude of 809m, it is still the starting point for an exhilarating journey through the mountains, beginning in the Monts du Cantal and ending in Béziers on the Occitan coast.

STANDING ON THE SHOULDERS OF GIANTS

Patience isn't a virtue you need to possess when travelling on the Ligne des Causses. Within minutes, this line offers passengers a superb vantage point over the plateaux and mountains in the Cantal. Many people will know this area primarily for its cheese, not its scenic beauty, but it's safe to say that it hides its light under a bushel in the landscape stakes. Our first stop in the town of Saint-Flour is a prime example: constructed on a rocky outcrop, it is barely higher than our departure point but stands out for a whole host of reasons. As the religious capital of the Haute Auvergne and seat of the diocese since 1317, this ancient town, christened the 'City of Wind' by poet Camille Gandilhon Gens d'Armes (1871–1948), has an upper and a lower town, both very different. By climbing the Sentier des Chèvres (goat track) that links the two, you'll be able to explore the quirky medieval upper town with its cathedral hewn from volcanic rock and its statue of Christ, otherwise known as the Beau Dieu noir or 'Beautiful Black God'.

Just a few kilometres further down the line, our train emerges onto one of the most incredible engineering structures on the French rail network: the Garabit Viaduct. Designed by Léon Boyer and built by Gustave Eiffel in 1884, this mammoth wrought iron and steel structure is 565m long. When it was constructed, this viaduct was the tallest in the world; at its highest point, it towers 122m above the steep Truyère gorge. The view from the apex takes your breath away: standing on the shoulders of giants seems a very suitable epithet. We should all feel humbled in the face of such beauty, as befits those who take the time to contemplate the splendour of the heavens and reflect on the infinite scale of the Universe.

• *Saint-Flour, perched on its rocky outcrop.*

44

NEUSSARGUES → BÉZIERS

• Grazing land on the Aubrac plateau.

IN THE VALLEY OF HELL

We barely have time to recover our composure before the train reaches its highest point, at Val-d'Acormie, 1,087m above sea level. It then drops back below 1,000m before stopping in the pretty village of Saint-Chély-d'Apcher, after which it climbs again above this symbolic plateau to an altitude of 1,041m at Aumont-Aubrac. In the meantime, the department of Cantal has been replaced by Lozère. Although not as high, this department is no less rugged and it marks the start of the line's slow descent through the Crueize gorges, also known as the Valley of Hell. Its steep sides, narrow gorges and sheer depth contribute to form a true jumble of precipitous landscapes, sculpted by thousands of years of erosion and spanned by a viaduct itself regarded as devilish in its complexity.

• Millau Viaduct, 2,460m long.

Soon afterwards we come to the Chanteperdrix viaduct, the Sainte-Lucie tunnel, Marvejols station, the Colagne valley and Le Monastier-Pin-Moriès. The line cuts through the huge gashes in the landscape created over time, effortlessly mastering their contours and setting its own gradient. It runs alongside the River Lot, which links the Sauveterre plateau with the Monts d'Aubrac, then diverts off before climbing again to the plateau of Sévérac. From here, it plunges into a series of tunnels, then skirts along cliff edges until it reaches Millau, where even committed train buffs can't help but admire the colossal Millau road viaduct, which opened in 2004. Then on through the town to yet another plateau: this time Larzac. Deep valleys alternate with karst plateaus, or 'causses', from which the line takes its name, before eventually petering out.

WHAT'S IN A NAME?

The Ligne des Causses hasn't always been so named. It was previously known as the Neussargues-Béziers line, but its name was changed for commercial reasons. The idea was to attract tourists to this part of the notorious 'empty diagonal' that bisects France, a wide tract of land with a very low population density and minimal economic activity.

THE SCENT OF THE SEA

Eventually we arrive in Bédarieux, less than 200m above sea level, and quite close to the Mediterranean. There's a subtle shift in the atmosphere and the southern way of life pervades the air, affecting how people speak and the way they behave. Like the locals, we are inexorably drawn to Lake Salagou with its reddish-orange earth and reed beds, almost Martian in appearance. It is surrounded by undulating banks studded with plants whose roots extend way below the 750 hectares of its deep blue waters. Flag irises thrive in the sunshine, children's laughter fills the air and water sports enthusiasts indulge their passion to their heart's content. Back in Bédarieux, we board the train one last time to continue our descent to Béziers, just 17m above sea level and not too far away at all. This is a quiet city, far too laid-back to wonder how we came to be here, whether by pounding down the motorway, or by braving the limestone plateaux of the Causses.

• Madeleine Church (11th century), in Béziers.

Miramas → L'Estaque
The 'other' Painters' Trail

on board the
CÔTE BLEUE

If you love the seaside, this train is for you.

Originally constructed as a relief route, the line known as the Côte Bleue is now one of the prettiest railway lines in France. From the little town of Miramas to the Marseillais port of L'Estaque, it winds between the calanques (rocky inlets) and lagoons of Provence.

Opposite page: *Côte Bleue, between Ensuès-la-Redonne and Niolon.*

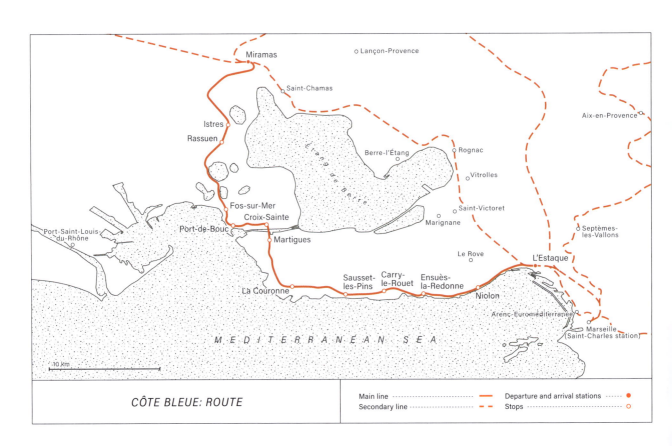

CÔTE BLEUE: ROUTE

EUROPE

① MIRAMAS	② ISTRES	③ RASSUEN	④ FOS-SUR-MER	⑤ PORT-DE-BOUC	⑥ CROIX-SAINTE

Old town — Istres
Étang de Lavalduc — Fos-sur-Mer

10km — 3km — 9km — 8km — 4km

CONSTRUCTION BEGAN IN
1879

JOURNEY LENGTH
1 hour 22 mins

DISTANCE
61km

COUNTRIES VISITED
France

VESSE VIADUCT, CONSTRUCTED
1915

LENGTH OF MÉJEAN VIADUCT
143m

- *Miramas, near the Étang de Berre.*

AN ELEGANT KIND OF DRYNESS

Miramas station appears a sleepy little place when we enter through its automatic doors. This ordinary little building is almost deserted and makes the heat of the Provençal summer a little more bearable. Nonetheless, we can only linger a few minutes as our train is already at the platform. As its name suggests, the Côte Bleue train is set to carry us along the Mediterranean coastline to the well-known port district of L'Estaque on the outskirts of Marseille.

As the regional train gets underway, the sea has yet to put in an appearance. Miramas, a small Provençal town, disappears from view; history tells us little of the origins of its name. Its houses blend into the rocky landscape and the parched vegetation. Spindly pines and thick clumps of bamboo conceal the last buildings from sight. We're left with the South in its purest distillation. It's an elegant kind of dryness, burning gold as far as the eye can see, offset with a dark green glaze. As we pull into Istres, a little station comes into view, serving a pretty town with some 40,000 inhabitants. Yet, to all appearances, we might as well be in the back of beyond.

- *The Côte Bleue crossing the Vesse Viaduct, built in 1915.*

AN IRIDESCENT LAGOON

Just a few minutes further down the line, we get a glimpse of this journey's first natural wonder. To our left is the Étang de Lavalduc, with its 3.54km^2 of iridescent rose-pink water due to the presence of the endemic *Artemia salina*. These small crustaceans also account for the pinkish hue of the flamingos to be found on the opposite bank. Lavalduc, forming a ring with five other lakes – Pourra, Citis, Engrenier, Rassuen and Estomac – is one of the places where these extremely rare and endangered birds take refuge, in surroundings as beautiful as their own stunning plumage.

The stations at Fos-sur-Mer and Port-de-Bouc are even more modest, yet groups of young people board the train at each port of call. Some sport merely a beach towel and a happy-go-lucky smile. The sun seems to slow down time. The sky is so blue that any sense of urgency seems futile, any worries can be shelved for the time being. Surely real life can wait until it's not quite as hot? This notion has been the subject of many books and films, so fascinated have writers and film-makers been with the underlying premise.

- *Étang de Lavalduc, near Fos-sur-Mer.*

48

MIRAMAS → L'ESTAQUE

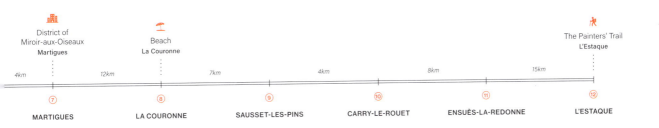

- The district of Miroir-aux-Oiseaux, Martigues.

- Port of Ensuès-la-Redonne.

A CERTAIN KIND OF BEAUTY

The lagoons are now a dim and distant memory. We're in a land where the Mediterranean rules all it surveys. From Sausset-les-Pins to Carry-le-Rouet, then on to Ensuès-la-Redonne, our carriage windows are full of sea, sea and more sea. Its presence can be felt everywhere. From the cliffs sculpted by seawater over thousands of years to the

A COOL DIP IN THE SHADE OF THE PINE TREES

The Mediterranean starts to feel ever closer. As we approach Croix-Sainte, a district of the large town of Martigues, you can smell the sea spray permeating the train. All of a sudden, we can see the beach, just a hop, skip and a jump away from where we are sitting. Sadly, we don't have time to feel the sand between our toes because we're approaching the Pont de Caronte, a wonderful feat of engineering. This railway viaduct was constructed between 1908 and 1915, then blown up by the German army in 1944, before being rebuilt in the early 1950s. It crosses the canal linking the vast Étang de Berre with the Mediterranean. Despite carrying the railway line, the

sea-sprayed buildings clinging steadfastly to the hills. As we press our noses to the windows, we can see tiny fishing boats bobbing up and down on the waves as they strain against the ropes tethering them to their pontoons.

This windblown, sun-scorched landscape is our companion until we arrive at our final destination, L'Estaque. Time seems to have stood still in this modest fishing port in the wider Marseille area. Whether it's the people, the wooden boats, the bustling bars where patrons sip aniseed-flavoured drinks, or the little stalls selling 'panisses', delicious fritters made with chickpea flour. Yet appearances can be deceptive: life most certainly has not passed this place by. Oh no, this is a lifestyle choice, a decision to opt for

central span of the bridge is able to pivot to allow tall ships to pass through.

After almost skimming the surface of the water, the track plunges into the rock, every metre making it only too clear what man had to do to excavate a passage along this route: wielding pickaxes, smashing through rock, dynamiting obstacles, building earthworks, then back to the pickaxe. As our train emerges from its rock-hewn cutting, we are already nearly at Carro-La-Couronne, another part of Martigues renowned for its idyllic beaches, tucked away between rocky outcrops. Here you can swim in crystal-clear water before drying off in the shade of the tall pine trees perched atop the rocky cliffs.

aesthetics over all else. An anachronism maybe, but who cares? If it was good enough for Paul Cézanne, Georges Braque and Auguste Renoir, who are we to disagree?

- View from the train: the Mediterranean coastline and the deep blue sea.

📣 MY CORNER OF THE WORLD

The author of this book grew up near the lakes around the Étang de Berre and the Gulf of Fos-sur-Mer. His childhood home lies on the shores of the Étang de Citis; it's said that you can even see the roof from the Côte Bleue train. A favourite family stroll included a visit to the lake to watch the birds enjoying the delights of this stretch of water.

49

Bastia → Ajaccio

From the capital of the North to the coral city

on board
U TRINICHELLU

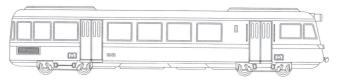

Two rickety little carriages.

Corsica is often described as the 'mountain in the sea' and is famous for its thousand kilometres of beaches, each equally stunning. However, anyone who loves travelling by train will be more interested in the mountainous terrain, culminating in the summit of Monte Cinto at an altitude of 2,705m. The railway line between the island's two major cities is particularly appealing.

Opposite page: The citadel of Corte, known as the Eagle's Nest.

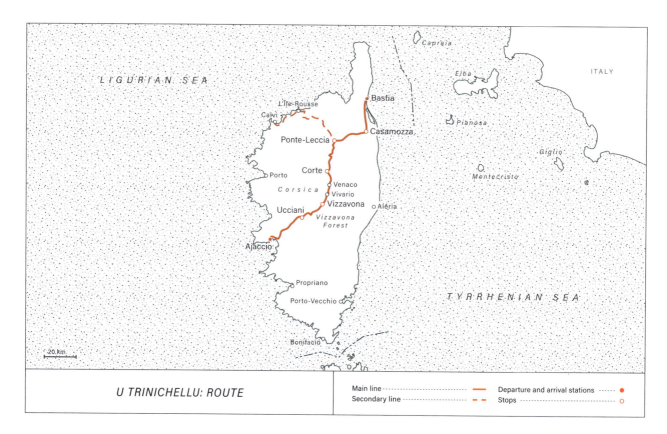

U TRINICHELLU: ROUTE

CONSTRUCTED
1888–1894

JOURNEY LENGTH
3 hours 41 mins

DISTANCE
157.4km

COUNTRIES VISITED
France

LENGTH OF THE PONT
DU VECCHIO VIADUCT
171m

📣 THE GR20, LEGENDARY HIKING TRAIL

The GR20 has a reputation for being one of the toughest and most scenic hiking trails in Europe. It leads walkers over a 200-km route through the Corsican mountains. It is divided into 16 stages and can be walked in its entirety or in part, taking anything from 5 to 16 days according to each hiker's level. If you really want a challenge, the current record stands at 30 hours, 25 minutes, set by Lambert Santelli in June 2021.

• *Bastia, Corsica's second town after Ajaccio.*

TWO COMPACT, CLATTERING CARRIAGES

Our journey on the Island of Beauty begins in Bastia, the pretty but reserved capital of Northern Corsica. After sampling a local beer in one of the town's sun-drenched squares and strolling around the narrow streets of the Terra Vecchia district with their colourful buildings, we climb on board U Trinichellu. Made up of two surprisingly simple carriages, the little train leaves Bastia station at a gentle pace reminiscent of the old-fashioned age of rail. Admittedly, it could hardly do otherwise, as the line between Bastia and Ajaccio requires the driver to be alert at all times. Winding around bend after bend, it snakes along the coast, clinging to the mountainside and traversing escarpments via impressive engineering structures.

LOOPS AND SWITCHBACKS

After running alongside a stretch of the Bastian coastline, our train passes Furiani, Biguglia and Casamozza before it braves the wild mountain landscape proper – the very soul of the island. The railway provides the key to a secret world, one that the locals usually keep to themselves; tourists generally prefer to stick to the beaches. To enter this special place, U Trinichellu undertakes a series of loops and switchbacks until it reaches Ponte-Leccia, starting point for a second route heading for Calvi.

• *Chapelle Santa Maria, high above Furiani.*

• *Picturesque street in Corte, at the very heart of Corsica.*

CORTE, MOUNTAINSIDE CITADEL

After admiring the 17th-century bridge straddling the River Golo, we continue our pleasantly bumpy ride to Corte, a beautiful fortress city perched high on a mountain top. Formerly the island's capital, where Pascal Paoli declared the territory's independence in 1755, this mountainside town is a must for its staggering beauty alone, to say nothing of its cultural heritage and the role it has played in Corsican history. We carry on through the villages of Venaco and Vivario, each more Corsican than the other, before reaching Vizzavona where it's well worth stopping to explore the stunning natural park of the same name, visit the now abandoned Grand Hôtel de la Forêt or join the GR20 at the halfway point. Then back on board where we plunge into the Vizzavona Tunnel, some 4km long, which links North and South Corsica. Legend has it that the weather can change completely from one end of the tunnel to the other.

A STONE'S THROW FROM THE PORT

In order to journey through these rugged landscapes concealed in the island's very heartland, U Trinichellu weaves its way calmly between retaining walls with rough stone arches, through 30 or so tunnels and over some 50 bridges and viaducts. But one of the latter surpasses everything else on the journey: the Pont du Vecchio. Designed by Gustave Eiffel himself in 1891, the 171-m length of this engineering tour de force towers 90m above the river that bears its name. Crossing the bridge is non-negotiable if you want to reach Bocognano and its waterfall, known as the Voile de la mariée (Bridal veil), then on to Mezzana, and finally a run along the coast before we pull into Ajaccio station, just a stone's throw from the port and its beaches. Time for a quick glance at your watch to decide how to round off this enchanting trip: a dip in the sea? Or should you sample the many distractions that are bound to be on offer on a long summer's evening by the seaside?

• *Col de Vizzavona, near Bocognano.*

• 1 – Bastia, port and citadel. 2 – Bigulia lake, south of Bastia. 3 – The area around the village of Venaco. 4 – Entrance to an old residential building in Corte.

EUROPE

Ponte-Leccia → L'Île-Rousse → Calvi
From central Corsica to the coast

on board
U TRINICHELLU

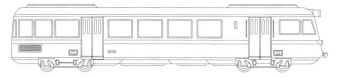

Shake, rattle and roll.

This is the second route covered by this modest Corsican railway, this time the line between Ponte-Leccia and Calvi via L'Île-Rousse, offering another take on the Island of Beauty. From the extremely arid landscapes in the nation's hinterland to the fun-filled beaches of the coast, the train slowly makes its way through the natural wonders of this varied terrain with their many different shades of beauty.

Opposite page: The citadel of Calvi, perched high above the turquoise sea.

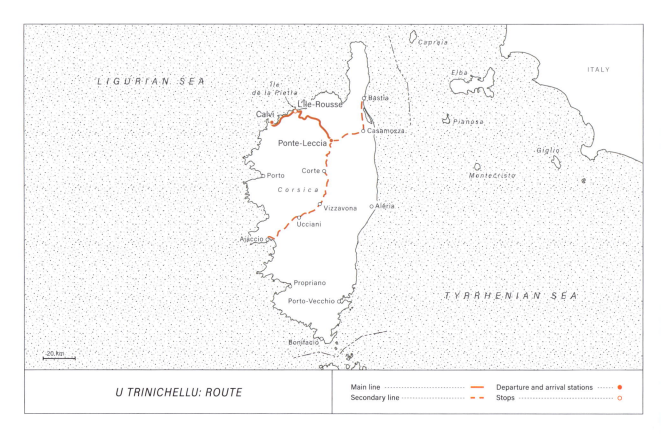

U TRINICHELLU: ROUTE

CONSTRUCTED
1889–1890

JOURNEY LENGTH
1 hour 50 mins

DISTANCE
73.2km

COUNTRIES VISITED
France

• Monte Cinto from Ponte-Leccia.

TAKING THE SLOW TRAIN

Some 73.2km long, this route actually starts in Ponte-Leccia, right in the centre of the island, in an arid and undulating landscape where, as the miles slip past, the sea can occasionally be sighted from behind the reassuring bulk of the mountains. Overwhelming in its peace and quiet, this view transforms our leisurely rail journey into a slow form of meditation, disturbed only briefly by the sight of a passing village, a herd of cattle or a mother wild boar guiding her babies, or *marcassins* as they're known in French. Gradually, the sea starts to make its presence felt – the tang of the sea spray inveigles its way into the surrounding countryside.

🎧 CALVI ON THE ROCKS

The 'Calvi on the Rocks' Festival was set up by a group of friends in 2003 and has since become one of the unmissable events of the summer cultural scene in France, and, of course, in Corsica itself. Dedicated to the electronic music genre, it now welcomes international artists every year, along with over 20,000 festival goers living it up across the beaches right up to the Citadel district.

HOMAGE TO THE MERMAID

U Trinichellu heads tantalisingly towards the coast, then appears to change its mind and doubles back inland instead. Fortunately, it can't keep up the pretence for too long and our rattling little monster soon returns to follow the coastline until we reach L'Île-Rousse, where we hop off for a short walk. With a population of a few thousand, this little village on the north side of the Island of Beauty certainly isn't one of the most frequented. Which is precisely why it's worth stopping. Why not amble along the pretty little streets and explore the covered market? Or wander the length of the Marinella promenade to pay homage to the bronze statue of a mermaid as she sits watching over passing sailors and looking out to the horizon. If you happen to have more time on your hands, you could even go as far as the Île de la Pietra, a little island mainly taken up by its lighthouse and semi-ruined Genoese watchtower.

• Tiny Île de la Pietra, linked to L'Île-Rousse by a causeway.

• U Trinichellu leaving Calvi.

CAT AND MOUSE

Twenty or so kilometres of our journey to Calvi remain, a good hour on U Trinichellu, and the train hugs the coast for the duration – at least where Mother Nature allows. Rather like a large blue mouse evading a miniature metal cat, the Mediterranean disappears from sight, only to pop up again a few minutes later. Even when Calvi station comes into view, we are convinced the sea has once again escaped our grasp. But anyone who enjoys a dip needn't worry; for as long as Corsicans can remember, the sea has always been a constant presence in this town, now famed for its electronic music festival.

IN THE SHADOW OF THE CITADEL

Calvi is renowned for its balmy climate and now attracts a large number of tourists while losing none of its old-world charm. It is divided into two main sections – the lower part on the seafront, and the upper part, reached by a short climb. You can explore the town on foot, wandering where you will. You might be tempted by a particularly attractive alleyway, or get carried away reading the names on the little boats moored in the marina. Then again, perhaps you'd rather explore the area around the citadel to find the house where Christopher Columbus is alleged to have been born? A perfect setting to round off this varied journey by investigating the surrounding area. Who knows, you might even discover a new island...

• Port and citadel of Calvi.

PONTE-LECCIA → ÎLE-ROUSSE → CALVI

• *Zilia, village on the fringes of the Corsican Regional Natural Park.*

Venice → Istanbul
From lagoon to strait

on board the
GOLDEN EAGLE DANUBE EXPRESS

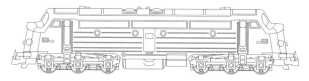

Luxury train with a laid-back vibe.

Of the many trains that have attempted to pick up where the legendary Orient Express left off with its long-distance luxury rail journeys, the Golden Eagle Danube Express stands head and shoulders above many of its rivals. Crossing eight countries as it travels from Venice to Istanbul, its Balkan Explorer tour is a particularly fine example of this rail heritage, offering a phenomenal railway excursion over 12 days and 11 nights.

Opposite page: The Grand Canal, Venice's main artery.

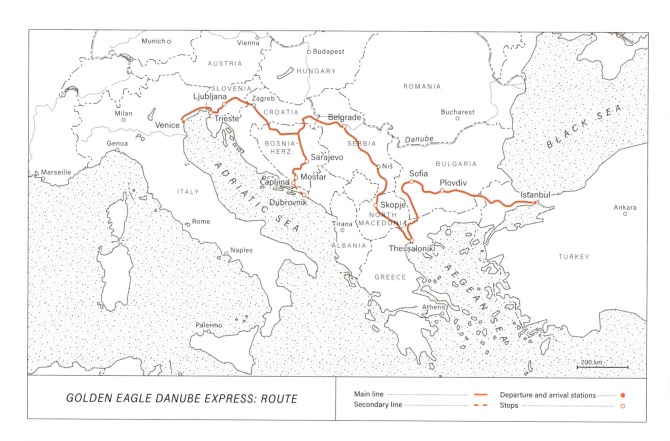

GOLDEN EAGLE DANUBE EXPRESS: ROUTE

EUROPE

1	2	3	4	5	6	7
VENICE	TRIESTE	CAVES OF POSTOJNA	LJUBLJANA	ZAGREB	SARAJEVO	MOSTAR

Castello di Miramare — Trieste
Dragon Bridge + Central Market — Ljubljana

162km · 47km · 58km · 117km · 400km · 125km

OPERATING SINCE
2008

JOURNEY LENGTH
12 days, 11 nights

DISTANCE
3,106km

COUNTRIES VISITED
Italy
Slovenia
Bosnia and Herzegovina
Croatia
Macedonia
Greece
Bulgaria
Turkey

NUMBER OF SUPERIOR DELUXE CABINS
12

▪ Santa Lucia station in the background.

▪ Venice, City of the Doges.

VISIT VENICE AND TAKE THE TRAIN

Our journey begins in Venice. After browsing the stalls in the Rialto Market, we find a spot on St Mark's Square to soak up the splendours of the nearby Basilica and the Doge's Palace, the seat of the city's former rulers. We arrived yesterday, and tomorrow, after spending two days on the shores of the lagoon, we'll board our train and head eastwards.

In the morning, we travel by boat along the Grand Canal to Santa Lucia station where the Golden Eagle Danube Express is ready and waiting for its next complement of passengers. On the platform, a hostess in the train's royal blue uniform leads us to our cabin: 8.6m² of luxury including a sofa that converts into a king-size bed, a table, two chairs, a shower and WC, a wardrobe, Wi-Fi, power sockets, USB ports, air conditioning and, best of all, two picture windows to enjoy views of the scenery and catch a breath of fresh air.

Very content with our stylish accommodation for the next few days, we leave behind the Venetian lagoon and travel to the port city of Trieste. We spend the afternoon strolling around the spectacular main square, Piazza Unità d'Italia, Miramare Castle and enjoying the architectural wonders of San Giusto Hill. After which it's time to get back on board our hotel-on-wheels to head off to neighbouring Slovenia. Dinner awaits us in the train's restaurant car, where, despite the mix of sophisticated local and international cuisine, the elegant tables laid out for each meal and the attentive service, the atmosphere is very relaxed. Unlike some luxury trains, there is no mandatory dress code here other than basic propriety. On the fourth day, after a good night's sleep lulled by the gentle hum of the train and a hearty buffet breakfast, we visit the caves of Postojna. With 20km of galleries and underground chambers, this cavern system also has its own 3.7-km-long rail track, a 5-m-tall stalagmite known as Brilliant and is home to *Proteus Anguinus*, unworldly animals that were long thought to be baby dragons. We then carry on to Ljubljana, the country's capital, with its Dragon Bridge, central market and bustling quayside areas.

▪ Mostar on the River Neretva.

AN EXHILARATING AND WONDERFUL SHOW

Every day, this exhilarating show plays out all over again. The waiting staff serve a selection of fine food and wine, each tasty morsel more delicious than the last, as the train bowls on to Sarajevo, the magnificent yet overwhelming capital of Bosnia and Herzegovina. Its scars in no way detract from the charm of its old buildings, markets and narrow cobbled streets. From here, we travel to Mostar, climbing back into the mountains and along the banks of the River Neretva lined with ancient houses and minarets.

60

VENICE → ISTANBUL

THE HEART OF THE BALKANS

And the show goes on. Dubrovnik, stunning real-life inspiration for King's Landing in *Game of Thrones*. Belgrade, the tranquil yet light-filled capital of Serbia with its city walls, beaches and underground passageways. Skopje, in North Macedonia, with its iconic fortress built on a hill that has been occupied since the Neolithic era, an old bazaar, a 15th-century stone bridge and any number of monuments commemorating Alexander the Great. Thessaloniki in Greece, with its labyrinthine walled old town, a fortress with seven towers, more succinctly referred to as the Heptapyrgion, a seafront and ancient ruins. On arrival in Sofia, Bulgaria's pleasant and laid-back capital, we realize it's been nine days since our epic journey began. We explore sections of the city's Roman walls, continuing right to the heart of the magnificent Alexander Nevsky Cathedral, passing by the Soviet Army monument, often given a cheeky makeover by street artists, and arrive at the steps of St George's Church, which was built back in the 4th century. Then it's on to Plovdiv, regarded as the oldest city in Europe still to be inhabited today. Its history dates back several millennia, as demonstrated by its archaeological sites and Roman amphitheatre, medieval ramparts and Turkish baths.

📢 **EYE-WATERINGLY EXPENSIVE**

With tickets coming in at over 15,000 euros per person in a twin cabin, travelling on the Golden Eagle Danube Express is reserved for those with deep pockets. The tracks used by this top-end outfit are not owned exclusively by this company, however, and if you're organized, it's perfectly possible to travel this route yourself at significantly less cost.

• *Thessaloniki, Greece.*

• *Skopje, North Macedonia.*

• *Domes and minarets of Istanbul.*

INCREDIBLE ISTANBUL

All too soon it's time to say farewell to our spacious cabin and its soothing splendour, the restaurant car and its unerring good taste, the lounge bar with its comfortable armchairs where cocktails disappear far too quickly. Now we're off to our final destination: Istanbul. Formerly Byzantium, then Constantinople, this sprawling megalopolis extends from the Black Sea to the Sea of Marmara and straddles the Bosphorus Strait. It will be our last, but by no means least, port of call. From the towering mosques in the Sultanahmet district to Topkapi Palace and the thousands of little shops making up the Grand Bazaar, plus the narrow streets of Cihangir, this city is an unadulterated joy, in a permanent state of flux. An epic in every sense of the word...

• *Istanbul, sprawling megalopolis and gateway to the East.*

61

Monterosso al Mare → Riomaggiore

The heart and soul of Italy – in glorious technicolour

on board the
CINQUE TERRE EXPRESS

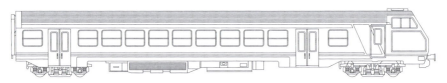

Winding its way between the villages.

Just 28km separate the start and end points for this Italian train. Nonetheless, this is a wonderful way to explore one of the world's most amazing regions, the Cinque Terre National Park, which runs along the Ligurian coast.

Opposite page: *Vernazza – just 700 souls and the sea.*

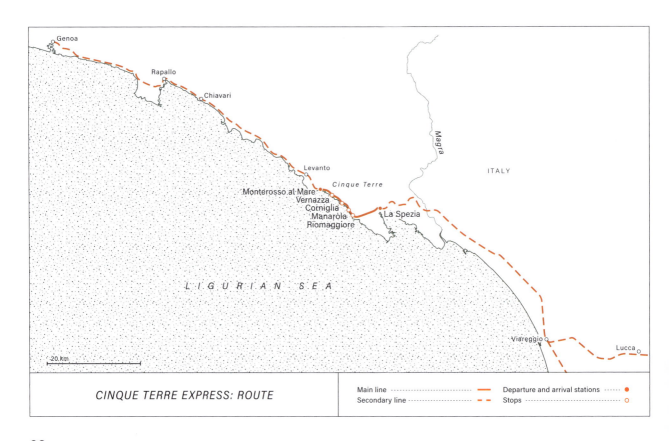

CINQUE TERRE EXPRESS: ROUTE

Main line
Secondary line
Departure and arrival stations
Stops

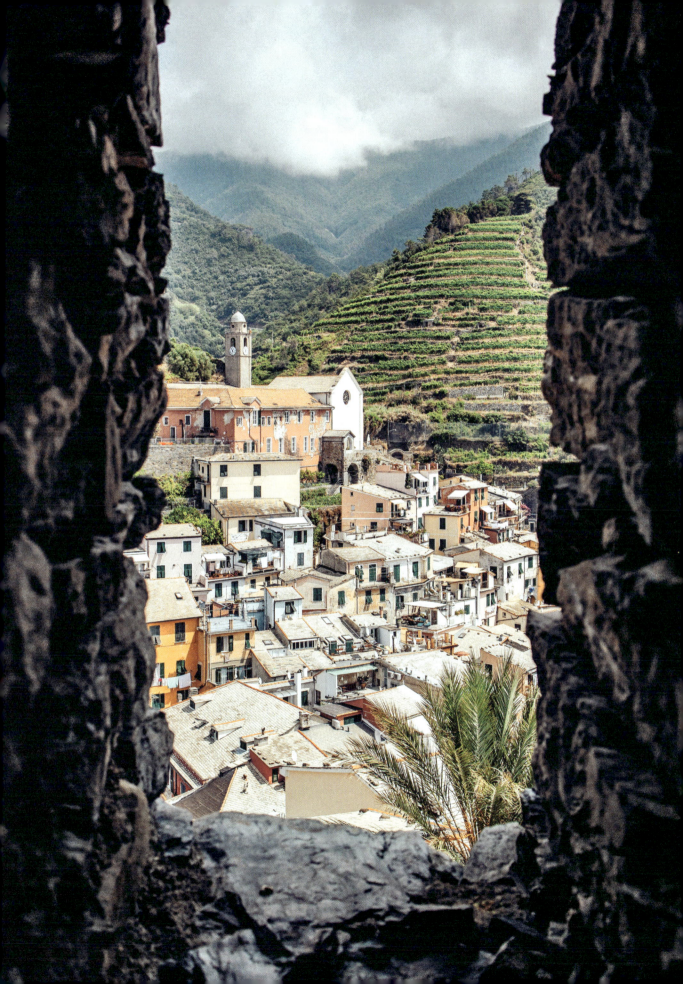

EUROPE

OPERATING SINCE
1874

JOURNEY LENGTH
**20 mins,
without stops**

DISTANCE
28km

COUNTRIES VISITED
Italy

📢 **UNDER THE GAZE OF THE MADONNA**

The Cinque Terre National Park lies between two railway stations and can also be explored on foot via a selection of hiking trails. The most scenic (and steepest) of these paths is from Vernazza to Foce Drignana, with views of both the valley and the sea. It passes through vineyards and also takes in the thousand-year-old Sanctuary of Nostra Signora di Reggio, home to a painting of the black Madonna, said to have been brought back from the Holy Land by the Crusaders.

THE ESSENCE OF ITALY

If you were asked to paint the very essence of Italy, you might very well come up with something resembling the Cinque Terre villages. Worthy holders of UNESCO World Heritage status since 1997, each village surpasses every expectation. Monterosso al Mare, Vernazza, Corniglia, Manarola and Riomaggiore now combine to form one of Italy's most popular tourist destinations. However, there is another way of appreciating the beauty of the villages and the surrounding areas: jump on the Cinque Terre Express, which, despite its name, is a slow train through the mountains linking the individual villages over a 28-km stretch of track.

We board the train at Monterosso, the biggest of the villages and perhaps the least attractive, but nonetheless an excellent starting point and good preparation for the visual delights ahead. Nestled at the foot of hills clad in a heady mix of wild flowers, olive groves and vineyards, the town's medieval castle is separated from the newest part of the village by the hill of San Cristoforo. This most recent development grew up around the long beach of Fegina, the perfect spot for a dip in the sea before you catch the train.

• *Monterosso al Mare and its beach.*

• *Multicoloured houses in Vernazza.*

SISYPHEAN TERRACES

Since we're taking the train from west to east (although you can do it in the opposite direction), our first stop will be at Vernazza. But before we arrive in the second village, make sure you enjoy the scenery on the journey from Monterosso. Each terrace on the route is the result of a Sisyphean effort by the farmers of yore, who shaped nature with their own bare hands. They were also responsible for building the stunning array of multicoloured houses in Vernazza over many generations. Together these form a higgledy-piggledy collection of exquisitely picturesque buildings clustered around meandering alleyways and overhanging the majestic central square. Some are perched up high, surveying the turquoise sea.

Next stop: Corniglia. This is the only village not to be right on the seafront. Instead, this little hamlet was built at the top of a cliff, accessed by a staircase with some 380 steps (the number varies depending on the source and most people don't have enough breath to finish counting by the time they reach the top!). Well worth the effort though, as Corniglia is an experience not to be missed. No chance of a dip here but breathtaking views of the Mediterranean. No deckchairs on the sand either; instead you can take a leisurely stroll from shady nooks to café terraces, dropping into cool stone churches and charming little restaurants en route.

FROM THE SUBLIME TO THE INCREDIBLE

Our next port of call is Manarola, the fourth village on our tour though the Cinque Terre. Once again, this place has an indescribable beauty all of its own. It is shoehorned in between two rocky promontories and is an astonishingly tranquil spot. Make the most of the peace and quiet here before attempting to walk the Via dell'Amore, a jaw-droppingly beautiful footpath suspended high above the sea, which links to our final stop if you'd rather walk than take the train. The path was constructed to allow labourers easier access to the railway line between Genoa and La Spezia, although for many years locals tended to shun it in favour of the old route between Manarola and Riomaggiore. The latter is longer and eventually fell out of favour with the arrival of this kilometre-long walkway almost entirely on one level.

Whether or not you opt to give it a try, we would still urge you to take the train on this section to enjoy the fabulous views of the scenery on the approach to Riomaggiore. This is the final village in our Ligurian adventure, and no less stunning than the rest. A former fishing village with pretty, brightly coloured houses strewn in close formation across the hillside, it looks for all the world as if it's a cardboard stage set or a *trompe l'oeil* painting. Yet you only need to head down to the tiny fishing port set in a narrow inlet and dip your toes in the water to confirm that it isn't make-believe. Despite tourism on a huge scale, this is an area determined to preserve the beauty that has propelled it from a poor and inaccessible backwater to a bucket-list destination. Especially if you visit by train.

• *Riomaggiore, a former fishing village.*

• *Don't miss the beach in Monterosso al Mare.*

In Riomaggiore, the houses go right down to the water's edge. | Opposite page: Corniglia with its inviting blue waters.

Rome → Palermo

By rail and sea

on board the
INTERCITY NOTTE

A train that can go on the ferry – who knew?

As unlikely as it may seem, there is a night train to Sicily.
To cross the Strait of Messina, this magical train quite simply rolls onto a purpose-built ferry and then rolls off again at the other end.

Opposite page: Rome, capital of the Dolce Vita.

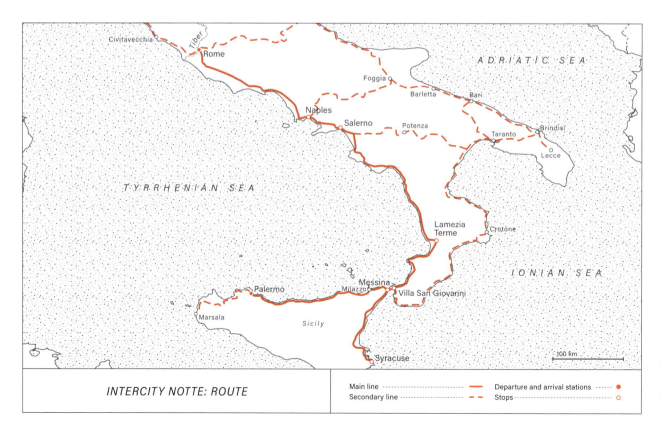

INTERCITY NOTTE: ROUTE

Main line — Departure and arrival stations ●
Secondary line --- Stops ○

EUROPE

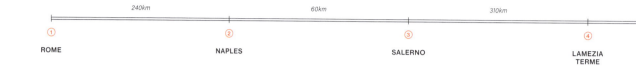

| ① ROME | ② NAPLES | ③ SALERNO | ④ LAMEZIA TERME |

240km — 60km — 310km

OPERATING SINCE
1896

JOURNEY LENGTH
12 hours

DISTANCE
426km

COUNTRIES VISITED
Italy

WIDTH OF THE STRAIT OF MESSINA
3.3km

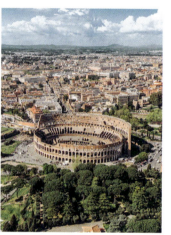

· *When in Rome... visit the Colosseum.*

LAST TRAIN FOR PALERMO

It's hot, stifling even, outside Rome's Termini main station. It's just before 11 o'clock at night and swarms of Vespas still fill the streets. The sound of backfiring pervades the air and their tail lights leave long red trails in the darkness. It's never easy to say goodbye to Rome, with its many grand monuments and unique atmosphere. But today the process is a little more bearable in the knowledge that we're about to embark on the night train to Sicily. Yes, you read that right: it's an island and there isn't a bridge from the mainland. This may seem unlikely, but it's an immensely fascinating proposition. In the meantime, while eager to see how this feat is brought about, we settle into our first-class cabin. Though only a few square metres in size, it's impeccably clean, with a thermostat, reading lamp, plenty of storage space, a banquette that converts into a bed and a second berth concealed behind the wall. As it's already late, we are getting ready for bed when the conductor drops by to bring us our travel kit containing earplugs, wet wipes, bottled water and other items, along with a slip of paper on which we can order breakfast and ask to be woken at a certain time. We request a wake-up call at half-past five so as not to miss the big event.

· *Villa San Giovanni, at the toe of Italy's 'boot'.*

· *Port of Messina on arriving in Sicily.*

THE CHARM OF THE ABSURD

We wake up to find we've arrived at Villa San Giovanni at the toe of Italy's 'boot'. But despite what you might think from looking at the map, this is not our terminus. Rather than requiring us to disembark, our train moves forward slightly, then reverses onto a track that leads straight to the ferry. Just before boarding, the rake of carriages is split into two halves and hauled by an old locomotive right into the ship's hold where there are designated tracks to position the carriages side-by-side. And this strange mechanical mish-mash, half-ship, half-train, is how we and our mode of transport get to cross the 3.5-km-wide Strait of Messina. When all's said and done, why build a bridge when you can load a train onto a ship?

This whole embarkation procedure takes place extremely slowly – quite surreal and pretty cool when you think about it. There's an ingenious craziness about the whole experience, a charming sense of absurdity going on around us, with the passengers remaining on the train throughout the process. Once on the ship, we are allowed to leave our carriage and finally beauty prevails over madness. Behind us, a dazzling sun rises over mainland Italy, while Sicily awakens ahead of us. Beneath us lies our train, soon to be restored to terra firma.

70

ROME → PALERMO

HEADING SOUTHWARDS

Once we're on the other side, the tracks diverge. One branch leads to Catania with the mighty Mount Etna, itself encircled by a railway line, then onwards to Syracuse and its chequered history. Founded by the Corinthians in the 8th century, this small town with a population of just over 123,000 is regarded as one of the finest in Italy. A genuine open-air museum encompassing the island of Ortigia, the San Giovanni catacombs and an amphitheatre, this should be on at the top of every visitor's wish list. It's almost as if the many layers of history are about to crash down around you at any moment. The town centre may be classified as a UNESCO World Heritage Site, but is that enough to protect so many wondrous artefacts? Not helped by the blazing sun, hot enough to melt the very structure of the marble.

- *Syracuse, port and open-air museum.*

📢 RAIL FERRIES ARE A RARE BREED

Although they date back to the 19th century, there are fewer than 10 rail ferries in the world. They are scattered across the Globe, including in the United States, China, Turkey and between Azerbaijan and Turkmenistan.

- *Cefalu, small town on the route to Palermo.*

WORDS OF PRINCELY WISDOM

Our train takes the other branch, setting off to explore Sicily's north coast. The greatest paradox of this island steeped in history becomes apparent as we progress. It's so beautiful, yet it's constantly crumbling away, falling apart before our eyes. There are buildings that bear witness to a splendid past but also show signs of future collapse. Ancient palaces reminding us that great noblemen once lived here, though even they were unable to make the wholesale changes necessary to ensure that everything stayed the same, despite the advice proffered by the Prince of Salina in Luchino Visconti's film *The Leopard*. These villages may seem idyllic to city-dwellers in their cramped concrete tower blocks, but poverty has reigned in these rural areas for many a year.

While human beauty is transient, the Mediterranean and its lush vegetation remain just as beautiful as ever. From our train, as we tuck into the breakfast we ordered the night before, the views never cease to delight. Brightly coloured little fishing boats bob on the blue waters off the coast, while gently rounded hills provide a soothing backdrop as we flash by. When we move inland, we are greeted by abundant perennial plants and shrubs, perfectly suited to the dry conditions.

A SICILIAN FATE

Eventually we approach our actual destination, the majestic city of Palermo, which epitomizes the splendours and sorrows of this beautiful island. The palaces here are more opulent than anywhere else on Sicily, yet they contrast even more starkly with the dilapidation that surrounds them. The difference between ancient relics and rubble is clear to see. Uncannily, our thoughts turn to the strange rail ferry by which we arrived on the island. One day, it too will disappear, to be replaced by something more efficient, more logical. A truly Sicilian fate.

- *The Sicilian coastline near Palermo.*

71

Catania → Riposto
In the fumaroles of Etna

on board the
FERROVIA CIRCUMETNEA

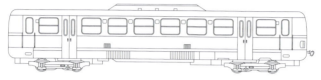

Round trip past the volcano.

The name Ferrovia Circumetnea is both crystal-clear and slightly misleading. First commissioned in 1895, this single narrow-gauge railway line does a virtually complete loop of Sicily's Mount Etna, still very much active to this day. It starts in Catania and ends in Riposto, passing through dark landscapes created by previous lava flows, with views of distant fumaroles and their wisps of steam.

Opposite page: Catania, popular Sicilian city destroyed several times by Etna.

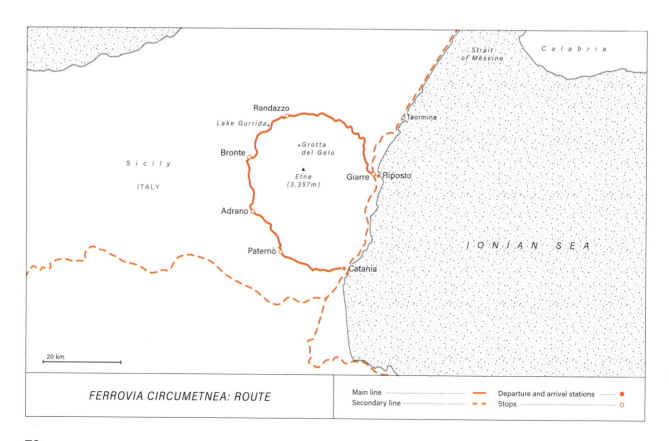

FERROVIA CIRCUMETNEA: ROUTE

EUROPE

CONSTRUCTION BEGAN IN
1895
JOURNEY LENGTH
3 hours
DISTANCE
111km
COUNTRIES VISITED
Italy

- *Catania with Etna in the distance.*

- *Etna, towering 3,357m above sea level.*

IN THE SHADOW OF THE VOLCANO

Anyone who has been lucky enough to visit Catania cannot fail to have noticed Etna, that wrathful, brooding presence dominating the entire city. Inexorably drawn by the fire that burns deep in the heart of the mountain, many visitors also seek to conquer the volcano on foot, by bike, bus, car or by hybrid methods. However, few people are aware of the little train linking the many villages surrounding this immense cauldron of fire. Let's climb on board for a fabulous 111-km circuit at a very gentle pace.

Contrary to what you might expect, the Ferrovia Circumetnea was certainly not conceived as a tourist attraction. It was originally built between 1889 and 1895 to help farmers in the region gain access to their land and to enable them to sell the fruits of their labours to the surrounding towns and villages. And while some tourists do take advantage of the train these days, it's still very much in use by locals going about their daily business without having to take to the roads.

TYRANTS AND ANCIENT CITIES

We set off from Catania's Borgo station on Via Caronda. A tiny, old-fashioned train awaits us on the platform, ready to tackle the slopes of Mount Etna in a clockwise direction. There's no sense of urgency. Instead, the train pulls away slowly, first passing through the western parts of the city at an average speed of just 35km/h, a pace it maintains throughout the three or so hours of our trip. Impossible to be precise about timings when the actual duration depends on the number of stops it makes! Some are request stops; the train won't stop unless a passenger wants to get on or off.

And while each stop is well worth a visit, some are rather more rewarding than others. The first of these is most definitely Paternò. With a population of some 50,000, this municipality is rumoured to have been the ancient city of Hybla Gereatis, the seat of the Sicilian King Hyblon, back in the 8th century BC. Nowadays it's a town with a rich architectural heritage including little-known treasures such as a Norman castle and several churches, often very much the worse for wear, as is the case across much of Sicily. Our next stop is Adrano, a town of 36,000 inhabitants, said to have been founded by Syracusan tyrant Dionysius the Elder in the 5th century BC. Once again, this is a little gem of a place with any number of architectural delights: the castle dating back to the Norman era (14th century), the 16th-century Chiesa Madre, the Monastery of Santa Lucia (12th–16th century), the last vestiges of Cyclopean masonry and, a little further afield, the Ponte dei Saraceni (Saracens' Bridge) as well as an archaeological site going back to the 10th century BC.

- *The Ferrovia Circumetnea train at the foot of the volcano.*

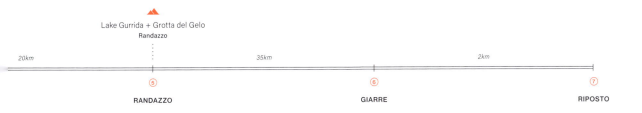

VOLCANIC WILDERNESS

After Adrano the landscape changes, becoming wilder, with more signs of the black volcanic earth we have come to see. This takes the form of huge dried-up lava trails in various shapes, some jagged, others curiously smooth. Pistachio and fig trees flourish between them, ready to be harvested, their fruit often sold to passengers by hawkers.

After stopping at Bronte, the train climbs to 1,000m, reaching the Maletto plateau where there's a stupendous view of Mount Etna. The hilltop village of the same name is worth a visit if only to see its ancient fortified town and castle, or even to take a stroll through the surrounding fields. Nourished by the volcanic earth and the favare, jets of water vapour that run together to form little streams, this land produces the finest strawberries in Italy.

- *Etna: sparse vegetation above 800m.*

- *A hiker at the summit of Mount Etna.*

📢 LIFE AND DEATH OF A LAKE

Etna experienced dozens of eruptions over the course of the 20th century and is regarded as one of the most active volcanoes on Earth. However, the most famous and probably most destructive eruption occurred in 1669. On this occasion, rivers of lava wiped out entire villages and managed to breach Catania's city walls before filling the castle moat and Lake Nicito. Formed by lava centuries earlier, the lake is said to have vanished in less than four hours.

FRUITS OF THE FIRE

Last stop of any note: Randazzo. Located to the north of Etna, this town is notable for the astonishing concentration of lava stone façades and buildings in its medieval centre. It's also renowned for dishes like pork with almonds and hazelnuts, or buccellati, pastries stuffed with dried figs, as well as being a good spot from which to access Lake Gurrida and the Grotta del Gelo cave. The former was created in 1536 when a stream of lava bisected the bed of the Flascio river. Surrounded by willows and poplars, it's a haven for migratory birds and pond turtles. The Grotta del Gelo, which translates as 'Frost Cave', is thought to be the most southerly glacier in Europe. The

- *Randazzo, medieval town built largely of lava stone.*

- *Motta Camastra, in the Alcantara valley.*

Ferrovia Circumetnea eventually completes its tour around the volcano by following the Alcantara valley. Citrus groves and vineyards abound along the track, perfuming the air and changing the colour of the landscape. The passengers' role is merely to lean back and savour every last minute of the remaining stretch to Riposto, filling their eyes, nose and ears with sensory pleasures.

75

Arbatax → Gairo
Sardinia: from sea to sky

on board the
TRENINO VERDE

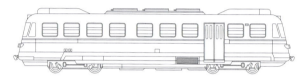

A super-slow transition from coast to mountains.

Dotted around the Sardinian mountains, strange little trains add a different shade of green to the verdant hues of the surrounding countryside. Known collectively as the Trenini verdi, these charming, old-fashioned chariots of the rails travel at an average speed of 20km/h so their passengers can admire the wonderful views of the island. Slow travel at its best – or a magnificent waste of time?

Opposite page: The rocky shoreline of Arbatax.

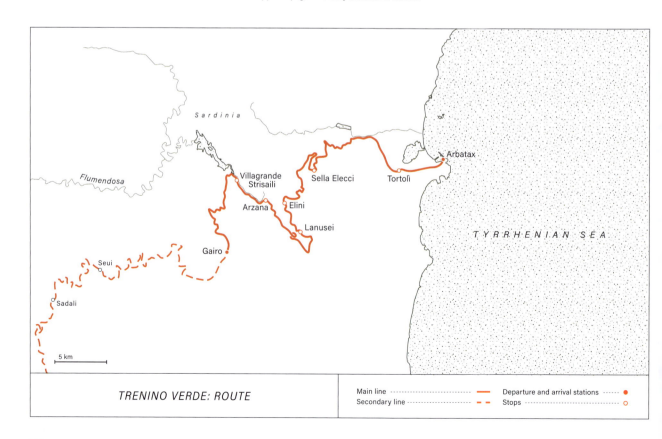

EUROPE

CONSTRUCTED
1980–1984

JOURNEY LENGTH
3 hours 30 mins
–4 hours

DISTANCE
62km

COUNTRIES VISITED
Italy

📢 THE MYSTERIOUS NURAGHI

Sardinia has at least 8,000 nuraghi. Despite their numbers, these remarkable stone structures date back to the second millennium BC but their purpose is shrouded in mystery. Were they religious centres, military buildings or astronomical observation towers? Archaeologists may speculate, but no consensus has been reached. One thing is certain: the civilization that built them has vanished without trace, leaving us clueless.

• Wooden carriages, inside and out.

IN PRAISE OF SLOW TRAVEL

When 19th and 20th-century engineers built the 438 kilometres of Sardinian railway lines used by the Trenino Verde, they were not short of grand ideas. Their aim was to revitalize Sardinia, open up the hinterland and connect the most remote villages to the vast modern rail network. It wasn't to be and Sardinia has never really managed to become part of the global economy other than as a holiday destination. Its utilitarian railway became nothing more than an excuse for a leisurely outing. In 1980, 130 years after the railway was constructed, little trains consisting of a steam locomotive and a single wooden carriage entered into service for this purpose. Along with diesel locomotives and railcars, this modest fleet provides unique access to the hidden heart of Sardinia. Travelling one of the five routes covered by this service isn't merely a journey but a homage to the long-forgotten goddess of slow travel. Let's hope you're in a religious frame of mind as we've selected three of the routes on your behalf. The local authorities have significantly shortened two of these (Macomer-Bosa and Tempio-Palau) for the time being.

• The red porphyry rocks of Arbatax.

THE RED ROCKS OF ARBATAX

This route starts in the Ogliastra region, at Arbatax, a stunning seaside resort famous for its intensely blue water and the rich red of the porphyry rocks. The station is also located very close to the marina; perhaps an opportunity for a boat trip before we board the Trenino verde? The train heads away from the coast towards the mountains, soon leaving the village of Tortoli in its wake.

RUINED NURAGHI

For a while, the coastal scenes and mountain views vie for our attention. Almost desert-like to the right, forests on the left. But before we arrive in the village of Lanusei, the latter gain the upper hand. While of limited interest to tourists, this little place has all the charm of authenticity, as though it has been conceived for no other purpose than to answer practical needs. It also grants access to the archaeological site of Bosco Seleni, where you can take refuge under the trees as you explore the remains of the mysterious Nuragic civilization, dating back to around 1800 BC.

Our little train continues to climb before surprising us with a breathtaking view of the coast we left behind some hours earlier. Did we mention that it takes between three and a half to four hours to cover the 62km of this journey at our leisurely speed? A long time with absolutely nothing to do but enjoy the rugged beauty of the scenery. Forget what you could otherwise be doing, sit back and enjoy it.

• Lanusei, a village of many colours.

RUGGED BEAUTY AND TRACES OF HUMANITY

This area has a rugged beauty so pure that only traces of human life are evident. One example is Gairo, our final destination, which has two very different tales to tell. The village is split into two halves, one picking up the baton from the other. The first half takes the form of Gairo Vecchio, which was abandoned in the 1950s after a landslide. This ghost village is virtually intact but should be viewed with caution and a keen sense of curiosity. The second is the present-day village, where life now goes on.

78

▪ *The village of Lanusei, starting point for visiting the archaeological site of Bosco Seleni.*

Zermatt → Saint Moritz
Take the slow train

on board the
GLACIER EXPRESS

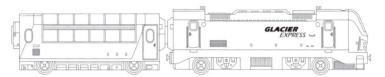

The world's slowest express train.

Dubbed the 'world's slowest express train', the Glacier Express links the chic Swiss ski resort of Zermatt to the equally prestigious resort of St Moritz. Passengers can enjoy the staggering views of the Swiss mountains at an average speed of 36km/h from the train's dedicated observation cars. An unforgettable way to travel at leisure though the very heart of the Alps.

Opposite page: See the mountains by train.

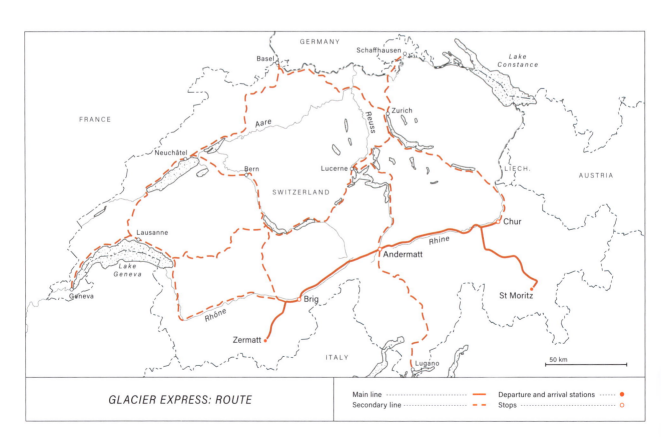

GLACIER EXPRESS: ROUTE

OPERATING SINCE
1930

JOURNEY LENGTH
8 hours

DISTANCE
approx. 300km

COUNTRIES VISITED
Switzerland

NUMBER OF BRIDGES AND VIADUCTS
55

TERMINUS ALTITUDE
1,775m

🔊 **THE GRAND CANYON OF THE OLD CONTINENT**

The Ruinaulta, also known as the Swiss Grand Canyon, is a gorge formed by a landslide 10,000 years ago sending 10 billion tonnes of rock tumbling into the Rhine valley. It can now be viewed quite easily from Valendas station, which is linked to Chur by the Rhaetian Railway.

A PANORAMIC TOUR

Our journey begins at an altitude of 3,883m in the village of Zermatt. Nestled in the valley of the same name, this internationally renowned winter sports paradise sits at the foot of the impressive rocky mass of the Matterhorn (also known as Mont Cervin in French-speaking countries), 4,478m above sea level. With the highest ski area in Europe, Zermatt is a favourite haunt of snow and mountain sports enthusiasts. But for us, its main claim to fame is that it's the starting point for one of the most impressive rail journeys on the Old Continent.

• *The ski resort of Zermatt, at an elevation of 1,600m.*

• *The Simplon Pass, near Brig.*

• *Andermatt, a resort in the Urseren valley.*

HIGH IN THE MOUNTAINS

The first thing to do when you board the Glacier Express is to choose your window seat. Although all seats offer superb views, those near the oversized panoramic windows can give passengers the feeling of soaring high up in the mountains looking down at the void below. If you want to be sure to enjoy these prime views, the most prestigious seats on the Glacier Express are in Excellence Class. These will guarantee your position right next to the windows along with a private bar, concierge service and personal travel guide. This exceptional service, with a few exceptions, also extends to the rest of this immaculate and ultramodern express train.

As soon as the Glacier Express pulls out of the station, the wonders of the journey open up before our eyes. The view from the village of Zermatt is already jaw-droppingly beautiful, but the vista of the surrounding peaks is even more spectacular when seen from a moving train. The Glacier Express trundles serenely along at a very modest speed of 36km/h past Brig and its stately mansions, family-friendly Fiesch, the pretty ski resort of Andermatt in the Urseren valley, Disentis with its 8th-century Benedictine monastery and the vibrant and attractive city of Chur. All these places look to have stepped right out of the pages of a fairytale, but although they all offer a range of outdoor activities (hiking, canoeing, cycling, etc.) in summer, they are not all regular stops during the winter months. Like many alpine railways, the Glacier Express line offers a gateway to two completely different sides of Switzerland depending which season you decide to travel: either a snow-white winter wonderland or a predominantly green vision of loveliness in the spring and summer months.

THE MAGICAL ALBULA LINE

Whatever the season, the most impressive part of our route has to be when the Glacier Express joins the Albula Line at Thusis. Opened in 1904 and awarded UNESCO World Heritage status in 2008, the line starts at an altitude of 641m, climbs to 1,815m, then drops down slightly to its terminus in St Moritz at 1,775m. This vertiginous ascent is only possible thanks to the unrelenting efforts of the engineers and labourers who between them created no fewer than 39 tunnels, some of them helical, and 55 bridges and viaducts. As well as being quite simply the most extraordinary of alpine jaunts, this section also tells the story of the great railway builders.

• *St Moritz, an upmarket ski resort.*

View of the Swiss Alps in springtime, near Fiesch.

Chur → Tirano

Cheek by jowl with the glaciers

on board the
BERNINA EXPRESS

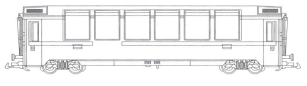

Across the Alps by train.

Constructed later than the Albula line, the Bernina line was initially conceived in the early 20th century for exclusively summer use. This preposterous idea was abandoned in 1913, with the result that nowadays it's possible to get up close and personal with the glaciers and lakes of the eponymous mountain range in both summer and winter.

Opposite page: The lake at St Moritz lies at an altitude of 1,768m.

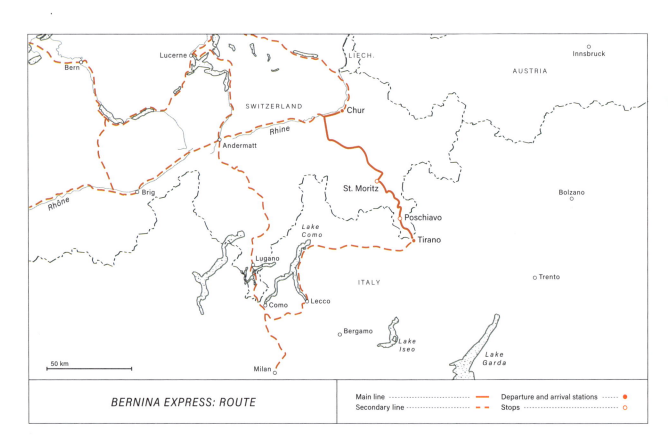

BERNINA EXPRESS: ROUTE

EUROPE

CONSTRUCTED
1896–1909

JOURNEY LENGTH
4 hours

DISTANCE
144km

COUNTRIES VISITED
Switzerland
Italy

LENGTH OF THE
SOLIS VIADUCT
164m

LENGTH OF THE
ALBULA TUNNEL
5,864m

LENGTH OF THE
HELICAL LOOP OF THE
BRUSIO VIADUCT
110m

📢 **THE WORLD'S LONGEST PASSENGER TRAIN**

On 29 October 2022, the Albula line, home to the Glacier and Bernina Express trains, witnessed a new world record. It played host to the longest passenger train in the world: 1,906m long, weighing 30,000 tonnes, it was made up of 25 rakes and had 150 passengers on board.

• *Alpine chalet, Chur.*

ALPINE CROSSING

A whistle pierces the air in the station at Chur, the oldest town in Switzerland and headquarters of the legendary Rhaetian Railway. On the platform, a pretty red train is about to depart for Tirano, an Italian town on the other side of the Alps: the Bernina Express. Though not quite as swish as its cousin, the Glacier Express, it follows some of the same route and is capable of an even more remarkable feat.

CHEEK BY JOWL WITH THE GLACIERS

The first section of the Albula line is used by both trains, but there's no question of competition, just a breathtaking introduction to the splendour of the Alps opening up before us. The train has already gained some height, crossing the Solis Viaduct, soaring above the Landwasser gorges via a second curved viaduct, 136m long and 65m high, then vanishing straight into a tunnel in the mountainside. It goes on to follow a series of spiral galleries by which it climbs even more by turning on itself: a mind-blowing ascent. After all this exertion, the Bernina Express stops briefly at Bergün station, where rail history buffs might like to linger to visit the Albula Railway Museum.

Surrounded by mountains, their presence becoming more and more imposing with every minute, we continue over another set of stunning engineering structures until we reach the most famous of them all, the Albula Tunnel, which is an incredible 5,864m long. When we exit the tunnel, we are already at an altitude of 1,800m, leaving St Moritz on our right before embarking on the *raison d'être* of this route, the Bernina line, which starts at Pontresina. The Bernina Express steadfastly continues to climb on this line with gradients of up to 7 per cent and no assistance from either rack or pinion. Ensconced in our comfortable seats, our noses pressed firmly against the panoramic windows, we marvel at the peaks of the Bernina glacier, towering over a metallic blue lake.

• *The old Romansh village of Bergün.*

• *Bernina Express, on the shores of Lake Blanc.*

• *Alp Grüm, 2,091m above sea level.*

UP, UP AND AWAY
– AND BACK DOWN AGAIN

This almost extraterrestrial landscape is where our rail journey reaches its highest point at Ospizio Bernina, at an altitude of 2,253m. Then it's downhill to the station of Alp Grüm, 2,091m above sea level, after which the train negotiates a 180° bend before starting its descent to Tirano. To lose height as quickly as possible, the Bernina Express enters a series of switchbacks. One of these is the spiral Brusio Viaduct, a loop in open country that typifies both the constraints and fixes inherent to this extraordinary line.

No stranger to unusual solutions, the Bernina Express completes its journey running side-by-side with cars, then rubbing shoulders with houses before it finally arrives at Tirano station.

• *Brusio spiral viaduct.*

• *The train crossing the curved Landwasser Viaduct.*

Alpnachstad → Pilatus-Kulm
In the land of dragons

on board the
PILATUSBAHN

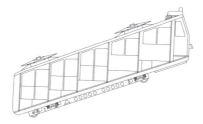

The world's steepest train.

Despite its diminutive size, Switzerland is an important rail nation and since 1889 it has been home to a very special train that epitomizes this paradox. This miniature red railcar scales the steep track from the village of Alpnachstad to the summit of Mount Pilatus on a gradient that can be as much as 48 per cent in places. This is a world record for a 'rack' railway line, so-called because of the rack-and-pinion system used to help the train climb steep inclines.

Opposite page: The Pilatusbahn reaches an altitude of 2,132m in just 30 minutes.

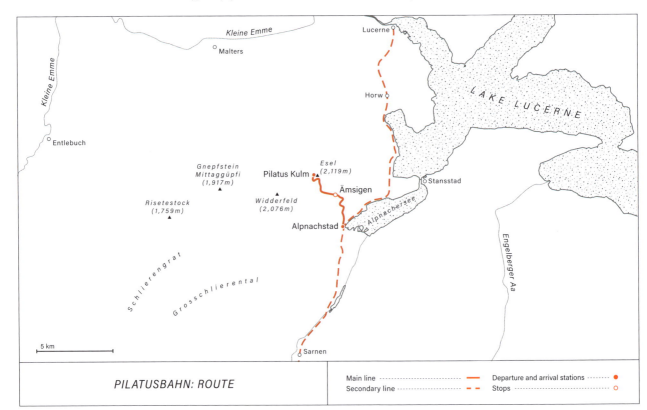

PILATUSBAHN: ROUTE

OPERATING SINCE
1889

JOURNEY LENGTH
30 mins

DISTANCE
4.6km

COUNTRIES VISITED
Switzerland

GRADIENT (PER CENT)
48

HEIGHT OF MOUNT PILATUS
2,132m

📢 **THE GORNERGRAT BAHN**

In Switzerland, there's another little rack-and-pinion train that's also well worth seeking out: the Gornergrat. This one starts from Zermatt and climbs to an altitude of 3,089m with uninterrupted views of the Matterhorn throughout.

OFF TO MOUNT PILATUS!

This short trip by train – just 30 minutes on the outward leg and 40 minutes for the return journey – begins at the Swiss station of Alpnachstad. You can't go wrong in this pleasant, flower-bedecked building on a cobbled square. It's only served by one small train, rather austere and spartan in its appearance. The bright red of its carriages is its sole redeeming feature. But don't be deceived: this little railcar with its sights set on Pilatus-Kulm, an activity centre perched some 2,132m above sea level, has many surprises in store for us.

▪ *Alpnachstad, village on the shores of Lake Lucerne.*

THE DRAGON'S LAIR

Unlike many other mountain trains, the rack railway on Mount Pilatus does not merely adapt to the contours of the landscape; it confronts them head-on. It climbs virtually straight up through forests and rock faces, tackling extremely sheer inclines with an average gradient of 35 per cent. At the steepest point, the gradient is as much as 48 per cent; in other words, the train climbs 48 metres for every 100 metres it travels. Inside the train, this is a truly thrilling sensation. We can almost feel the effort made by the mechanical creature transporting us to our destination. Did this beast's breath cause the mist hovering between the treetops? Or is it from the dragons as we disturb their lair? If local legend is to be believed, nothing is impossible.

▪ *Summit of Mount Pilatus (2,132m).*

▪ *View of Mount Pilatus.*

RELAX AND ENJOY THE VIEW

It's too late to turn back in any event, so we continue on our way. The surrounding vegetation becomes sparser, hugging the ground, then ultimately peters out to leave just a few patches of green plastered to the side of the mountain. From this point onwards, we pass through a kingdom of distorted rocks with ancient and convoluted folds. Take a look behind you – the view is staggering: the breadth and depth of the panorama quite simply takes your breath away. The pretty alpine cows we passed earlier are now merely dots in the distance. Turning back to face the direction of travel, we realize that we are about to arrive at Pilatus-Kulm. This isn't a town or even a village, but a rocky ledge, a starting point for a number of mountain trails such as the Flower Trail, the Dragon Path or a selection of more challenging hikes. This incredible vantage point also offers access to other cultural and sporting activities, but only one is mandatory: spend a few minutes soaking up the panoramic views, allow the beauty of the Alps to imprint itself on your memory and offer heartfelt thanks to the delightful little train for bringing us up here.

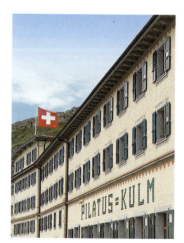

▪ *Hotel at the summit of Mount Pilatus.*

ALPNACHSTAD → PILATUS-KULM

• *Mount Pilatus cable car station.*

San Sebastián →
Santiago de Compostela
A pilgrimage by rail

on board the
TRANSCANTÁBRICO CLÁSICO

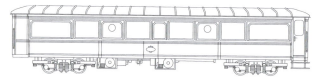

A luxury pilgrimage by train.

Covering eight days and seven nights, the route of the Transcantábrico Clásico feels more like a slice of life than a simple train journey. Over the course of slightly more than a week, this train whisks its passengers through a succession of towns, sights and fascinating discoveries, where the Spanish way of life, art and luxury are key.

Opposite page: Church of the Universidad Laboral, Gijón.

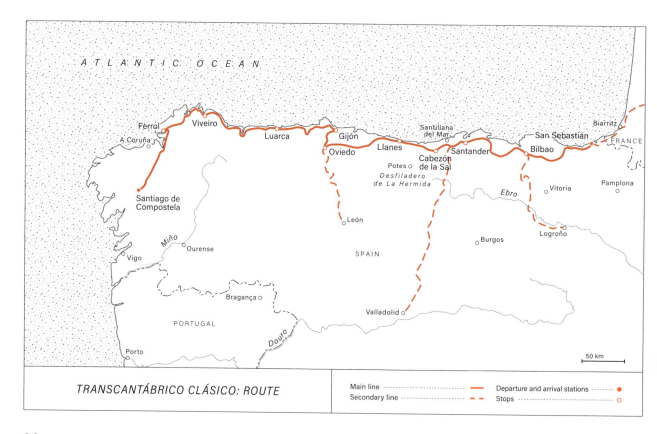

TRANSCANTÁBRICO CLÁSICO: ROUTE

EUROPE

OPERATING SINCE
1983

JOURNEY LENGTH
8 days, 7 nights

DISTANCE
667km

COUNTRIES VISITED
Spain

RANKING AMONG THE 25 BEST TRAINS IN THE WORLD
25

🔊 ONE OF THE WORLD'S BEST LUXURY TRAINS

Established in 1983, the Transcantábrico Clásico was ranked by the Society of International Railway Travellers as one of the 25 best trains in the world in 2009. What sets it apart from the rest? The rich and varied points of interest on its itinerary, the stylish 1920s carriages and the impeccable service offered throughout.

• *Playa de la Concha, in San Sebastián.*

ALONG THE COSTA VERDE

Exceptionally, this particular train journey begins with a coach trip. After greeting us in San Sebastián in the contemporary comfort of the Hotel Barceló Costa Vasca and showing us around this glorious town set around La Concha bay, the Transcantábrico Clásico team then transport us to Bilbao in a luxury coach. It is here we join our train, now raring to explore the four autonomous provinces of the Costa Verde – the Basque Country, Cantabria, Asturias and Galicia – and sample their delights, *maravillas* in Spanish.

A LUXURY TRAIN – SPANISH-STYLE

The feeling of relief we experience on boarding the train after a welcome drink is immense. The fine wood-panelled walls, sumptuous carpets and beautifully curated furniture of the four lounge cars immediately vanquish the memory of that surprise coach journey. Once settled in our suite, the feeling of relief is even ousted by a sudden surge of pleasure. Clad from floor to ceiling in marquetry, our cabin inspires the urge to lie back on the delightful damask-covered sofa or the enormous bed with its many cushions. Or even to jump in the shower. Like many of the world's inhabitants, this is something we've probably never done on a train before. Eventually, our luxury convoy departs for Carranza, enabling us to enjoy our first dinner on board, followed by an evening's seasonal entertainment. Next morning, after breakfast in our cabin or in the buffet car, we go back to Bilbao for another guided tour. In the professional hands of the train's personal guide, our day includes a visit to the famous Guggenheim Museum, stunning both inside and out. We then return to the Transcantábrico Clásico and continue on to Santander, capital of Cantabria, where we also have the chance to explore. After visiting the cathedral, the Royal Palace and the intriguing Centro Botín, we can't resist trying our luck in the Grand Casino or relaxing on the splendid beach.

• *Bilbao, large port and financial centre.*

• *Carranza Valley in the Basque Country.*

• *As Catedrais beach near Ribadeo.*

A MANY-SPLENDOURED ROUTE

Over the next few days, the *maravillas*, or delights, of our route will become apparent – all very different. The medieval village of Potes, tucked away in the Hermida Gorge and its nearby thermal baths. The Palace of El Capricho, designed by renowned Catalan architect Antoni Gaudí in Comillas. The incredible historic town centre of Santillana del Mar. The Cave of Altamira, home to outstanding examples of cave art dating back to the Upper Paleolithic era. Then there's the Principality of Asturias, also stunning but not widely known, fittingly represented by its two main cities: Oviedo, an elegant inland centre, and Gijón, its laid-back coastal counterpart.

The train then continues along the Costa Verde to the town of Ribadeo, from where a short bus ride takes us to As Catedrais (Cathedrals) beach. Hugging the shores of the Cantabrian Sea, this is no place of worship, however. The beach's romantic name originates from the spectacular rock structures hewn out of the cliff. The next day, the Transcantábrico Clásico takes us to Viveiro where the River Landro flows into the sea. It's also our last night on board the train. The following morning, the train will reach its terminus at Ferrol, where another coach will be waiting to take us to Santiago de Compostela. This final stage is no less beautiful than the rest of this pilgrimage to the wonders of Northern Spain.

• *The prehistoric Cave of Altamira.*

94

▪ *Gijón, famous for its port and old fishing district.*

EUROPE

Lleida → La Pobla de Segur
The magic of the lakes

on board the
TREN DELS LLACS

Explore the splendours of Catalonia by train.

Covering a distance of just 89km, the Tren dels Llacs (Train of the Lakes) crosses 40 bridges, goes through 75 tunnels and passes four huge lakes. An extraordinary route through the spectacular natural countryside of the little-known regions of Segrià, Noguera and Pallars Jussà.

Opposite page: Sant Antoni, a man-made lake.

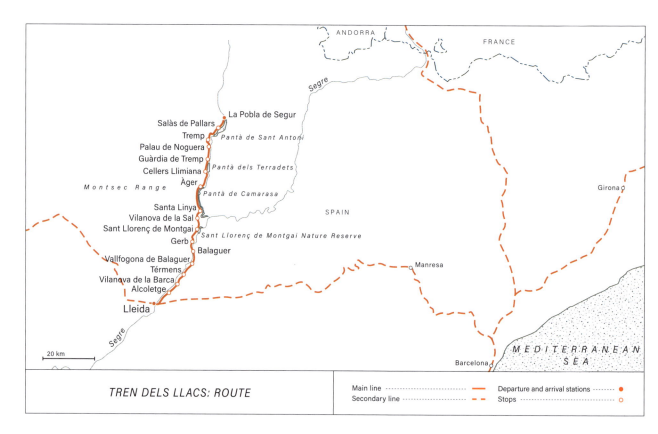

TREN DELS LLACS: ROUTE

EUROPE

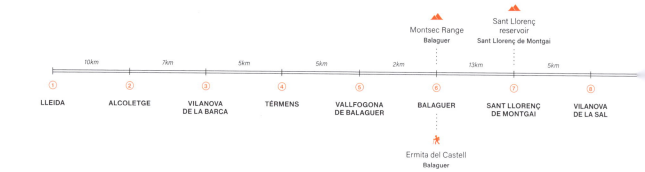

OPERATING SINCE	
2005	
JOURNEY LENGTH	
2 hours	
DISTANCE	
89km	
COUNTRIES VISITED	
Spain	

MOUNTAINS AND WATER

While some trains have names that give you pause for thought, others are crystal-clear. The Tren dels Llacs falls into the second group as, true to its Catalan name, it transports its passengers to an area where lakes are the rule rather than the exception. The Catalan government, in the form of Ferrocarrils de la generalitat de Catalunya, took control of the line in 2005, but the glorious views played no part in their decision. It was merely regarded as one section of the international rail project between Andalusia and Ariège. The project was never completed and the line was restricted in length to a handful of stunning lakes – very much to our advantage. Lleida or Lerida? Catalan or Castilian Spanish? This ongoing debate has its roots in the depths of contemporary Spanish history but needn't bother us unduly. Whichever you opt for, the town is well worth a second glance. Work on building the cathedral began in the 8th century, on the ruins of a mosque; its fortress is said to date back to the Knights Templar and its sloping terraces make it a perfect place to feast your eyes and your taste buds. As we board this train from another era, we are greeted by a troupe of actors in costume – the perfect relaxing start to our journey.

▪ *Lleida, on the River Segre.*

▪ *Plaza de Sant Joan, Lleida.*

▪ *Colegiata de Santa Maria, Balaguer.*

▪ *The Montsec mountain range, bisected by the River Noguera.*

WATER, WATER, EVERYWHERE

The first leg of our trip follows the River Segre. This tributary of the River Ebro is 265km long and will accompany us for the first part of our two-hour journey. There are 15 other stations on the route in addition to its departure point and terminus. Some we pass without stopping: Alcoletge, Vilanova de la Barca, Térmens, Vallfogona de Balaguer. Don't expect to see any urban sights on this line. It is not called the Tren dels Llacs for no reason; there are lakes and mountains as far as the eye can see.

The scenery changes as we reach Balaguer, with the plains filled with fruit trees irrigated by the waters of the Segre giving way to the jagged Montsec mountains, bisected by the Noguera Pallaresa. Like the Segre, this river used to define the train's route back in the days when its engineers were hoping to connect the South of Spain with the South of France.

LLEIDA → LA POBLA DE SEGUR

LAKES A-PLENTY

The first lake we see on our journey is the reservoir of Sant Llorenç de Montgai. This forms an integral part of the nature reserve of the same name and was dammed to store 10 cubic hectares of water at a very high level. This ample water supply and the presence of a number of reed beds attract many species of aquatic birds to the area. Human visitors will also find plenty to keep them busy, since the mountainous terrain around the lake lends itself to cycling, rock climbing or hiking and the lake itself is perfect for kayaking. An honourable mention should go to the trail (not for beginners!) that leads to the Ermita del Castell, a late 12th-century hermitage with stunning views of the mountains and the mist below.

Sant Llorenç de Montgai reservoir.

Next in line is Lake Camarasa, some 20km in length, running along the Montsec mountain range to the confluence of the Segre and Noguera Pallaresa rivers, our watery companions until this point. This lake is not unlike a Scottish loch; in its waters you might be lucky enough to spot the shadows of huge carp, largemouth bass and barbels. You may even hit the jackpot and see a couple of otters playing in the shallows, under the patient gaze of Eurasian griffon vultures. The train chugs along at its own pace, a clunky but charming old thing, without the slightest ambition to be a record breaker.

🔊 SALT MINING HISTORY

This Catalan region was previously home to many salt mines and was known for being as poor as it was difficult to access. When the Tren dels Llacs was first built, this injected fresh blood into the area and boosted its image. However, this resurgence came at a price; the countryside had to be reshaped to fit the new brief. Labourers had to drain wetlands, excavate entire valley sides and blast their way through mountains to construct the necessary bridges and tunnels.

MARSHLAND

The Tren dels Llacs' next port of call is Lake Cellers, which shares its name with the only urban settlement on its shores. It is also known as Terradets reservoir, mainly because the gorges with the same name are also located here, closeby this 330-hectare body of water. Man's footprint is once again in evidence here, with the construction of a dam, but the marshy end of the reservoir bucks the trend, firmly resisting human attempt to tame it.

The lake covers an area of some 112 hectares of abandoned meandering waterways and tiny wayward lagoons fringed with willows and poplars, home to huge catfish, dainty egrets and ruthless marsh harriers.

Last but not least, the Sant Antoni reservoir. Regarded as one of the largest freshwater resources in Catalonia, it is 11km long and surrounded by dense and beautiful forests. There are a number of beaches too, where you can walk, fish, swim or just work on your tan. You can never tire of this superb view; make the most of it as we cover the final few kilometres to La Pobla de Segur.

Terradets reservoir, on the River Noguera.

Sant Antoni reservoir, created by human hand.

Porto → Pocinho
The promise of a vineyard

on board the
LINHA DO DOURO

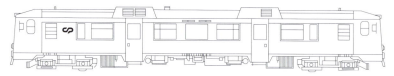

Train ride along the Douro valley.

The Linha do Douro is all that remains of an ambitious rail project dating back to the end of the 19th century. Opened in individual sections that the Portuguese authorities closed and reopened as the state of the economy dictated, nowadays it forms the gateway to one of the most scenic regions in this small Iberian country.

Opposite page: Terraced vineyards at Peso da Régua.

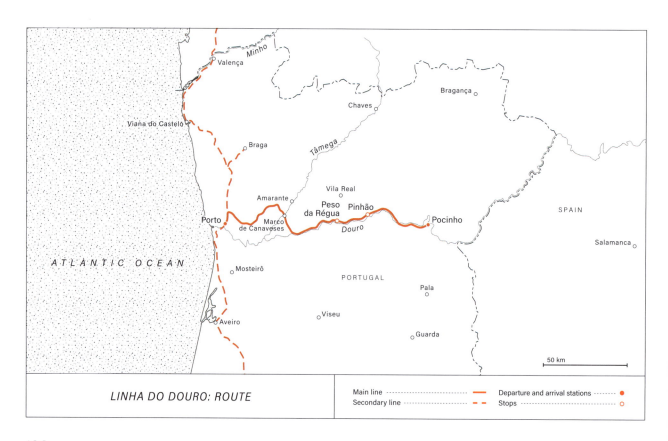

EUROPE

① PORTO

② PESO DA RÉGUA

100km

CONSTRUCTION BEGAN IN
1887

JOURNEY LENGTH
3 hours 20 mins

DISTANCE
170km

COUNTRIES VISITED
Portugal

LENGTH OF THE FERRADOSA BRIDGE
375m

NUMBER OF BRIDGES
40

NUMBER OF TUNNELS
75

- *Bird's eye view of Porto.*

PORTO, CITY OF MANY BRIDGES

The Douro is part and parcel of Porto's identity. This river has been inextricably linked with the city since time immemorial, criss-crossing it, providing it with water and bringing it to life. The city has returned the favour many times over. It reserves its finest treasures for the riverside, such as the unforgettable Ribeira district. Then there are the bridges, so many bridges, all serving to glorify the river. The grandest of them all has to be the Ponte Dom Luís I, closely followed by the Ponte Maria Pia, both constructed by Gustave Eiffel and one of his disciples, Théophile Seyrig, during the 1880s. So it's hardly surprising that we'll be following the course of this river as we leave Porto.

Our journey begins in a station that is an attraction in its own right: Porto São Bento. Inaugurated in 1896, it really is a sight to behold. With its high ceilings and beautiful glazed arches, the station concourse is clad in large azulejo tiles representing scenes of daily life and episodes in Portugal's history. Our heads filled with pretty pictures, we board our train, which sets off at a modest pace, but before too long, a sudden jolt makes us look up to behold a magnificent view. Behind us we can see the Ponte Dom Luís I and the Ponte Infante Dom Henrique. Ahead there's the Ponte Maria Pia and the Ponte de São João.

- *Vintage trams in Porto.*

- *The Douro Valley, centre of the port-producing industry.*

- *Above the Douro.*

THE INEXORABLE APPEAL OF THE RIVER

For the first part of the journey, the train trundles through Porto's vast residential area. This urban sprawl is only alleviated every now and again by little flashes of nature, like when we cross the Tâmega, just before the city of Marco de Canaveses, but green starts to dominate the further we travel. At Pala, the Douro suddenly comes into view and we remain with it until Pocinho. At Mosteirô, the line succumbs to the inexorable call of the river and plunges deep into the wine region that bears its name, which became a UNESCO World Heritage Site in 2001. This is where the magic begins.

Before us, the blue river appears vast, bottomless. We can almost touch it as we run alongside. Just a few more centimetres and a final push and we'd be able to trail our fingers in the water as we pass... On the other bank, a vast forest descends right to the shoreline. Hamlets and villages vanish as fast as they appear in the midst of its all-encompassing green swathe. Same story on the other side, but we'll never know as our eyes are glued to the river. From time to time, the Douro becomes wider, only to narrow again a few kilometres upstream. Are the mountains yielding to let the mighty river past or is the river carving out their lower slopes? Geologists are sure to have an answer, but for us the question remains unresolved – a poetic conundrum.

PORTO → POCINHO

PINHÃO

POCINHO

25km   45km

• Peso da Régua station with its decorative azulejo tiles.

THE RIVER AT OUR FEET

After two hours or so we arrive at Peso da Régua and its pretty little station clad in the distinctive azulejo tiles with their geometric patterns. There's a sudden influx of passengers at this point, keen to see what's set to be the finest section of the line. The Douro is still omnipresent, virtually at our feet. From time to time, a cruise ship tries in vain to race our train before vanishing from view. Just as we arrive at Pinhão station, a second ship comes into sight. We may not be going quite as fast as when we set out, but the ship is still no match for our train as we pull into the charming station, where large canopies protect 20 or so friezes of azulejo tiles depicting local landscapes.

📢 ALL YEAR ROUND

Trains operate on the Linha do Douro all year round, but there's a steam train between Régua and Pocinho during the summer months. The perfect way to slow down and turn back the clock as you enjoy this fascinating and scenic route.

VINEYARDS AS FAR AS THE EYE CAN SEE

As you look further afield, beyond the River Douro, the hillsides are no longer untouched by human hand. They have been crafted to form wide terraces where the renowned vineyards of this region thrive. Their distinctive ridges populate the horizon, for all the world like the striped furry coat of a giant sleeping animal. The Douro appellation goes back to 1756 and two wines are produced in the region: port and Douro.

As the valley narrows further, it begins to resemble a canyon, the perfect setting for an adventure film. Rock makes its presence increasingly felt and the vegetation becomes sparser, more suited to arid conditions. Adaptation is key and as soon as the conditions become more propitious, it explodes into growth once again. When the landscape permits, terraces burst forth between the trees and shrubs. The train, however, crosses the river via the Ferradosa railway bridge, 375m long and 7m wide, but there's no need to worry: the stunning scenery we've been enjoying for the past hour or so, keeps on coming, ringing the changes as we progress. Rock, trees, terraces, more trees, rock, glimpses of mountains in the background... with the river flowing through the middle of it all. Here and there, another pretty little station with its azulejo tiles, boats tooting their horn

• Pocinho station, the end of the line.

as we pass. Our final destination lies in the middle of nowhere, at Pocinho, fulfilling the promise of our journey.

103

Kalavryta → Diakopto
A view that rocks

on board the
ODONTOTOS RACK RAILWAY

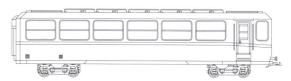

Snaking along the rock face.

With its 0.75m gauge, the Odontotos Rack Railway is currently regarded as the narrowest public railway line in the world. This is due to the extraordinary way it links Kalavryta and Diakopto through the mountains of the Northern Peloponnese.

Opposite page: Vouraikos Gorge, home to the river that ultimately flows into the Gulf of Corinth.

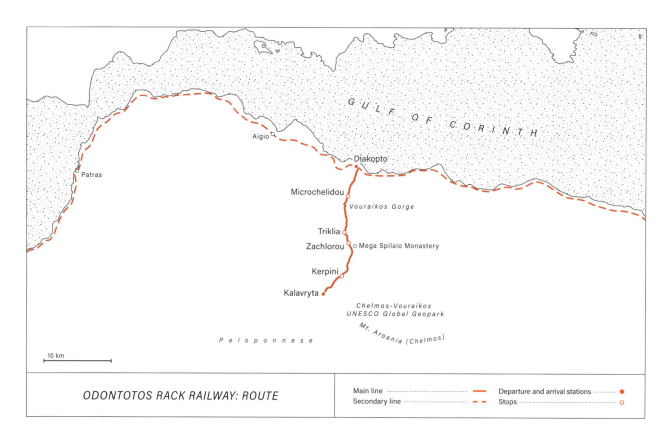

ODONTOTOS RACK RAILWAY: ROUTE

Main line ———
Secondary line - - - -
Departure and arrival stations ●
Stops ○

OPERATING SINCE
1896

JOURNEY LENGTH
1 hour

DISTANCE
22.35km

COUNTRIES VISITED
Greece

📢 **GATEWAY TO THE GREEK UNDERWORLD**

In Greek mythology, the River Styx, which separates the Underworld from the world of the living, rises in the Chelmos mountains. Bold explorers may well be able to track it down during this voyage of discovery.

GREECE'S BEST-KEPT SECRET

Unless you spend all your holidays exploring Greece, it's very unlikely that you'll have come across Kalavryta. Located in the heart of the 544-m² Chelmos-Vouraikos National Park, this village is one of the best-kept secrets of this country so beloved of tourists. When the mercury climbs, its cooler climate can be a boon, but in the winter months it becomes a winter sports resort the minute snow arrives in the Chelmos mountains. With fewer than 2,000 residents, the village has a tranquil atmosphere and a selection of little tavernas squeezed between the usual tourist traps; it also boasts UNESCO World Heritage status for its surrounding natural environment. As a bonus, this peaceful little holiday destination has a most unusual and attractive railway that makes its way to Diakopto every single day of the year, no matter what the weather or the season.

• *Chapel in the Kalavryta ski resort.*

• *The Odontotos line in the Vouraikos Gorge.*

A GORGE-SIDE VIEW

When the little train leaves the modest, tree-shaded station in Kalavryta, most passengers probably don't have a clue what lies ahead of them on the Odontotos Rack Railway. After all, the stats don't give anything away, merely suggesting a 22.35-km journey taking just over an hour. In theory, just enough time for a little snooze before we reach the coast. Yet it would be a big mistake to doze off on this train, as the narrowness of the track makes it quite simply spectacular.

The Odontotos Rack Railway really is one long close encounter between metal and the rock of the Vouraikos Gorge. The two elements seem to become one, moving apart now and again only to resume their embrace shortly after. During the descent, the train plunges into six tunnels, emerging briefly to skirt the mountain as it snakes along the steep slopes overhanging the waters of the river way down below. Some passages are so narrow that they appear to be plummeting into the very bowels of the Earth before the train sees the light of day once more, offering us a welcome glimpse of the rugged beauty of the landscape, so very different from the cerulean blue waters of traditional Greek beach scenes.

• *Church of the Assumption of the Theotokos, Kalavryta.*

• *Station in the tiny village of Zachlorou.*

A PILGRIMAGE FULL OF GRACE

Suddenly, we are plunged back into the human world as we arrive in the tiny village of Zachlorou. Although there are no roads of any note leading here, this humble human enclave surrounded by Nature's glory is worth a stop purely to immerse yourself in its other-worldly atmosphere and visit the Mega Spilaio Greek Orthodox monastery. Regarded as the oldest in the country, this sanctuary is said to have been built in the 4th century in a cave where monks are alleged to have discovered an icon of the Virgin Mary painted by Luke the Evangelist. Whether you're religious or not, the grace embodied in this beautiful place is sure to touch your soul.

Then it's back to the train for the last stage of the journey to Diakopto, savouring every last glimpse of this exquisite landscape. On arrival, after a bite to eat to take the edge off our hunger – the Greeks do this so well – we have two choices. Hardy souls may be inspired to head for the port, surrounded by towering mountains, to continue their journey by sea. Others, still stunned by the formidable beauty of their rail excursion, may be tempted to stretch out on the long beaches fringing the Gulf of Corinth. As we said at the outset, this may be a short trip, but no less sweet for all that.

Steep sides of the Vouraikos Gorge.

EUROPE

Belgrade → Bar
In the heart of former Yugoslavia

on board the
BELGRADE-BAR RAILWAY

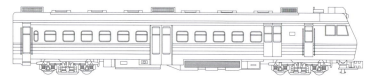

A legendary train of no name.

Unlike many of its counterparts, the Belgrade-Bar railway has never been referred to as anything else: no romantic names or nicknames here. Some put this down to its origins in the heart of Yugoslavia, ruled with a rod of iron by dictator Tito, who certainly wasn't renowned for his love of poetry. No matter, this line is an absolute must for lovers of rail travel on the Old Continent.

Opposite page: The Morača valley, near Podgorica in Montenegro.

BELGRADE-BAR RAILWAY: ROUTE

108

EUROPE

Tito's blue train
Belgrade

① BELGRADE — 60km — ② LAZAREVAC — 35km — ③ VALJEVO — 80km — ④ POŽEGA — 130km — ⑤ PRIJEPOLJE

OPERATING SINCE
1976

JOURNEY LENGTH
11 hours

DISTANCE
476km

COUNTRIES VISITED
**Serbia
Bosnia and
Herzegovina
Montenegro**

NUMBER OF TUNNELS
254

NUMBER OF BRIDGES
435

LENGTH OF MALA
RIJEKA VIADUCT
498.80m

• *Belgrade's railway station.*

DAY OR NIGHT?

There are two ways of travelling by train from Belgrade, capital of Serbia, to Bar, on Montenegro's Adriatic coast: by day or by night. During the summer season, the daytime train – which departs at 9am and arrives at 8pm – is by far the best option as it means the journey takes advantage of the beautiful Balkan light from start to finish. Paradoxically, in winter, the night train is the better bet. Leaving at 9pm and getting in at 8am, this service shows the finest parts of the 476-km journey in their best light. This is good to know as the route between Belgrade and Bar is packed with treasures. As is often the case when a train departs from a large town or capital city, the first part of the journey inevitably involves passing through the urban outskirts. Belgrade's are no different from many others, but they do have one notable feature. During the first few kilometres, if we look carefully, we may be able to spot the personal train of Yugoslavia's dictator, Josip Broz, otherwise known as Tito, alongside the track – a metallic hulk bearing witness to the excesses of the former ruler of Yugoslavia.

• *Belgrade, capital of Serbia.*

DEEP IN THE MOUNTAINS

We have to wait until we pass Valjevo, start of the mountainous stretch, before the natural splendours of our route start in earnest. From this point on, they fill every inch of our gaze, imposing in their stature. Sometimes, they're so close that we have no choice but to negotiate them via one of the 254 tunnels or 435 bridges on the line. At other times, they are so far away that the sky is barely visible on the horizon above these verdant giants. After exiting one of these splendid engineering masterpieces, the Zlatibor tunnel, we pass through Bosnia and Herzegovina for 9km without any sign of passport control.

We then trundle rhythmically on to Potpeć Lake, formed by a dam on the River Lim, its waters varying from a tropical turquoise to a stormy petrol blue according to the season. Still deep in the mountains, a church might occasionally appear in a cluster of buildings making up a village, or a monastery with the typical architecture of this region. The very fact that they are there seems to halt time for all that surrounds them, but our train manages to escape, continuing its climb to the highest point on the line.

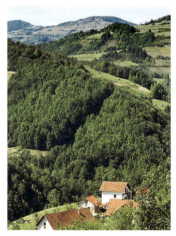

• *Mountainous terrain in Serbia.*

110

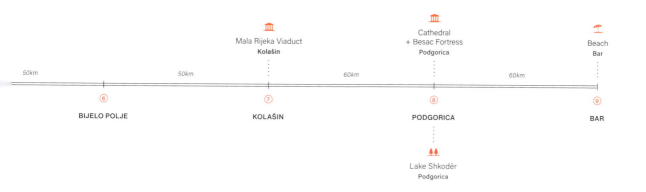

A GIANT ON THE RIVER

After crossing the border to Montenegro, we finally reach the highest point, just over 1,000m above sea level, a mere stone's throw from Kolašin. Now our field of vision is taken up by spectacular grey mountains, punctuated only sparsely by narrow green corridors, becoming denser as they near the blue ribbon of the river. As we head back down, we end up crossing the river by a veritable giant, some 498.80m long and 200m high: the Mala Rijeka Viaduct. With a tunnel on each side, this feat of engineering is impressive not only due to its height, but also its antiquated design. It was once the highest railway viaduct in the world, measured from the valley floor.

We carry on downwards, a peaceful, languorous descent. The mountains are not as tall here as we leave the peaks further and further behind. One last glimpse, then the mountainous landscape disappears for a while, giving way to the city of Podgorica, the little-known capital of Montenegro, with its ancient Ottoman-influenced centre, ultra-modern cathedral and notable bridges, including the distinctive Millennium Bridge and the lesser-known Ribnica.

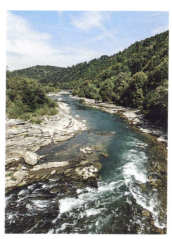

▪ The wild reaches of the River Lim in Montenegro.

📢 INCORRECT MATHS OR AGE-OLD DISPUTE?

A mathematical mystery hangs over the Belgrade-Bar line. Officially 476km long, the route winds through Serbia for 301km and covers a further 175km in Montenegro. There's just one problem: the line also clips a corner of Bosnia and Herzegovina for 9km. Miscalculation or age-old dispute between the relatively new states? It doesn't really matter – but it says a lot about the deep-rooted ties between the various Balkan territories.

▪ The Crnojevica valley, near Lake Shkodër.

SEA AND MOUNTAINS

Our route continues, this time past the breathtakingly beautiful Lake Shkodër, also known as Lake Skadar. One superlative too far, you might think? By no means: just take a tour of the national park around the lake to realize this is a very fitting epithet. This is an absolute paradise for keen birdwatchers and nature-lovers with waterlily-strewn lakes and forest-clad hills. For a bird's eye view of this European jungle, a gentle climb up to the fortress of Besac will suffice. Constructed by the Ottoman settlers, this structure became a prison in the Second World War.

Then it's back to our train for the final stage of our journey along the Adriatic coastline. The vegetation on this stretch is very different to what we've seen before. Mediterranean culture starts to hold sway, becoming omnipresent. The blue of the sea, the shape of the houses, people's faces – fascinating to see as we approach our destination. And finally, 11 hours after we set out, we arrive in Bar, with its long beach and ruined buildings with their mountainous backdrop – still with us after all this time.

▪ The Ottoman fortress at Besac.

111

Africa

9 TRAIN JOURNEYS
10 countries
Nature at its well-preserved and beautiful best – by train
FROM CAIRO TO VICTORIA FALLS

① **Cairo → Luxor → Aswan**
CAIRO-ASWAN SLEEPER
p. 114

② **Cairo → Alexandria**
CAIRO-ALEXANDRIA LINE
p. 118

③ **Tangier → Casablanca**
AL BORAQ
p. 122

④ **Choum → Zouérat**
DESERT TRAIN
p. 126

⑤ **Cotonou → Parakou**
EBONY TRAIN
p. 130

⑥ **Nairobi → Mombasa**
MADARAKA EXPRESS
p. 134

⑦ **Dar es Salaam → Lobito**
TRAIL OF TWO OCEANS
p. 138

⑧ **Pretoria → Cape Town**
BLUE TRAIN
p. 142

⑨ **Pretoria → Victoria Falls**
PRIDE OF AFRICA
p. 146

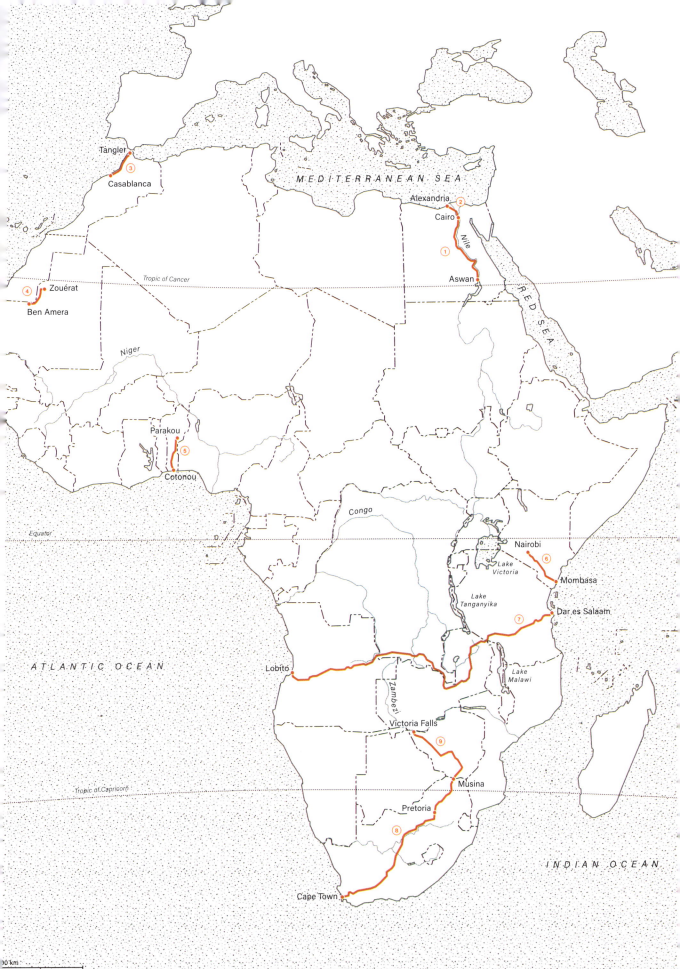

Cairo → Luxor → Aswan
A railroad through ancient Egypt

on board the
CAIRO-ASWAN SLEEPER

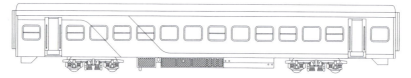

By train through the Wonders of the Pharaohs.

There are very few countries with a cultural heritage as globally renowned as Egypt's. An endless source of inspiration for artists, this place and its unparalleled history exert a magnetic force on the rest of us. You might think the only way to visit is via tour operators or guided tours – but you'd be wrong. There just happens to be a train that links three of the main cities in Egypt; the perfect introduction to the country.

Opposite page: Cairo, largest megalopolis in Africa.

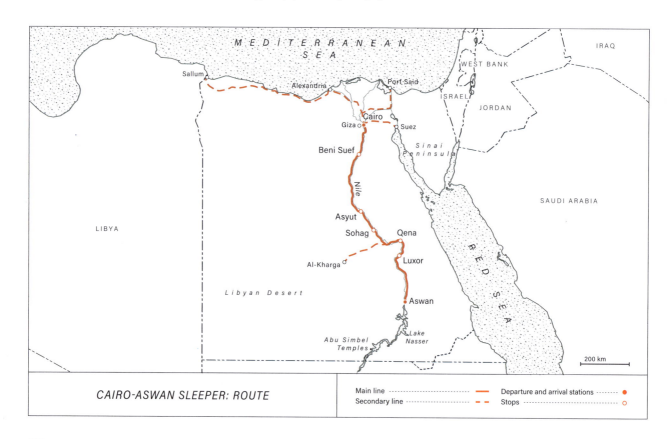

CAIRO-ASWAN SLEEPER: ROUTE

Main line ·············· —
Secondary line ·············· – –
Departure and arrival stations ·············· ●
Stops ·············· ○

114

AFRICA

CONSTRUCTED
1856

JOURNEY LENGTH
13 hours (1 night)

DISTANCE
472km

COUNTRIES VISITED
Egypt

📢 **TOURISM IS VITAL BUT CAN BE DANGEROUS**

Tourism may be one of the country's main sources of income, but it has long been the source of dubious and rather dangerous practices to the detriment of Egypt's cultural legacy, to say nothing of tourists themselves, animals and local people. This is why, in recent years, the government took the decision to ban anyone from climbing on the monuments and visiting the sites on animals in a bid to promote animal welfare. It goes without saying that it's down to visitors to back up this stance.

IN THE FOOTSTEPS OF THE PHARAOHS

Cairo is a hectic city by day and by night with its incessant noise and traffic jams – enough to make anyone feel like a tiny worker bee in a huge hive. In the distance, a few kilometres beyond the last shanty towns of the Egyptian capital, is the famous site of Giza, its noble pyramids, forgotten burial grounds and of course the famous Sphinx, font of all wisdom. This city is where we commence our journey to Luxor and Aswan.

• The Nile, Cairo's main artery.

• A felucca, one of the traditional Nile sailing boats.

A SLOW PASSAGE ALONG THE NILE

After the mandatory and unforgettable tour of the famous monuments mentioned above, we spend the late afternoon fighting our way through the barrage of street vendors surrounding the station before we can board our train. The train itself is fairly simple, by no means luxurious, but certainly not spartan either. The cabins have two bunk beds, the lower berth turning into seats during the day. They are on a par with the night trains found in Europe, America or Asia. The atmosphere on board is very different to the bustling city alongside. It takes us some time to leave the city limits, so vast is its sprawl – and when we finally escape, nightfall is almost upon us. Just as we espy a few palm-tree-fringed fields in the gloom, darkness falls over our train and the Nile Valley.

At 6 o'clock the next morning, we awaken to find the delights of Luxor beckoning beyond our carriage. After a tasty breakfast in one of the city's many cafés and a gentle stroll along the banks of the Nile, we head straight for the Temple of Amun. This monument is missing an obelisk, now to be found on the Place de la Concorde in Paris. Time permitting, there are a number of options to choose from, all wondrous in their own right: the Karnak temple complex, the tombs in the Valleys of the Kings and Queens, the temple of Ramses II and the Memorial Temple of Hatshepsut, and, last but not least, the Colossi of Memnon. Those with more time on their hands may even consider taking a cruise on a felucca, one of the traditional sailing boats that ply their trade along the river.

• Temple of Abu Simbel, built by Ramses II.

AN ETERNAL STRUGGLE

New destination, new train. This time we are bound for Aswan. Ensconced in comfortable seats with plenty of room to stretch our legs, we watch plantation after plantation of sugar cane pass by, along with fields of a luminous green, the crops flourishing in this soil nurtured by the sacred river of the ancient Egyptians. Insatiable monster that it is, the desert is never far from view. From time to time it makes its presence felt, dry, crouching under the sun's burning rays, ready to engulf anything created by mankind. Tall trees flash before our windows at irregular intervals, providing shade for men and animals in search of respite from the scorching sun.

Then it's back to the sand monster: desert everywhere, as far as the eye can see. Lofty palm trees are the only vegetation able to withstand its grip, providing small green oases. Otherwise, just rocks and extreme aridity: stereotypical Egypt as it appears to the rest of the world, be it in books or documentaries. An eternal struggle between the forces of luxuriant nature and those of aridity. Eventually, we arrive at Aswan station. As we leave the train, we are assailed by light and heat. The sound of the muezzin calling people to prayer ricochets off the light-coloured walls of the houses and pursues us as we head for the city's treasures. While slightly less well known than the sights in Cairo and Luxor, the temples of Abu Simbel and Philae are still hugely important and unmissable monuments to Egyptian history.

• The Egyptian desert alongside the Nile.

116

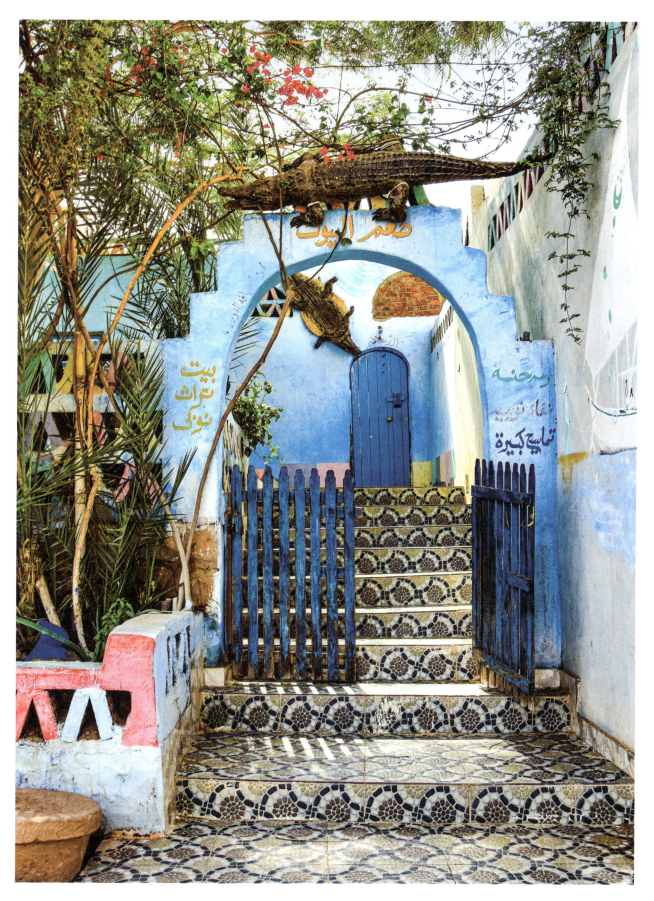

Nubian house, Aswan.

Cairo → Alexandria
The fast train to Alexandria

on the
CAIRO-ALEXANDRIA LINE

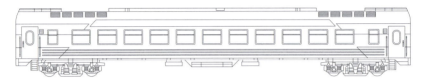

A train journey across Egypt's fertile plains.

While Alexandria's lighthouse and library are no more, the city itself still stands. Founded in 332 BC on the orders of Alexander the Great, for many years it was one of the greatest cultural and intellectual centres in the Mediterranean basin. Nowadays it's an attractive and cosmopolitan city that has lost none of its historical charm. Just two and a half hours from Cairo, it is a delightful choice for an excursion by train.

Opposite page: The River Nile in Cairo, a vibrant and well-used river.

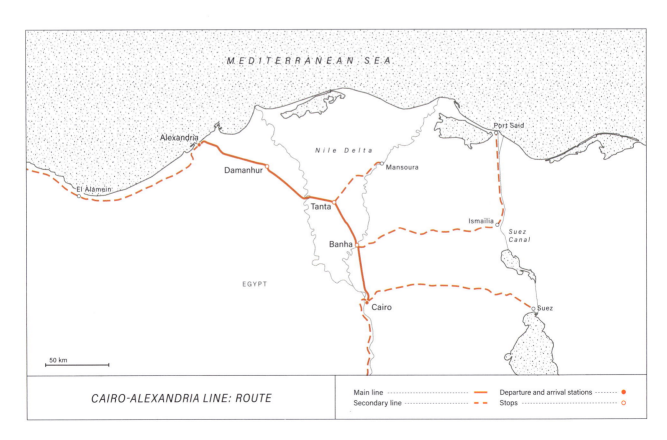

CAIRO-ALEXANDRIA LINE: ROUTE

Main line — Departure and arrival stations ●
Secondary line -- Stops ○

CONSTRUCTED
1856

JOURNEY LENGTH
2 hours 30 mins

DISTANCE
220km

COUNTRIES VISITED
Egypt

LOSS OF A WONDER

Commissioned in 297 BC by Ptolemy I and completed under the reign of Ptolemy II, the Lighthouse of Alexandria was one of the Seven Wonders of the Ancient World before it was destroyed by a series of earthquakes. It was reckoned to be some 130m high and its name, Pharos, is still the base of the words used to refer to lighthouses in many parts of the world. It was in fact located on the former island of Pharos, now a peninsula.

• *Ramses station in Cairo.*

AN ANCIENT JOURNEY

This journey between Egypt's two most iconic cities starts in Cairo's Ramses station. Beneath the inverted pyramid suspended from the ceiling of the concourse, surrounded by walls as magnificent as they are pretentious, a departure board shows platform information for our train. In its white livery bearing stripes in the three colours of the Egyptian flag, the train looks a little old-fashioned, but what it lacks in style, it makes up for in the comfort of its crimson seats.

All around us, the outskirts of Cairo seem interminable, almost as though they are moving with us. On they go, district after district, building after pastel-coloured building, offering glimpses of everyday Egyptian life. Children playing on waste ground, men weighed down by heavy loads, women firmly at the helm of their family units. Eternal images, caricatures even, but with their roots in reality. Our urban daydreaming comes to an abrupt halt when two affable gentlemen pass through the carriage to check our tickets, closely followed by another sporting a waistcoat in the exact same shade as the seats and pushing a trolley laden with food and drink.

FERTILE GROUND

After leaving the urban sprawl of Cairo, we are now passing through the vast agricultural region between the two cities. Fields in various shades of green and yellow disappear into the distance. From the train windows, they appear to be divided entirely at random, but this is doubtless down to crop rotation, common law, disputes between neighbours or even the presence of a long-forgotten wall. In this part of Egypt, agriculture has been in existence since time immemorial. We are in the area known as the Nile Delta, acknowledged as one of the most fertile regions on the planet. All the more reason why one of the world's greatest civilizations should have grown up here.

• *The Nile Delta, a fertile farming area for many thousands of years.*

• *New Library of Alexandria.*

• *Ras El Tin Palace, jewel of Alexandria.*

A BEACON IN THE DARKNESS

This vast expanse of farmland is our companion for most of the journey. It too offers us a window onto the country's way of life. Here we see farms and isolated buildings, people working in the fields and evidence of water management. The towns here are no longer suburbs of the capital; they are simply oases in a sea of green. And yet the sea and Alexandria are just around the corner. We can sense their presence by the increasing urban density and the sudden sighting of a motorway between the rail tracks and the farmland.

This time, Alexandria, with its many towers and minarets, is upon us in a matter of minutes. As we leave the train, we can smell the sea, its presence on the horizon unmistakeable from the square outside Alexandria's elegant station. Now all that remains is to stride out to the coast, take a walk along the seafront and explore the 15th-century Citadel of Qaitbay , the fascinating catacombs of Kom el Shoqafa (dating back to the first century), Ras El Tin Palace (1847) or the new Library of Alexandria, opened in 2002 and built on the ruins of its predecessor. It contains some four million titles.

• Alexandria, city of many parts, home to 4 million inhabitants on the Mediterranean coast.

Tangier → Casablanca
The shining light of Morocco

on board
AL BORAQ

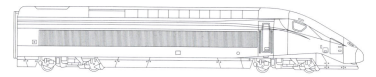

Africa's first high-speed train.

Launched in 2018, Al Boraq hurtles through Morocco from Tangier to Casablanca on a line covering 350 kilometres, 200 of which are passable at a speed of 320km/h. This is the first genuine high-speed line on the African continent, using rail technology that could transform mobility in this part of the world, while still offering a beautiful journey through the Kingdom of Morocco.

Opposite page: Hassan II Mosque, Casablanca, completed in 1993.

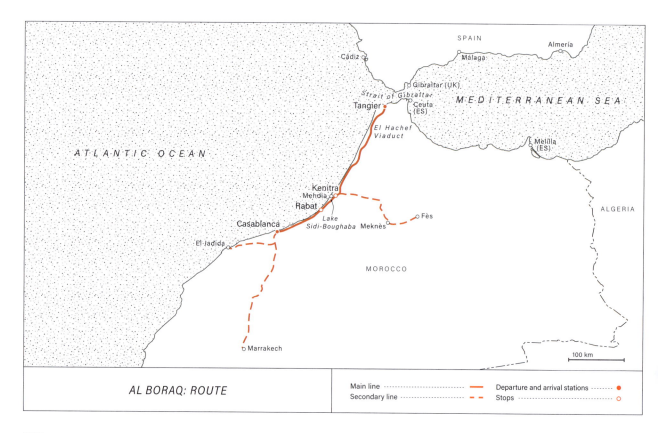

AL BORAQ: ROUTE

Main line ——— Departure and arrival stations ●
Secondary line – – – Stops ○

AFRICA

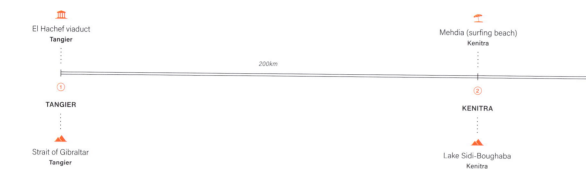

El Hachef viaduct	Mehdia (surfing beach)
Tangier	Kenitra
① TANGIER	② KENITRA
Strait of Gibraltar	Lake Sidi-Boughaba
Tangier	Kenitra

200km

CONSTRUCTED
2018

JOURNEY LENGTH
2 hours 10 mins

DISTANCE
350km

COUNTRIES VISITED
Morocco

LENGTH OF
EL HACHEF VIADUCT
3.5km

• *Cape Spartel, on the Strait of Gibraltar.*

FROM THE WHITE CITY OF TANGIER TO CASABLANCA

Where to start with Tangier? There's so much to say, it's hard to know what to mention first. Poised between the Mediterranean and the Atlantic Ocean, religious yet with freedom of choice, light-filled yet with precious shade, deeply Moroccan, with a hint of Spanish and a profoundly international outlook, the white city of Tangier embodies all the different identities of the Moroccan nation and Mediterranean culture, in all their different nuances. It has inspired artists, offered food for thought for philosophers, welcomed outsiders and sheltered ocean-going smugglers. Tangier is more than a place to visit; it's a place to be experienced.

So it's a wrench to pull ourselves away from this vibrant city, saying goodbye to the narrow alleyways of the medina, the sturdy kasbah, the views over the Strait of Gibraltar and the little Spanish bars on the ground floor of apartment buildings. Fortunately, the station itself is rather out of the ordinary and serves to lift our spirits: streamlined architecture, rectangular towers, flat roofs, lofty glass façades and geometric structures. On a brand-new platform, its dazzling white expanses softened by small pockets of planting, our train awaits, a broad green and red stripe extending backwards from it's aerodynamic nose. Inside the carriage, all is immaculately clean and it's with a sigh of pleasure that we slip into one of the large ruby or emerald-coloured seats (according to ticket class).

AT LIGHTNING SPEED

Off we go. The air conditioning makes for a cool and calming atmosphere, almost studious in its serenity. The name Al Boraq, on the other hand, means lightning and harks back to the winged creature that bore the Prophet Muhammad to the heavens and back. As the train picks up speed, we see Tangier disappearing past the windows, its suburbs gradually giving way to a desert-like landscape. Not quite sand just yet, but low-growing vegetation, tough enough to withstand the blazing Moroccan sun. In the distance, light-coloured buildings are strewn across far-off hillsides. Then suddenly, something changes. Lines become a little less distinct, colours a tad

stretched out. Our metal lightning bolt is on the verge of reaching its maximum speed of 320km/h.

We maintain this speed, a record for the African continent, for about an hour, the panorama changing as we hurtle on. The arid landscape transforms into a network of narrow green valleys and vast cultivated fields. As we approach Kenitra, we start to see the shores of the Atlantic Ocean. Almost without realizing, we are upon the enormous El Hachef viaduct, 3.5km long, regarded as one of the longest bridges in the world capable of carrying trains travelling at such a high speed.

• *Al Boraq, waiting to depart Tangier station.*

TANGIER → CASABLANCA

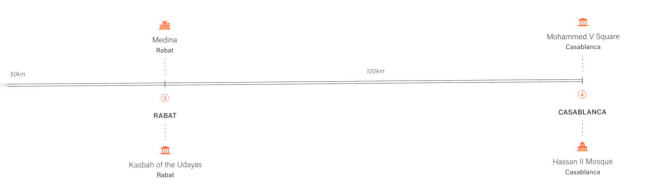

- *The walled Kasbah of the Udayas in Rabat.*

SURFING BY RAIL

Just before we reach Kenitra, our surroundings change again, becoming even more agricultural. Large commercial farms, dominated by their pale-coloured farm buildings, extend into the distance from the wall running alongside the tracks. We have now left behind the high-speed track and are making our way into Kenitra station at a more leisurely speed.

As in Tangier, this station is another superb example of modern architecture on a vast scale. Beyond its doors lies a pretty and relatively unknown coastal city. We make our way to Mehdia Beach, acclaimed Moroccan surfing hotspot, then on to the magnificent and protected Lake Sidi-Boughaba. Between Kenitra and Rabat, the scenery outside Al Boraq's windows changes again: this time, tall trees jostle for space with sprawling residential districts and industrial areas where work never ceases. We reach Rabat, another ultramodern station. Never let it be said that Morocco's capital has failed to understand the modern railway brief. Just like the rest of this line, every aspect of this building demonstrates the local authorities' determination to show off their power and their understanding of the modern world. As for the city itself, it would be a travesty to miss out on its tranquil atmosphere, to say nothing of the Kasbah of the Udayas, the labyrinthine medina and its wide and peaceful avenues. Not to mention Rabat's incredible cultural life and all those cosy restaurants...

- *Maamora Forest, near Rabat.*

📢 REIMAGINING THE LANDSCAPE

Before building this high-speed line through Morocco, the landscape first had to be remodelled. In particular, the construction crews had to stabilize the subsoil and drain various other areas lying on the line's path. In total, they also used some 700,000 sleepers, 7,400 overhead wire masts and 1,600 tonnes of ballast to support the rails.

- *Hassan II Mosque, star Casablanca attraction.*

ONWARDS TO CASABLANCA

We finally get back on board our high-speed train for the short final stretch between the country's official capital and its economic and business centre, Casablanca. Once again, the train travels at a standard speed as it leaves Rabat, passing through the suburbs, and then the fields, industrial districts and small towns that separate the two cities. The intention is that one day this too will be a high-speed link, demonstrating just how far Morocco has come in the field of rail technology.

Until these epic projects come into being, we have plenty of time to enjoy a slower pace of arrival in one of Morocco's tourist meccas – and to gird our loins before we are launched into its legendary hustle and bustle. Our final perambulations of the trip take us from the exquisite Hassan II Mosque to the narrow alleyways of the ancient medina, and from Mohammed V Square to the luxury boutiques along the seafront Corniche, and of course the city's famous sunrises and sunsets.

125

AFRICA

Choum → Zouérat
Blue snake in the sand dunes

on board the
DESERT TRAIN

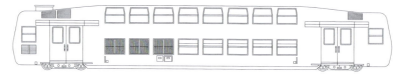

Tiny train among the iron ore behemoths.

Deserts aren't always empty; in fact, they very rarely are. To the east of the largest of them all, the mighty Sahara Desert, a railway line has been slicing its way through the sand dunes for the past 60 years. Constructed by the French in 1963, this track is used by the world's largest iron ore trains to carry this valuable commodity from the Zouérat mine to Nouadhibou on the Atlantic coast. Overshadowed by these laden heavyweights, a tiny blue train takes tourists on a voyage of discovery into the desert.

Opposite page: Palm grove in the Adrar region of Mauritania.

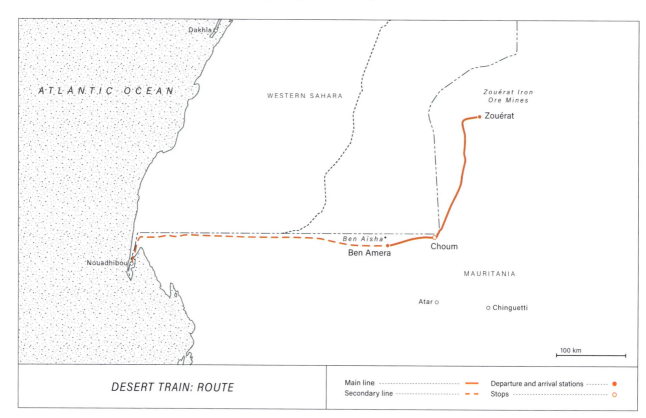

DESERT TRAIN: ROUTE

Main line — Departure and arrival stations •
Secondary line --- Stops ○

AFRICA

① CHOUM — 250km — ② ZOUÉRAT

🏛 Zouérat mine
Zouérat

CONSTRUCTED
1998

JOURNEY LENGTH
6 days

DISTANCE
approx. 700km

COUNTRIES VISITED
Mauritania

LENGTH OF
IRON ORE TRAINS
2.5km

TRACKS IN THE SAND

At Choum station, we are suddenly assailed by doubts. Is this really where we depart from? Is it even a station? Is it even a place? There's nothing here to suggest we are in the right spot. A few scattered buildings, the distant sound of a generator and, thankfully, rails on the ground. Then we hear the distinctive clattering noise of a train. We stand back to watch as its metal hulk passes by, going on and on and on. This is the longest iron ore train in the world: 2.5km of rail wagons laden with iron ore. And right on top of it all, perched on the mine's black gold, Mauritanians ferrying livestock and handmade goods.

- *The Desert Train line, near Choum.*

- *The blue locomotive of the Desert Train.*

BLUE AND BATIK CLOTH

Once this Leviathan has passed through en route for Nouadhibou, we can see our train, blue from top to tail, made up of one locomotive and two carriages, one for daytime and one for the night. If anything, the interior is even more colourful than the outside. Lined with brightly coloured batik cloth, there are comfortable bench seats to sit on while an employee, swathed in a turban to protect him from the worst of the desert weather, serves tea. And thus commences our spectacular journey across the Sahara with all the gifts it has in store for us. The overwhelming endlessness of the landscape, jagged mountains, wild camels searching for sustenance in the sand.

THE BOWELS OF KEDIET EJ JILL

This part of the journey takes over four hours. Desert on repeat, magnificently constant in its aridity, although by no means devoid of living things, the Sahara is ever present throughout the day. It exerts an unwavering fascination over us, holding us so spellbound we can barely tear our eyes away to eat lunch. On arriving at Zouérat station, we finally see the huge iron ore mine that accounts for the lion's share of the local economy. No time to visit this evening, just long enough for a quick walk, dinner, then bed in our hotel.

The following day begins with an unorthodox tour of the world's biggest iron ore mine. Abuzz with thousands of workers scurrying between mechanical excavators, the mine plunges into the dark bowels of the mountain, Kediet ej Jill. We may be visiting as tourists, but these workers are responsible for excavating just some of the 12 million tonnes of iron ore produced by the mine each year. A disturbing thought for those of us willing to put ourselves in others' shoes and acknowledge our privilege.

- *The Desert Train at Zouérat station.*

CHOUM → ZOUÉRAT

THE MONOLITHS OF THE SAHARA

After lunch among the dunes, shielded from the relentless sun by acacia trees, we climb back on board our tiny railcar and return to Choum, where we continue on to Ben Amera. As before, the desert, mountains and their one-humped inhabitants are a constant fixture, completely oblivious to our fleeting presence. From time to time, we see a truck in the distance, invariably weighed down with food supplies or large containers of drinking water.

Located 250km further south, Ben Amera only comes into view after we've spent a night in our bunks in the second carriage, stargazing though the windows at a sky like no other. In the early morning light, the reason for our trip is only too evident. Just a stone's throw from our halt, a village made up of Mauritanian tents, also known as *khaimas*, nestles at the foot of the 633m-high monolith. This is the largest natural structure of its kind in Africa and the third largest on the planet after Uluru and Mount Augustus in the Australian outback. We carry on to another monolith, Ben Aïsha. Slightly smaller, this one has rock paintings that date back to 5,000 years before trains arrived in the desert.

- *Ben Amera, a monolith 103km from Atar.*

- *Ben Aïsha, another monolith, home to rock art.*

🔊 RIDING WITH THE IRON ORE

If Mauritanians choose to trust their luck on top of the wagons filled with iron ore, they are entitled to travel free of charge. The poorest and/or bravest among them make good use of this opportunity to transport a wide variety of goods such as craft items, fish and livestock, even quite large animals in some cases!

- *Mosque in Chinguetti, Holy City of Islam.*

- *Market in Atar, capital of the Mauritanian Adrar region.*

THE SEVENTH HOLY CITY

Our train sets off again for Choum 24 hours later, giving us plenty of time to explore the village and tour Ben Amera. On arrival, we jump into a four-wheel drive to visit somewhere completely out of this world: Chinguetti. Said to be the seventh holy city of Islam, hidden in the dunes, it is also known as the City of Libraries and has the faded beauty of towns that were once great. Ghosts of the past jostle on its sandy streets between buildings hewn from golden stone. It may no longer attract the thousands of pilgrims of bygone days, but the many Koranic schools and libraries bear witness to their passage.

Awestruck by the old manuscripts and ancient texts tucked away in the corners of this ancient caravan town and UNESCO World Heritage Site, we eventually turn our backs on Chinguetti as we head for Atar. And so our journey comes to an end, as we attempt to take in the beauty of the Mauritanian Adrar region with its mountains and canyons – most people are completely unaware of their existence.

129

Cotonou → Parakou

The two faces of Benin

on board the
EBONY TRAIN

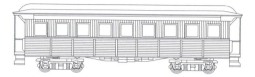

The one and only passenger train in Benin.

As the only passenger train operating on the railway line between Cotonou and Parakou, the Ebony Train chugs along at 40km/h or so from the Atlantic coast into the country's heartland. Its route through the Beninese countryside offers a multifaceted, complex and in-depth vision of a country where multiple influences have held sway.

Opposite page: Cotton field on the forest fringes.

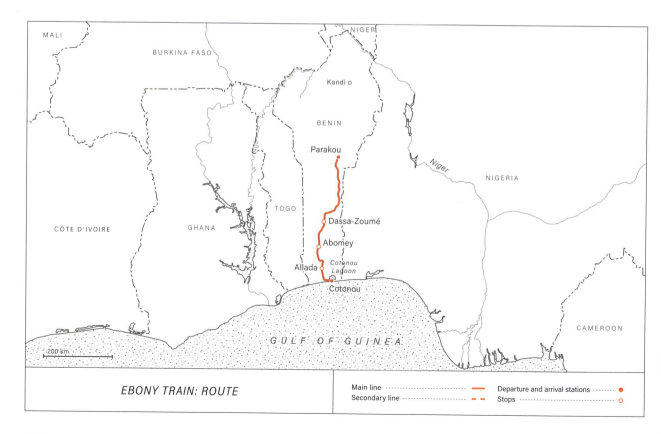

AFRICA

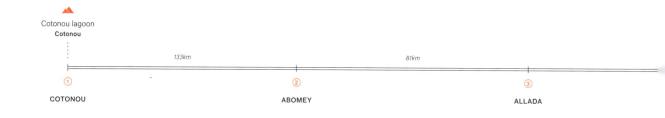

CONSTRUCTED
2005

JOURNEY LENGTH
2 days, 1 night

DISTANCE
436km

COUNTRIES VISITED
Benin

• *The village of Ganvié on Lake Nokoué.*

IN THE BENINESE COUNTRYSIDE

A huge pillar, at the foot of which the five arms of a red star extend in all directions. At the top of the pillar, a man with a hoe in his right hand, a rifle on his shoulder and a bundle of wood under his left arm. Wide, open avenues and swarms of scooters that seem to move as one. A vast market covering some 20 hectares where families take a leisurely stroll. Long beaches, tranquil streets lined with coconut palms, a canal and a lagoon flowing into a large lake. Can you guess where we are? No? I thought not – this is Cotonou, the undeservedly little-known capital of Benin.

GREEN AND YELLOW LOCOMOTION

This amazing city, a melting pot of influences as diverse as French, Soviet, Voodoo, Christian and Islamic, is our departure point for the next journey on our list. Our train is also rather special: an old yellow locomotive with two wooden carriages dating back to the 1920s, now fully refurbished and painted green. Once our little group are on board, the train sets off slowly, heading for the north of the country. Sitting on

• *The 1920s-style Ebony Train.*

the open deck at the rear of the second carriage, there's no doubt that we're in completely different terrain. Lush greenery swaying gently in the wind borders the track on both sides. The little road running parallel with the railway line is the province of two-wheelers bound for Cotonou, now left far behind us. As our guide had promised, children wreathed in smiles run up and wave as we pass by – a spectacle that is both moving and disconcerting at the same time. This train, running on rails that date back to colonial times, is only used by tourists in search of just this kind of touching scene.

THE RAILWAY TAKES CENTRE-STAGE

In Allada, we stop to allow the nation's only freight train to pass by. Our driver takes the opportunity to check out the engine while we wander around the open-air market just a few metres from the track. Large blankets are used to display fruit and vegetables, soon to be balanced on the heads of women dressed in gaudy colours. Swathes of fabric, also known as batik cloth, hang on racks out of the glare of the sun.

Back on board, we realize something: despite there being no other passenger train on the country's only railway line, economic activity has sprung up all along the tracks. Tiny restaurants, groceries, little shops and even houses have been built on this ochre land. Scooters are everywhere, whizzing along dirt roads or parked away from the heat under huge, brightly coloured parasols, patiently waiting for their owners to return.

• *Traditional Beninese market.*

COTONOU → PARAKOU

- *Façade of an old building in Dassa.*

VOODOO TRAIL

After lunch is prepared on board by one of the train staff, Dassa station appears on our right. With its yellow walls, tin roof and well-worn wooden shutters, the building resembles a saloon bar. This is where we will stop for the night, sleeping in a small hotel in this town with a population of just over 100,000.

Next morning, the heat is sufficiently bearable for us to climb the surrounding hills, where our guide takes us to see villages where the local form of the Voodoo religion is still practised. The cult is very much alive in this country, the only place on Earth where it is officially recognized as an everyday part of life. Its followers maintain that the religion is worlds away from satanism or black magic. It has been practised on the continent for centuries and serves to protect the local people.

📢 A RELIC FROM COLONIAL TIMES

Now purely for tourists, a journey on the Ebony Train is usually included in trips that also offer tours of the northern part of the country by bus or four-wheel drive. It's impossible to go any further by train, despite the ambitions of the original French colonists to extend the line to Niamey, capital of Niger.

WHEN THE HARMATTAN BLOWS

We return to the Ebony Train with weary legs, our muscles feeling the strain of climbing all those hills. Due to the rugged terrain, our ascent was rather more than a constitutional, but we were rewarded by the beautiful scenery and forests made up of African birches (ngálǎma), baobabs, African locust beans and many other species. The Harmattan wind, which blows in from the Sahara, creates eddies of dust that fall in silence, settling on the carriages.

From the comfort of our wicker armchairs, we look on as the lush vegetation of the south transforms into savannah, and semi-arid mountains start to appear on the horizon. On reaching Parakou, our terminus, we say farewell to our little train as we plunge into a completely different atmosphere to anything we've experienced thus far. Desert influences mean drier air and earth. The buildings are low and some distance from one another, all the better to withstand the suffocating heat. There's certainly no shortage of space.

A roaring noise in the background turns out to be the engines of trucks laden with cotton, making their way to the port of Cotonou.

- *Benin, the forest kingdom.*

- *The ticket office at Parakou station.*

THE GATEWAY TO THE NORTH

Regarded as the gateway to the north of the country, Parakou is an important stop-off for any traveller wishing to visit this region's wildlife parks. The city also shows a completely different side to Africa. A world away from the tiny villages, enchanting countryside and smiling children, it's a busy place, where people work hard, determined to escape from the economic doldrums. Of course, this would be so much easier if the infrastructure was better – the railways, in particular.

133

Nairobi → Mombasa
Under the watchful gaze of elephants

on board the
MADARAKA EXPRESS

An extraordinary express train in Kenya.

Completed in 2017 and inaugurated by the then President of the Republic in 2018, the Madaraka Express links Nairobi, Kenya's capital, with the major port city of Mombasa, in just four hours. The line in question runs alongside and replaces the Lunatic Line, constructed under British rule, which took 15 hours to cover the same distance. This colossal project sought to boost the country's economy for the benefit of travellers on a voyage of discovery, especially as it passes through Tsavo National Park.

Opposite page: Mount Kenya National Park, established in 1949, to the north of Nairobi.

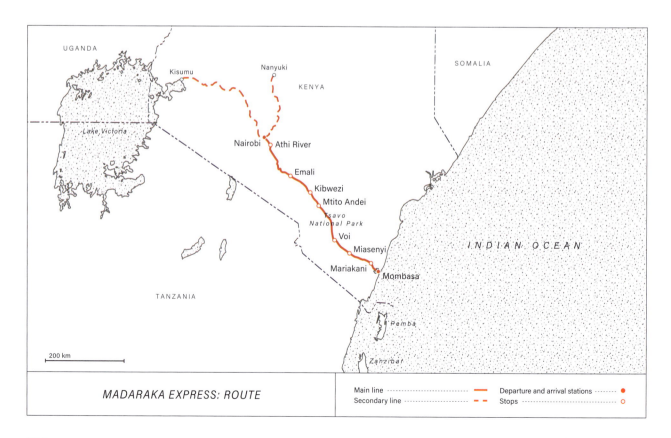

MADARAKA EXPRESS: ROUTE

CONSTRUCTED
2017

JOURNEY LENGTH
4 hours

DISTANCE
472km

COUNTRIES VISITED
Kenya

NUMBER OF MAIN STATIONS CONSTRUCTED FOR THIS LINE
9

📣 ELEGANT STATIONS INSPIRED BY LOCAL THEMES

Nine new main stations were built to accommodate passengers on this line, each with architecture inspired by a natural or cultural feature of the country. The concentric circles of Mombasa station represent the ocean's waves, while the stripes on Miasenyi station are intended to resemble the zebra's distinctive coat. Emali station, on the other hand, is designed in the shape of a fist, symbolizing unity, whereas Nairobi station takes the form of two trains, one on top of the other.

FROM THE HEART OF KENYA TO THE INDIAN OCEAN

Nairobi's vast central station rears up before us. Its remarkable Brutalist architecture dwarfs everything in its vicinity, but the treat awaiting us inside certainly won't disappoint: the Madaraka Express. This long orange and white train gleams as it waits at the platform. A uniformed attendant stands at each door, checking passengers' tickets as they board. The interior is equally modern, rather like a corridor in an enormous spaceship with blue stripes against the orange seats.

• *Nairobi railway station.*

• *Zebras spotted on leaving Nairobi.*

NATURE AT LARGE

Despite looking like a high-speed train, the average speed of the Madaraka Express is just 120km/h, allowing ample time to appreciate the urban cityscape as we leave Nairobi. Memories of our stay in the city linger in our minds – Jamia Mosque, Uhuru Park, the Maasai street market, the city's national park, not forgetting the waymarked trails through the 1,000-hectare Karura and Sigiria forests.

Through the train's generous windows, the colours pop. Ochre earth contrasts with the vast blue expanse of the sky and its banks of stately clouds. The vegetation alongside our route varies: sometimes arid, it keeps us on our toes by randomly switching to grassland or even to clusters of gargantuan trees. Impossible to capture in just a few words; it's as though it's trying to show off everything the Kenyan landscape has to offer. The mountains are always there in the background, sometimes in the foreground, sometimes distant, but always the focal point of the train's panoramic windows.

• *Lily Lake in Karura Forest.*

WHAT TO LOOK FOR IN TSAVO NATIONAL PARK

By the time we reach Mtito Andei, our base for the next night or so, we have already passed Athi River, Emali and Kibwezi. Admittedly, the town itself is not our main objective; our real destination is the vast Tsavo National Park. Covering over 22,800km², it is larger than El Salvador or Slovenia and occupies about 4 per cent of Kenya's national territory. It is split into two parks (East and West) by the Nairobi-Mombasa highway and is home to around 10,000 elephants, some of which have tusks so long that they touch the ground. However, pachyderms are by no means the only animals to be seen here. This landscape reflects the very essence of African wildlife, with ostriches, oryx, zebras, impalas, giraffes, hippos, lions, cheetahs, leopards and crocodiles also sharing this habitat. It goes without saying that we need to take the time and trouble to watch, look and remain silent so as not to miss the tell-tale signs.

Back on the spotlessly clean train, we continue our journey towards the Indian Ocean. Tsavo National Park still keeps us company for quite some time until we reach Voi, but from this point onwards the earth outside is virtually the same shade of orange as our train. Diminutive buildings with red roofs enhance this colour palette, the stark brown of a rugged mountain providing the only contrast. Then the sky seems to recede into the distance and the savannah gives way to more landscaped greenery as we draw into Mombasa's extremely impressive station. More like a spaceship than a station, our terminus is surrounded by lush planting.

• *The verdant hills of Chyulu, near Kibwezi.*

Madaraka Express on the Nairobi Viaduct in Mombasa.

Dar es Salaam → Lobito
Africa – from east to west

on the
TRAIL OF TWO OCEANS

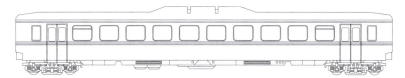

From the east to the west of a continent – by train.

The Trail of Two Oceans doesn't just take you on a journey; it's an adventure. Operated by Rovos Rail, a renowned luxury train operator in Africa, this train literally crosses Africa from coast to coast: from the Indian Ocean to the Atlantic Ocean, in 16 days. This is a deluxe and immersive experience, taking in no fewer than four countries on the African continent.

Opposite page: Udzungwa National Park, a haven for zebras, lions, elephants, giraffes and other animals.

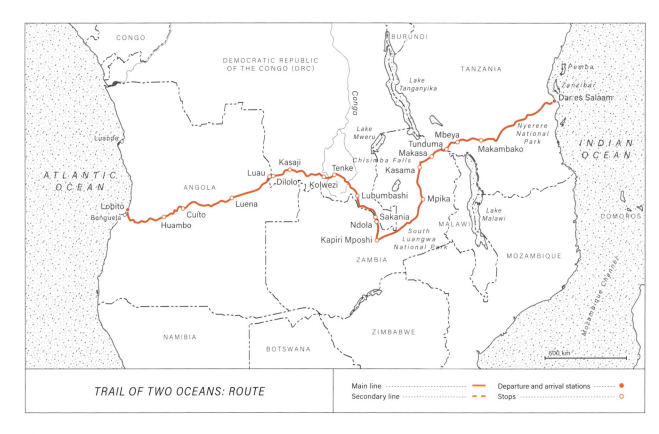

TRAIL OF TWO OCEANS: ROUTE

AFRICA

CONSTRUCTED
2019

JOURNEY LENGTH
16 days,
15 nights

DISTANCE
4,300km

COUNTRIES VISITED
Tanzania
Zambia
Democratic
Republic of
the Congo
Angola

IMAGINE AN ADVENTURE…

Across Africa. The mere act of saying those words conjures up such a range of images from popular culture, the media and rather hackneyed clichés. Adventurers in Hollywood movies hacking their way through the jungle with machetes, huge herds of elephants travelling from one watering hole to the next, car rallies rocked by scandal due to concerns about their colonial past, or the misery of mass human migration in the wake of war – we all recognize these images and they influence our view of reality accordingly.

By connecting the Tanzanian coastline of the Indian Ocean with the Angolan coastline of the Atlantic in 16 days, the Trail of Two Oceans gives a whole new meaning to the concept of crossing Africa. It takes a more direct route, with more rail travel, and is a much more deluxe offering than the journeys just described.

▪ *Dar es Salaam, Tanzania's capital and economic centre.*

▪ *Stretch of water in the Selous Game Reserve.*

MOUNTAINS IN THE MIST

Our adventure begins in Dar es Salaam, a name that translates as 'abode of peace'. With a population of over 4.3 million, Tanzania's capital and financial hub is a melting pot of Swahili, German, British and Asian influences. Lying on the wide estuary of the Msimbazi River, this city, or more specifically its substantial station, is where we join our train. As soon as we cross the threshold, it's like pressing the reset button: the hustle and bustle of the city and its modern buildings fade into distant memories. The train's wood-panelled walls, spacious armchairs, double beds, observation cars and dinky coloured curtains are mementos of bygone days. Time slows down.

Our first day is punctuated by splendid meals, including a very punctual afternoon tea, during which the myriad wonders of Tanzania never fail to delight. The following day we stop in the Selous Game Reserve, 55,000m^2 of nature at its best – only 8 per cent of which is allocated to tourist safari tours, while 92 per cent is set aside for hunting. The park is home to 800,000 large mammals. Lions, elephants, antelopes, hippos, African wild dogs and giraffes, to name but a few. Then there's Udzungwa National Park with its mist-shrouded mountains, thundering waterfalls and hundreds of endemic species. Mere words cannot hope to describe the beauty of this landscape – use them if you will, but you might as well whistle in the wind…

▪ *Sanje Falls in Udzungwa.*

140

DAR ES-SALAAM → LOBITO

Olduvai Gorge in the Great Rift Valley.

WELCOME TO THE *MIOMBO*

Our train continues to cruise along in style. Delicious meals follow delicious meals and our days on board run into one another, losing nothing of their deluxe appeal in the process. In contrast, the excursions on offer are all so different that our brains struggle to take in all this glory. The lakes in the Great Rift Valley, some of the deepest and most ancient anywhere in the world. The three sets of waterfalls making up the Chisimba Falls, behind which there is said to be a spirit that frowns on bad behaviour, along with their natural pools. This is *miombo* country, the typical woodland savannah found in this part of Zambia. We are allowed to enter after completing various border formalities. On the sixth day, we have a two-day stopover to visit South Luangwa National Park. This former hunting area turned game reserve also boasts the full spectrum of Africa's large mammals with the exception of the rhinoceros, which has been poached to extinction. The reserve's walking safaris allow keen birdwatchers to try and identify species as diverse as the African skimmer, the carmine bee-eater or that most elusive of creatures, Pel's fishing owl.

Desert-like landscape in South Luangwa National Park.

🔊 COBALT BLUE, BLOOD RED

With 3.5 million tonnes of cobalt in its territory, the Democratic Republic of the Congo has by far the world's largest reserves of this metal, a key component of batteries. Cobalt is often mined under inhumane conditions and attracts large-scale protests by human rights activists objecting to the involvement of the big tech giants in this industry.

OUR REWARD: THE ATLANTIC

After a quick hop by plane to Ndola, we rejoin the Trail of Two Oceans to cross the border between Zambia and the Democratic Republic of the Congo. Another checkpoint, another set of formalities, all made so much easier by the splendour and beauty of our surroundings. We tick off towns and cities as we go: beguiling Lubumbashi, often referred to as the 'Copper Capital'. Lukuni. The open-pit cobalt mine at Luishia. Kolwezi, where we get to tour a cobalt mine. Mutshatsha, Kakopa, Malonga and more besides.

On Day 12 we cross the Angolan border and put our watches back an hour for the second time since leaving Dar es Salaam. Although the scenery is still as

Copper mine in the Congo.

spectacular as ever, especially along the Kasai River, our last days on board focus on the culture of this part of Africa. First stop, Luena, where we take a deep dive into the recent history of Angola; then on to Cuíto, former capital of the forgotten kingdom of Ovimbundu, which was gradually wiped out by Portuguese colonists. Finally, after our 15th night, we arrive in Lobito on the opposite side of Africa, where the second ocean of our journey awaits us. A just reward for a classic expedition.

The Atlantic coast of Angola.

141

Pretoria → Cape Town
A blaze of blue in the rainbow

on board the
BLUE TRAIN

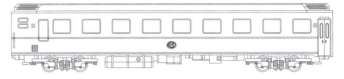

A train as blue as its name suggests.

With over 200,000 kilometres of railway tracks, South Africa is way ahead of other African countries in terms of rail density. The result of controversial historical, political and economic factors, this network is also the ideal way to discover the vast heritage of the Rainbow Nation and to understand the social chasm that divides it. Enter the opulent Blue Train, which travels from Pretoria to Cape Town.

Opposite page: Cape Town, the southernmost city in Africa.

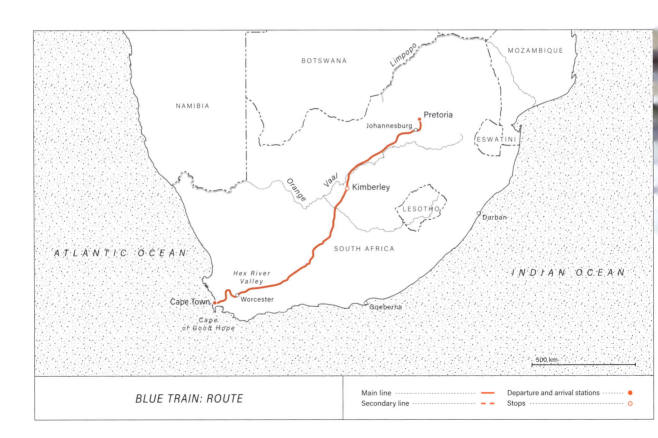

BLUE TRAIN: ROUTE

CONSTRUCTED
1946

JOURNEY LENGTH
3 days, 2 nights

DISTANCE
1,600km

COUNTRIES VISITED
South Africa

🔊 **SHOSHOLOZA MEYL, THE SOUTH AFRICAN PEOPLE'S TRAIN**

In a land of luxury trains, South Africa does not reserve its railways solely for the wealthiest travellers. The Shosholoza Meyl trains also allow those with shallower pockets to travel between the Rainbow Nation's major cities. Their rather romantic name alludes to their populist aspirations. Not only is it the title of a traditional South African song, the Zulu word *shosholoza* also means moving forward or allowing others to take your place. Meyl, the other half of the name, means long-distance train.

BLUE AND GOLD

You can't miss the Blue Train as it stands proudly alongside a platform at Pretoria station. Its locomotives and carriages are resplendent in royal blue, finished to perfection by the cream detailing and its logo, a large gilded letter 'B'. Unlike most other luxury trains in its class, this legendary symbol of the Rainbow Nation makes no claim to offer long journeys across South Africa and neighbouring countries. Instead, its sole purpose is to link Pretoria and Cape Town via Kimberley. Yet the standard of service on offer is commensurate with its prices.

The journey usually begins in the station lounge, reserved exclusively for passengers. There's a very Anglo-Saxon vibe with the roulette wheel spinning and champagne flowing to the soothing sound of a saxophone playing in the background. Once on board, the same vibe is evident. Butlers lead passengers to their cabins or suites to freshen up or get ready for dinner. Gentlemen are required to wear a jacket and tie, but heaven forbid that they should tell ladies what to wear... The clock is well and truly turned back.

• *Lavish bar on the Blue Train.*

EVENING DRESS AND SHANTY TOWNS

While we seek to abide by the dress code, the train leaves the station and, just like that, we find ourselves travelling through a strange mix of savannah and small urban settlements. Relaxation is on the agenda in the observation car at the rear of the train. Not everyone is in evening attire – yet! – but there's a glass in every hand. Champagne, South African fine wines, fruit juice or cocktails – take your pick.

What an unsettling national dichotomy: the line runs alongside the shanty towns, those infamous townships from the days of apartheid.

In the dining car, tables are immaculately laid with white linen, elegant silverware and engraved crystal glasses. There are five courses and a cheeseboard, then we adjourn to the club car where Cuban Cohiba cigars are served to those who partake. The champagne continues to flow and there's a genuine party atmosphere despite all those dark suits.

• *Soweto, South African township, remembered for the riots that took place here in 1976.*

• *Big Hole, former diamond mine at Kimberley.*

DIAMONDS ARE FOREVER

What a wonderful way to wake up: still half asleep, we remain sprawled on the comfortable beds in our cabins to better admire the unadulterated views of the mountains. For all the world like large cats, fluffy clouds brush against the distant peaks. We eat our breakfast, worthy of the grandest of hotels, against a backdrop of gold vegetation and the blue of the sky. The views continue until Kimberley.

We are transported by minibus across this forgotten epicentre of the South African diamond rush to visit the former open-pit mine. There are five huge excavations, the largest of which is simply known as the Big Hole. It is 240m deep and covers an area of 170,000m². Naturally, this will be the main topic of conversation at dinner that evening, as we enjoy another elegant black-tie extravaganza. What better way to discuss precious gemstones than with a cigar in one hand and a glass of cognac in the other?

WAKING UP TO THE *WINELANDS*

Second morning, second magical experience. The Blue Train is skirting the mountains of the Hex River Valley when a crew member suggests we might like to grab our cameras. Jagged rock monsters hold their pose, imperturbable, as the sound of digital flashes erupts over the scene. At the foot of these rocky outcrops, vineyards bask in the perfect conditions provided by the landscape, the sunshine and the nearby river. We can only promise to sample the products when we reach Cape Town, already more than just a dot on the horizon.

• *Vineyard in the Hex River Valley.*

PRETORIA → CAPE TOWN

1 – Street in Pretoria in the early hours of the morning. 2 – Blue Train at the platform.
3 – Cape Town, legislative capital of South Africa, with a population of 400,000. 4 – Desert landscape in Mpumalanga, east of Pretoria.

Pretoria → Victoria Falls
Steaming through Africa

on board the
PRIDE OF AFRICA

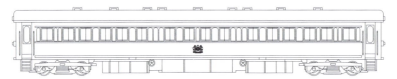

A luxury train between the choicest jewels in South Africa's crown.

The opulence of this train is on a par with the grandest of terrestrial palaces, making the Pride of Africa one of the most stunning trains in the world today. And yet, this particular journey takes in so many truly staggering wonders of the natural world that the elegance and refinement of this outstanding mode of transport almost pale into insignificance.

Opposite page: Matobo National Park, famous for its granite rock formations.

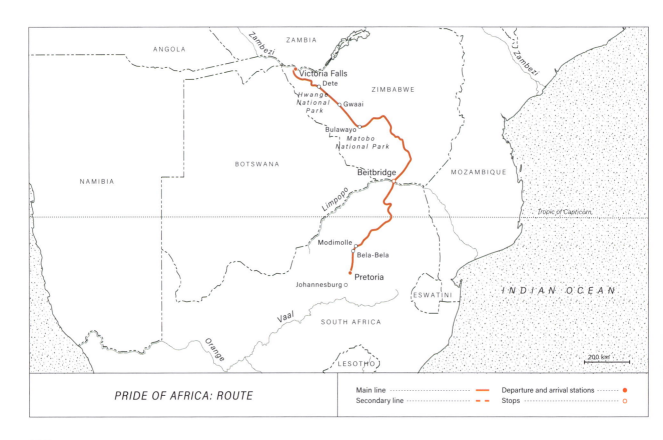

CONSTRUCTED
1989

JOURNEY LENGTH
5 days,
4 nights

DISTANCE
1,400km

COUNTRIES VISITED
South Africa
Zimbabwe

A BUSINESSMAN ON THE AFRICAN PLAINS

Ruthless businessman, high-ranking politician, diamond magnate and proponent of British imperialism, Cecil Rhodes was one of the architects of the railway intended to connect Cape Town, in South Africa, to Cairo, in Egypt. This project never came to fruition, but many sections of the line are still in use today, some by the trains we are discovering together.

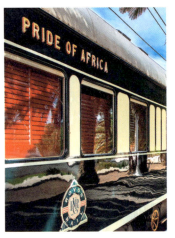

- *Pride of Africa at Pretoria station.*

STEAMING THROUGH THE SAVANNAH

One step inside the Rovos Rail Station is enough to realize that this journey will be unlike any other. With its red brick walls, white columns either side of the entrance and waiting room worthy of an English country house, this private station sets the tone. On reaching the platform, any further doubts are dispelled. The steam locomotive with its sumptuous carriages and the air of luxury it exudes come together to form the Pride of Africa, set to take us on a journey that promises to be a treat for all the senses.

After a tour of the station, guided by no less a personage than the founder of Rovos Rail himself, Rohan Vos, it's time to board the train and explore our quarters: a Deluxe Suite with a double bed, private shower, writing desk and comfortable chairs. Yet the armchairs of the observation car are where we settle to enjoy the views and chat to fellow passengers. Glasses clinking, tongues loosened, everyone has their own story to tell of how they came to be on this luxury train. Outside, the fabulous countryside around the town of Bela-Bela, renowned for its hot springs with healing properties, unfolds before our eyes. Next comes Modimolle: originally christened Nylstroom by the Boers, who believed it to be the source of the Nile, this town was renamed Modimolle after a substantial hill with a distinctive rectangular shape, not too dissimilar to the mountain in *The Lion King*.

IN THE SHADE OF THE UMBRELLA THORN TREES

Dinner time comes around, served, like all other meals, in the dining car with the pomp worthy of the world's finest gourmet restaurants. White linen, wooden chairs upholstered in dark green leather, the exact same shade as the Pride of Africa's external livery, fine dining, impeccable service and evening wear for the guests (dinner only). Between each bite, it's as though the savannah is sharing the table with us. Night falls over the vast golden landscape with its umbrella thorns, their foliage in the shape of an inverted shallow bowl. Early the next morning, the train crosses the Tropic of Capricorn, then shortly afterwards the Limpopo River, 1,750km long. According to Rudyard Kipling's *Just So Stories*, this is where the Elephant's Child has his nose pulled by a crocodile as he drinks from the waters. Assisted by a Bi-Coloured-Python-Rock-Snake, he pulled so hard to escape the predator's tenacious jaws that his nose turned into a trunk. Our heads full of stories, both old and new, we arrive at Beitbridge station in Zimbabwe. On the platform, a band playing traditional music helps pass the time as we wait to complete the usual border formalities.

- *Sunset over the savannah.*

- *Baobab tree in Zimbabwe's nature reserves.*

THE SHEER POWER OF THE FALLS

On the third day of our rail excursion we pass through baobab country before climbing up to Bulawayo, the country's second largest city at an altitude of 1,368m. Our route then takes us on to Matobo National Park, where we have another stopover. Located in the heart of the Matobo Hills (the word *matobo* means 'bald head' in the language of the Ndebele people), the park is famous for its huge granite rock formations, seemingly scattered by a giant, with caves containing rock paintings dating back to the Late Stone Age. Cecil Rhodes' tomb is also to be found in these parts.

On the fourth morning we travel between the towns of Gwaai and Dete along the 114km of one of the world's longest stretches of straight railway line. This runs along the eastern edge of Hwange National Park, the country's largest wildlife reserve and the Pride of Africa's last stop before the Victoria Falls. The park has no fewer than 107 species of mammals including lions, elephants, zebras and rhinos, as well as 450 bird species. The memory of their majestic and endangered beauty lingers on in our minds well into the next day, when we arrive at what is possibly one of the world's most stunning sights: Victoria Falls. The unadulterated power of nature, some 1,700m wide and 108m high. A breathtaking sight – in the truest sense of the word.

• A train with luxury cabins – who could ask for more?

Russia & the Middle East

8 TRAIN JOURNEYS
5 countries
Legendary journeys at the crossroads of cultures
FROM MOSCOW TO MEDINA

① **Moscow → Vladivostok**
TRANS-SIBERIAN RAILWAY
p. 152

② **Moscow → Sergiev Posad → Rostov → Yaroslavl → Kostroma**
GOLDEN RING
p. 160

③ **St Petersburg → Murmansk**
ARKTIKA
p. 164

④ **Moscow → St Petersburg → Tallinn**
RED ARROW
p. 168

⑤ **Ankara → Kars**
DOGU EKSPRESI
p. 172

⑥ **Eskişehir → Konya → Adana**
TAURUS EXPRESS
p. 176

⑦ **Bandar-e Torkaman → Bandar-e Emam Khomeyni**
TRANS-IRANIAN RAILWAY
p. 180

⑧ **Mecca → Medina**
HARAMAIN
p. 184

Moscow → Vladivostok
The soul of Russia, from one side to another

on the
TRANS-SIBERIAN RAILWAY

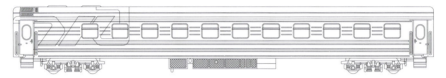

From one side of Russia to the other – by train.

Contrary to popular belief, the word 'Trans-Siberian' doesn't refer to a train, but to a network of railway lines. The most feted of them all is that served by the Rossiya (Russia), which covers 9,289km in the space of one week to travel from Moscow, in the west of the country, to Vladivostok, on the far eastern border of Russian territory. That's almost a quarter of the way around the planet! With or without stops, in individual compartments or open sleeper cars, travelling on this train is like taking a plunge into the unknown across the world's largest country. An encounter with the soul of Russia, if you will.

Opposite page: Lake Baikal, the most famous lake in Siberia.

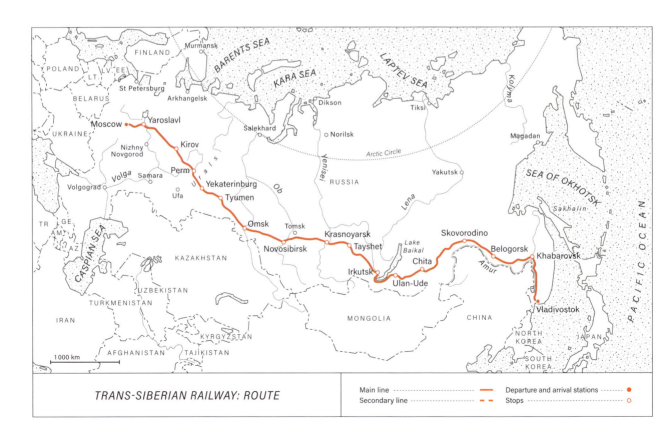

TRANS-SIBERIAN RAILWAY: ROUTE

Main line — — — — —   Departure and arrival stations ●
Secondary line — — — — —   Stops ○

RUSSIA & THE MIDDLE EAST

CONSTRUCTED
1916

JOURNEY LENGTH
7 days, 6 nights

DISTANCE
9,289km

COUNTRIES VISITED
Russia

NUMBER OF TIME ZONES CROSSED
8

DISTANCE TRAVELLED IN EUROPE
1,777km

DISTANCE TRAVELLED IN ASIA
7,512 km

▪ View of tundra from the train.

▪ The Trans-Siberian railway alongside Lake Baikal.

POETRY AND NUMBERS

The Trans-Siberian Railway. The very words send shivers down your spine. Whether you say them out loud or read them silently, they instantly bring to mind myriad images, be they fact or fiction. A seemingly endless journey, with barefoot passengers stretched out in vast open sleeping cars, piping-hot tea by the glassful, scores of Russian towns we've never heard of until they suddenly appear on the horizon, vast snow-covered forests, rosy-cheeked babushkas, lakes we imagine to be Lake Baikal – simply because we have no idea of their real names – churches with gilded domes and the magnificent desolation of a Siberia so icy cold, you can barely believe it supports any life at all.

It may have inspired reams of poetry, but the Rossiya's statistics are no less impressive. Over the course of the 1,777km it travels in Europe and the 7,512km in Asia, all in just seven days, this most celebrated of Trans-Siberian trains passes through 87 towns and cities, five of which have more than one million inhabitants, five federal districts and eight time zones. Then there's the fact that any number of people, probably hundreds of thousands, owe their livelihood solely to the existence of this train, which has in turn inspired countless literary masterpieces, such as the unparalleled *Prose on the Trans-Siberian and of Little Jehanne of France* by Blaise Cendrars. Any attempt to describe a journey of this scale kilometre by kilometre, or even stage by stage, would be bound to end in failure, as it can only hope to offer snapshots of the whole. The gigantic nature of the enterprise requires an element of restraint; rather than serving up the full menu, far better to provide a flavour of the whole.

▪ Moscow, starting point for the Rossiya.

A DAILY ADVENTURE

The first thing to understand about the Trans-Siberian Railway, and especially about the Rossiya, is that it wasn't designed to fulfil the dreams of travellers seeking week-long adventures. It's a Russian train providing a daily service to thousands of people, some of whom travel rather modest distances, while others go much further. They use it when they need to go and work on site for a while, or when they go and visit their children studying in one of the major cities, or simply to spend some time with ailing grandparents. They hop on board if they want to buy something special they can't locate in their home town, to attend a wedding, to go on holiday or for a job interview. Given the colossal size of the Russian Federation, these journeys might take several hours, or even a few days.

▪ Sleeping car on the Trans-Siberian railway.

MOSCOW → VLADIVOSTOK

COMFORT VERSUS IMMERSION

All these individual purposes inevitably determine how the Trans-Siberian is arranged – compartmentalized, if you prefer. In Russia, where there are huge differences in income, some can afford to pay for compartments sleeping just two or four people, whereas others travel in large communal carriages with rows and rows of berths. As a passenger, it's down to the experience you're hoping for: comfort versus immersion. Intimacy versus proximity and all that that involves. Peace and quiet versus murmured conversations, friendships as fleeting as they are intense, impromptu games of chess, occasional shouting matches, splendidly improbable encounters and late-night vodka sessions. The very fact that the Trans-Siberian is so accessible and so reliable is what makes it a meeting point for almost all strata of Russian society with its innate subtleties and stereotypes.

• *Krasnoyarsk, in Siberia.*

• *Seven days is a long time on a train...*

STANDING AROUND THE SAMOVAR

The different sides to Russia are only too apparent around the samovar. This is a kind of Russian tea urn found in every carriage and used day and night to supply boiling water to make tea, coffee or even pot noodles; the latter are by far the most popular form of sustenance consumed on the train. When you're travelling such long distances, getting enough to eat is a challenge that everyone tackles in their own way. The most organized travellers bring along a cool box stuffed with provisions, while others take advantage of short stops to buy food from the itinerant salesmen who hang around platforms selling hard-boiled eggs, meat-filled Russian buns, otherwise known as pirozhki, smoked fish, potato blinis, fruit and vegetables. Yet others, with more generous budgets, opt for the relatively expensive offerings from the dining car. By paying just a few roubles extra, these can be delivered to your seat. The Trans-Siberian experience is made up of different landscapes and cities. Impossible to do it justice without going into the detail these places undoubtedly deserve. Yet there are so many of them that sometimes we have to choose. A journey like this is only possible if we apply a little subjectivity, whether we're experiencing the real thing or reading about it second-hand.

• *Train station kiosk to refuel during the long travels.*

155

🔊 REVIVAL OF A FORGOTTEN BRANCH LINE

Nowadays, an abandoned section of the Trans-Siberian railway shows off Lake Baikal to its best advantage without the need for passengers to take to another mode of transport. Now known as the Circum-Baikal, this line runs over 89 kilometres between Slyudyanka and the village of Port Baikal. Over a five-hour excursion, passengers on board are treated to the delights of the 'Blue Eye of Siberia', with its captivating lakeside, woodland and hillside views, via tunnels, viaducts and retaining walls constructed by Russian engineers.

THE POWER OF NATURE

First of all come the landscapes. Processions of forests – birch, spruce, pine – cloaking the plains and mountains, valleys and gorges. Vast expanses of taiga where conifers reign supreme. The endless steppes. Sheer mountains, carved out by the elements, emerging from the tree canopy like huge animals breaking through a net. Rivers powerful enough to compete with the most fearsome ocean currents, including the Amur, site of the last bridge constructed on the Trans-Siberian line.

• *Navigation channel in Lake Baikal, near Irkutsk.*

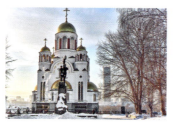

• *Church of All Saints, Yekaterinburg.*

DESTINATION: URALS

Then there are the towns and cities. Our starting point, the sprawling city of Moscow, power seeping through every street, Red Square, the imposing Kremlin building, St Basil's Cathedral with its multicoloured domes, rather like an extravagant many-tiered cake, the Cathedral of Christ the Saviour, Gorky Park, the esplanades along the Moskva River and the Metro, for all the world like a vast underground palace. Or Yaroslavl, founded in 1010 and awarded UNESCO World Heritage status in 2005, with its countless Russian Orthodox churches, the Monastery of the Transfiguration of the Saviour, its golden roofs, all on the banks of the Volga – is this where we start to realize just how vast Russia actually is? Yekaterinburg, standing on the slopes of the Ural Mountains, with the stunning Sevastyanov House and the Church of All Saints, also known as the 'Church on Blood in Honour of All Saints Resplendent in the Russian Land', built on the site where the last Tsar of Russia, his family and members of the imperial household were assassinated.

• *Sevastyanov House, Yekaterinburg.*

• *Dormition Cathedral, Omsk.*

THE END OF THE EARTH?

The Rossiya also passes through Tyumen, Omsk, Novosibirsk, Krasnoyarsk and many others, towns that conceal as many mysteries as they offer voyages of discovery for those who take the time to stop and look. Then on to Irkutsk, gateway to the indescribable Lake Baikal, the world's largest freshwater lake. Its statistics beggar belief: 636km long, with a surface area of 31,722km², a record-breaking 1,642m deep, 25 million years old, 22 islands, crystal-clear waters and legends telling of a humongous water dragon or the passage to the Underworld. It's one of those places that every human being should have the opportunity to visit at least once in their life.

Since even boundaries have boundaries, Lake Baikal isn't the end of the journey. Before reaching Vladivostok, the train still has many ports of call, not least Ulan-Ude, where the monumental sculpture of Lenin's head vies for attention with a large Buddhist temple, reminding us of Russia's multicultural heritage, and Chita, located 6,198km from Moscow and 3,090km from Vladivostok. Then on through Skovorodino, Belogorsk, Khabarovsk and Ussuriysk, before eventually reaching its terminus on the shores of the Sea of Japan. The end of the Earth, from a European perspective. Not quite for Americans perhaps, and not at all if you're in Tokyo or Pyongyang. The world doesn't always finish in the same place…

Fourteenth-century bell tower of the Belogorsky Monastery.

▪ Orthodox church and frozen landscape (opposite page), memories of a trip on the Trans-Siberian Railway.

Moscow → Sergiev Posad → Rostov → Yaroslavl → Kostroma

At the heart of the Russian Orthodox religion

in the
GOLDEN RING

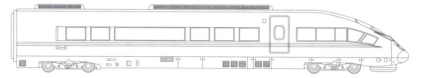

A plethora of trains linking the cities of princes.

Located north-east of the Russian capital, the Golden Ring consists of a number of royal cities with a vast architectural, cultural and religious heritage. Although not as well known as Moscow or St Petersburg, these cities nevertheless represent an important aspect of the country's history, along with its noble families and religious life. There are a number of trains covering this route, but you need to be flexible and adapt to the Russian pace of life.

Opposite page: Rostov Kremlin.

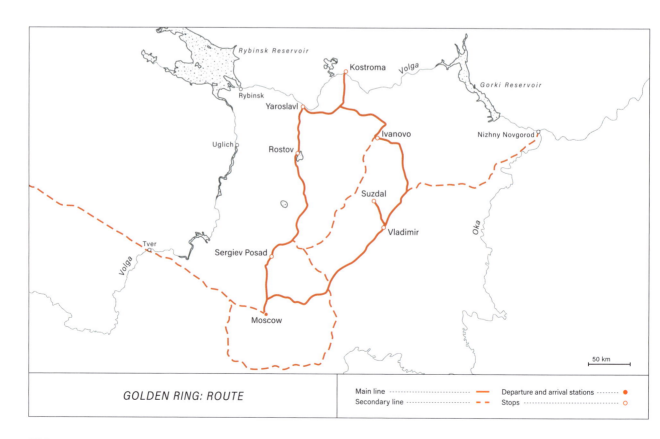

GOLDEN RING: ROUTE

Main line ———— Departure and arrival stations ●
Secondary line ---- Stops ○

① **MOSCOW** — 80km — ② **SERGIEV POSAD** (Trinity Lavra of St Sergius) — 160km

---

OPERATING SINCE
1887

JOURNEY LENGTH
3 hours, 20 mins

DISTANCE
Varies

COUNTRIES VISITED
Russia

A TRULY RUSSIAN EXPERIENCE

Although the Golden Ring has now become a popular tourist circuit, it certainly wasn't designed as such. Founded at different times during the Middle Ages, the princely cities that make up the Ring (Sergiev Posad, Pereslavl-Zalessky, Rostov, Yaroslavl, Kostroma, Ivanovo, Suzdal and Vladimir) grew up between Moscow and the Volga on a particularly fertile patch of black earth known as Opolye. Unless you use a tour operator or hire a car, visiting these cities requires the ability to navigate the foibles of the Russian rail network. Perhaps the final legacy of those capricious noble princes?

• *Lomonosov Moscow State University.*

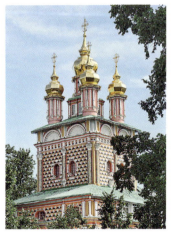

• *Trinity Lavra of St Sergius, Sergiev Posad.*

THE RUSSIAN VATICAN

For the first stage of our journey, we take an ordinary commuter train referred to by Russians as the *elektrichka*, as it's powered by electricity. With a red cab at both ends for the driver and long white carriages, clean and modern, the most recent examples of the elektrichka are not dissimilar to their equivalents the world over. Their main attraction is that they are the ideal way to reach the most popular of the Golden Ring cities: Sergiev Posad. Sometimes referred to as 'Russia's Vatican', this city is home to the spiritual centre of the Russian Orthodox Church: Trinity Lavra of St Sergius.

This architectural wonder, visited by throngs of pilgrims every year, is also a museum with an unparalleled collection of liturgical objects, and is renowned for the star-studded, midnight-blue onion domes of one of its churches. This monastery was founded in the 14th century by no less than the Patron Saint of Russia himself, Sergius of Radonezh, and spared by the Soviets when they came to power. The very essence of Russia.

MOSCOW → SERGIEV POSAD → ROSTOV → YAROSLAVL → KOSTROMA

• *Dormition Cathedral, Rostov the Great.*

ROSTOV THE GREAT (NOT ROSTOV-ON-DON!)

After returning to the capital to spend the night, we take the Moscow-Yaroslavl train to the city of Rostov the Great (Rostov Veliky in Russian), not to be confused with Rostov-on-Don, a city located near the Sea of Azov. For the most part, this route is served by fairly standard Russian trains which, though clean and comfortable, are primarily intended to get us from A to B as if we were regular commuters. They make no claim to be a tourist attraction and you'll see very few foreigners as they tend to prefer coach trips.

On arriving, we head straight for the shores of the shimmering Lake Nero, dominated by the citadel of Rostov Kremlin. The belfry of Dormition Cathedral, crowned by green teardrops, is a sight to behold. The cream walls and silver onion domes of the Church of the Resurrection are equally eye-catching and the painted walls of the Church of St John the Evangelist are simply breathtaking.

• *Monastery of St Jacob the Saviour, Rostov the Great.*

• *Kotorosl, one of the rivers in Yaroslavl.*

• *Ipatievsky Monastery, Kostroma.*

THE PRINCE'S CITY

Then it's back to the train for just over an hour before we reach Yaroslavl. Founded in 1010 by the legendary Yaroslav the Wise, Grand Prince of Kiev, at the confluence of the Kotorosl and Volga rivers, this city is regarded as the capital of the Golden Ring. Here too, the religious buildings are stunning in their splendour and sheer number: the dazzling Monastery of the Transfiguration of the Saviour, the stunning emerald-domed St Elijah the Prophet's Church, the unusual reddish hue of Saint Michael the Archangel Church with its choir, a moving sight for anyone who appreciates the fragile beauty of Orthodox liturgical art.

As the day draws to a close, we take another train, this time to Kostroma, our final stop. The atmosphere in the carriage is different. Night has fallen over Russia. Workers are travelling home, dozing in their seats with their headphones firmly in place, all the better to forget their hard day's graft. They are oblivious to the architectural treasures they pass every day, too familiar to raise an eyebrow. Tomorrow, more passengers will make the same journey, but in the opposite direction. We, on the other hand, are set to visit Kostroma, favoured by the Russian imperial family, the Romanovs, with its Church of the Resurrection, all blood-red walls and slate-grey onion domes, the Ipatievsky Monastery and the old Fire Tower.

📢 IT'S RAINING PRINCES…

Other cities in the Golden Ring are not as easy to reach by train, but are well worth a visit by bus or hire car. Should you wish to prolong the whole experience in this way, do stop in majestic Suzdal, Ivanovo, with its youthful, artistic vibe, and affluent Pereslavl-Zalessky.

163

St Petersburg → Murmansk
Ice and steel

on board the
ARKTIKA

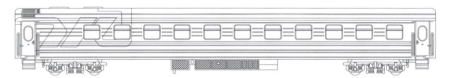

A train bound for the Barents Sea.

Whereas the Trans-Siberian Railway heads directly for Russia's eastern boundaries, the Arktika makes its way towards the far north. In just shy of 24 hours, it links the majestic city of St Petersburg with Murmansk, one of Russia's northernmost cities, on the Barents Sea. This is a rail adventure extending into the Arctic Circle, where ice and steel do battle.

Opposite page: Typical taiga landscape.

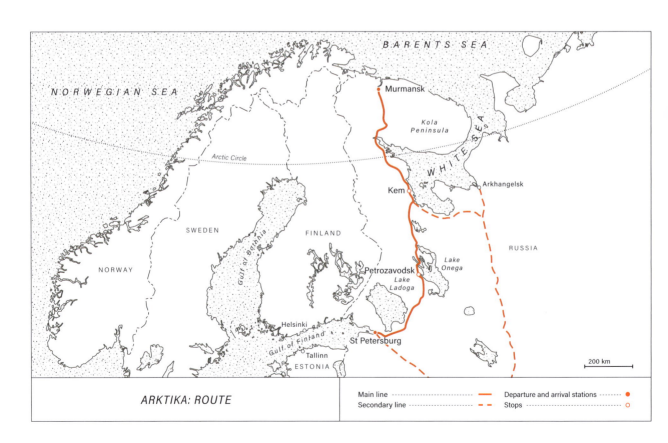

ARKTIKA: ROUTE

CONSTRUCTED
1917

JOURNEY LENGTH
23 hours, 57 mins

DISTANCE
1,274km

COUNTRIES VISITED
Russia

🔊 **TAKE A BUS TO THE ICE KINGDOM**

In many ways, Murmansk feels like the end of the Earth, the last piece of terra firma before the ice kingdom. And yet it's possible to go even further by taking a bus to Kirkenes, in Norway – a journey that lasts another four hours. A starting point whether you're returning to southern Europe, or keen to explore the further reaches of the far north.

• The Arktika en route for Murmansk.

ON BOARD THE ARKTIKA

St Petersburg is one of those cities that needs no introduction. Its 4.5-km-long main thoroughfare, Nevsky Prospect, the crazy multicoloured confection that is the Church of the Saviour on the Spilled Blood with its ornate onion domes, the prestigious collection in the Hermitage Museum with its elegant façade, or the colossal Mariinsky Theatre are just some of the delights that make this relatively new city, founded by Peter the Great in 1703, such a glorious place to visit. After taking in all the beauty and colour we can manage in one go, we find our way to Ladozhsky station. There, under a series of spectacular triangular plate-glass windows, our train, the Arktika, awaits.

By no stretch of the imagination can the Arktika be described as a luxury train. Its chunky red engine isn't designed to slice through the air but to plough its way through snow and ice. Inside the train, the first two classes offer compartments for two or four people. For a more immersive experience, the best option is to travel in third class, otherwise known as *platzkart*, where there are rows of bunks in vast communal carriages. This is where the *provodnitsa* rules the roost. With her immaculate blue uniform and bright red cap, this lady has many responsibilities throughout the long journey: she checks the tickets on the lookout for stowaways, settles passengers into their respective quarters, provides information, sells sundry provisions and brings passengers hot water from the samovar if they are unable to get there under their own steam. She also ensures that a tranquil atmosphere prevails in the carriage.

UNDER THE STERN EYE OF THE PROVODNITSA

The provodnitsa may be in charge, but the one thing she doesn't do is conversation. You have to rely on the other passengers for that. While some refuse to engage at all, others might suggest a game of chess, that traditional Russian pastime that can be played even if you don't speak the same language as your opponent. And yet the language barrier doesn't prevent people trying to communicate. Some locals struggle to make themselves understood by foreign passengers, especially as they are a relatively rare sight on this line, despite its formidable and underrated beauty.

For there can be no doubt that the scenery outside is staggeringly beautiful. The taiga, with its coniferous forests so typical of these latitudes, goes on for hundreds of kilometres. It defies the snow, imperturbably piercing its white cloak but permitting a snowy blanket to drift around the tree trunks. These two forces co-exist in a superb battle of brutality, neither capable of dominating the other. Next will come the tundra. No more statuesque tapering trees. Only spindly shrubs, grasses, mosses and lichen are able to survive in this environment where even the lakes are frozen.

• Taiga, coniferous forests so typical of these latitudes.

THE SECRETS OF THE BARENTS SEA

Surprisingly, there are human beings here too. In fact, Murmansk has a population of almost 300,000, jam-packed into sturdy apartment blocks. We arrive to dazzling light, a glass of steaming tea in our hands for warmth. One question springs to mind: why would you want to live in a place where the temperature rarely gets above 16°C, even when the sun is shining? There's a one-word answer: gas. Unlike much of the Barents Sea coastline, the port of Murmansk does not ice over. There is plenty of work here – hard work admittedly, but work nonetheless. Something to bear in mind when, after nightfall, we enjoy the glorious sight of the Aurora Borealis as we return from visiting the nuclear-powered ice-breaker, the Lenin.

• Typical snowy scene in Siberia.

Kola peninsula on the Barents Sea.

Moscow → St Petersburg → Tallinn
Flowers in the snow

on board the
RED ARROW

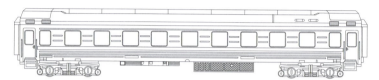

A legendary train caught in the geopolitical crosshairs.

Renowned for the beauty of its forest landscapes and flowering meadows, the rail journey between Moscow and Tallinn via St Petersburg can be travelled by a variety of routes. We have opted for a very special itinerary as an opportunity to ride on one of the most famous Russian sleeper trains, the Red Arrow. Yet this is merely the first step in an adventure full of unexpected twists and turns.

Opposite page: View over the rooftops of St Petersburg.

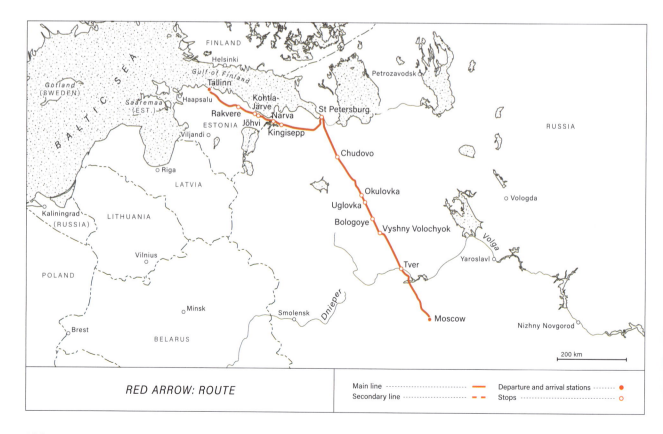

RED ARROW: ROUTE

①	②	③	④	⑤	⑥	⑦
MOSCOW	TVER	VYSHNY VOLOCHYOK	BOLOGOYE	UGLOVKA	OKULOVKA	CHUDOVO

OPERATING SINCE
1931

JOURNEY LENGTH
20 hours

DISTANCE
867km

COUNTRIES VISITED
Russia
Estonia

CITY OF NINE STATIONS

It's already late when we arrive at Leningradsky, the oldest of Moscow's nine railway stations. Beforehand, we'd spent time enjoying the best of the Russian capital with its legendary buildings, its largely underrated hospitality and its shamefully little-known cuisine. We were careful not to dawdle as our train, the famous Red Arrow, is known for its punctuality. Every evening it leaves Moscow on the stroke of midnight and arrives in St Petersburg at 8 on the dot. Inside its red carriages, there's a relaxed vibe. In Russia, sleeper trains are still very much the norm due to the country's vast scale and everyone knows the ropes. There's the *provodnik* or *provodnitsa*, who is in charge of each carriage and tells passengers where to find their compartment or berth. We remove our coats and snow-flecked shoes before stepping into the disposable slippers provided on board. Meanwhile, the Red Arrow begins its night-time journey through Moscow's huge urban sprawl.

• *Dining car on the Red Arrow.*

• *Winter Palace, St Petersburg.*

LANTERNS IN THE WIND

Conversation is flowing in the dining car. When you travel by train, especially at night, you're liable to mingle with people from nearly every walk of life. Only the very rich and those with urgent deadlines to meet tend to favour air travel. Outside, eerie landscapes are just visible, illuminated from time to time by moonlight or by the lights of occasional built-up areas. From where we sit, they resemble little lanterns swaying in the wind. We can tell it's cold, but it doesn't feel it on board. Russian trains are renowned for their reliable heating systems – sometimes just a little too efficient! Little by little, as people finish their glasses of tea and conversations wind down, the dining car empties and everyone returns to their berth.

We arrive in St Petersburg at 8 o'clock prompt. Vosstaniya Square (which translates as Uprising Square), right in front of the station, is ready for the day ahead and we can see the main street, Nevsky Prospect, stretching out ahead of us. The sun has yet to put in an appearance, leaving the sky a pretty, bluish-grey colour. Time for breakfast before we set out to explore the city and all its architectural and cultural delights. Hermitage Museum, the Church of the Saviour on the Spilled Blood, St Isaac's Cathedral and of course the canals and the River Neva itself.

• *The famous White Nights of St Petersburg.*

MOSCOW → ST PETERSBURG → TALLIN

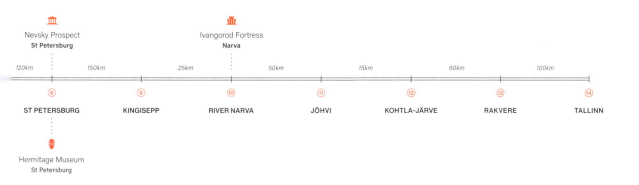

• *Moyka quay, St Petersburg.*

A CROSS-BORDER ADVENTURE

It's just after 10pm by the time we return to the station to catch our second train. This is also when our adventure starts to get a bit more hair-raising. Those in the know about geopolitical matters will be aware that relations between Estonia and Russia haven't exactly been cordial since the collapse of the Soviet Union. This doesn't mean that the rail link between the two capitals is no more, but the situation has definitely changed since the Covid-19 pandemic and the Russian invasion of Ukraine.

In the light of the international situation, it's not beyond the realms of possibility that we might be required to leave our train in the middle of the night and made to continue to the border (the River Narva) by bus. On one side of the river is the Russian town of Ivangorod and its 13th-century fortress; on the other side is its Estonian twin, which takes the name of the river on which it lies. This is a harsh reflection of the gulf, both gaping and hydrological, that separates two worlds that are becoming harder and harder to reconcile.

📢 AGE-OLD GRIEVANCES AND DEEP-SEATED TENSIONS

Geopolitical tensions are an ever-changing phenomenon, hard to pin down. Hence why crossing the border between Russia and Estonia means reporting to the competent authorities not only in your own country, but also in the countries in question. Under no circumstances should this be contemplated by travellers who are averse to queuing or hanging around to go through border checkpoints, and, by extension, the associated border controls.

• *Early morning on the Estonian plains.*

• *Wildflower meadow in Estonia.*

KALEIDOSCOPE OF FLOWERS

As surprising as it may seem, this cross-border adventure does have its compensations for those brave enough to risk it, especially in spring and summer. The fertile soil of Estonia is the backdrop for large-scale explosions of blooms. For months at a time, the countryside is carpeted in primroses, wood anemones, wonder violets, bitter milkwort and lady's smock, to say nothing of shy and mercurial orchids. These are just a few examples of the fragile treasures to be found in the fields and meadows, or scattered in woodland, according to their preferred habitat.

Eventually, sated by this kaleidoscope of flowers, our noses filled with the scents that manage to make it through the train's air-conditioning system, we arrive in Tallinn, capital of the small state of Estonia. While a modest size, the city is nevertheless a perfectly preserved historical masterpiece. Each alleyway, square and building in the old part of the city centre is evidence of this fact. We instinctively know what to do the moment we set foot on Estonian soil; it's the kind of city you can only truly appreciate by losing yourself in its narrow streets, drifting aimlessly until you come across any number of hidden treasures. So that's exactly what we do – it's what we're there for after all.

171

Ankara → Kars
The snows of Anatolia

on board the
DOGU EKSPRESI

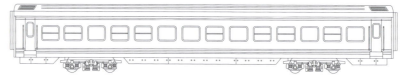

A train ride to the mountains of Anatolia.

The Dogu Ekspresi – which translates as the Express of the East, or even the Orient Express – runs on one of Turkey's most spectacular and most fabled rail routes. It links Ankara, the country's capital, with the town of Kars, close to the Armenian border, and is so popular that the government launched a second edition in 2019, the Turistik Dogu Ekspresi, specifically intended for tourists, which is both more expensive and more luxurious. However, the train's true soul remains in the local version.

Opposite page: White, with red and blue stripes: the livery of the Dogu Ekspresi.

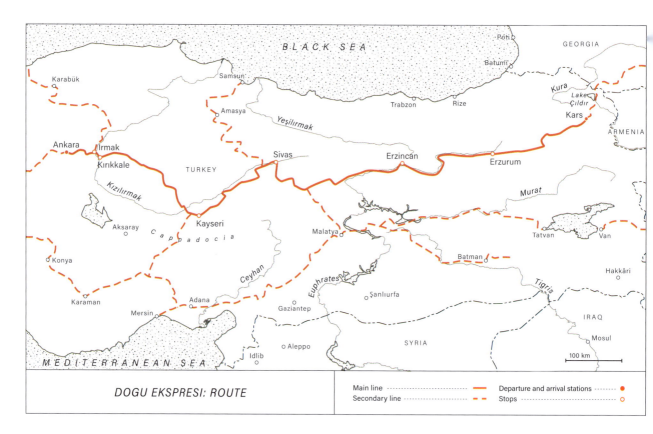

DOGU EKSPRESI: ROUTE

① ANKARA	② IRMAK	③ KIRIKKALE	④ KAYSERI	⑤ SIVAS
62km	20km	260km	200km	

Ataturk's Mausoleum — Ankara
Cappadocia — Kayseri

OPERATING SINCE
1936

JOURNEY LENGTH
26 hours

DISTANCE
1,360km

COUNTRIES VISITED
Turkey

A TRAIN IN WINTER

The Dogu Ekspresi adventure begins at Ankara station just before 6pm, our train's daily departure time. As we arrive, it's waiting patiently at the platform, white, with red and blue stripes along its entire length. The train is clean and basic, with no visible modern touches. People from all social classes head for the carriage doors, seeking information from the on-board crew. Those with the cheapest tickets turn towards the rows of blue seats, while others are directed to the four-berth compartments, simple yet practical. All passengers are equipped with substantial stocks of food since the buffet car only serves drinks and snacks.

• *Ankara, Turkey's capital, in winter.*

• *Dogu Ekspresi on its way to Kars.*

THE COMPLETE ANATOLIA EXPERIENCE

To enjoy this trip to the utmost, we are travelling in winter, which means the sun starts to dip below the horizon after just a few kilometres. Behind us, Ankara is already out of sight. The citadel, its construction dates lost in the mists of time, Ataturk's Mausoleum – burial site of Mustafa Kemal Ataturk, the founding father of modern Turkey – and the four minarets of the Kocatepe Mosque are no more than beautiful memories of our city tour. Outside, Anatolia is all around us. This name, coined by the Turks to describe the Asian part of their territory, holds the self-confessed soul of the nation. At this point on the journey, the landscape comprises vast cultivated plains in the foreground and gently rolling mountains in the distance. Anatolia also encompasses forests, rivers, villages and roads. The various components of the landscape alternate and merge into one another: a little town on the edge of the fields, dense clumps of trees beside a stream, little pockets of snow on the rocky slopes.

PLANET CAPPADOCIA

It's the middle of the night, around 1.30am, when we arrive in Kayseri, gateway to the legendary Cappadocia. Known across the world for its extraterrestrial landscapes, this region is home to some of the planet's most extraordinary sights. Its unusual topography, fairy chimneys, cave villages and churches make this an unmissable destination and one that can be accessed from Kayseri. Whether on foot, on horseback or in a hot air balloon, you need to explore this region with your eyes wide open and a healthy appetite. Because, as well as its tourist attractions, Cappadocia also has some unique wines and dishes including testi kebab, cooked in a clay pot.

• *Mount Erciyes (3,916m), Kayseri.*

ANKARA → KARS

- *Erzincan, a city with a population of 200,000.*

SNOW REIGNS SUPREME

When we wake up at around 7.30 the next morning, a glance outside is all it takes to see that we are surrounded by snow. Fields, mountains, villages – nowhere is safe from the permanent snowy onslaught. It falls so thickly, it's as if we're caught in a white-out. At first glance, the world appears to have stopped. On looking again, we see tiny indications that life is continuing after all: the headlights of a van following a winding road, the reassuring lights of a house and a farm vehicle heading to work. The people who live here really understand snow in all its many moods.

As we approach midday, the Dogu Ekspresi stops at Erzincan. Like many other passengers, we don our winter coats and rush to the little food stall on the platform, our stomachs grumbling due to the lack of more substantial fare on board. And of course this is definitely the weather for hot food. Gözleme perhaps, flatbreads stuffed with spinach or meat. Or maybe a cag kebab, a lamb skewer typical of the region around Erzurum, our next destination. Or even an islak burger, also known as a 'wet burger', traditionally sold on the streets of Turkey. Can't make up your mind? Then it's got to be a pide, a local pizza in the shape of a boat, with lashings of cheese, meat and onions.

- *Erzincan, on the banks of the Euphrates.*

📣 **A BORDER WHERE TENSIONS RUN HIGH**

Beyond Kars lies one of the most closely guarded frontiers in the world, the border separating Turkey from Armenia. Although neighbours and closely linked by the respective histories of their peoples, the two countries are in open conflict, although there is no direct military action. Between April 1915 and July 1916, two-thirds of the Armenians in what is now Turkey were massacred, deported or starved to death. An absolute human tragedy that Ankara still, to this day, refuses to acknowledge as genocide.

- *Lake Çıldır, near Kars.*

- *Kars, the line's terminus.*

THE WHITE CITY OF KARS

Replete once more, we resume our journey towards Kars. Snow is everywhere, imperious in its majesty – it's an indisputable fact of life here. Our adventure is starting to resemble the life of the characters in *Snowpiercer*, a French graphic novel and dystopian TV series, also available in English, in which the last surviving members of the human race take refuge on a train to survive a new ice age. Except our story also has a hint of Orhan Pamuk, living legend of the Turkish literature scene and recipient of the 2006 Nobel Prize for Literature, who wrote a novel entitled *Snow*, in which most of the action takes place in Kars. The latter eventually appears on the horizon after we've been travelling for over 24 hours. Located at an altitude of 1,754m, this city is remarkable for its feeling of peace and quiet. Over the centuries it has been occupied by the Seljuk Dynasty, the Mongols, the Ottomans, the Soviets and the Armenians. It has absorbed all these cultures and soaked up the blood of the battles and massacres that have shaped its evolution. What remains is a city that seems frozen in time, its own unique time. Despite the many tourists who travel here in winter, Kars is not overwhelmed. Ice fishing is still common practice here and horses are still used to draw sleighs over the snowy landscape. This is our reward.

175

Eskişehir → Konya → Adana
The remnants of a legend

on board the
TAURUS EXPRESS

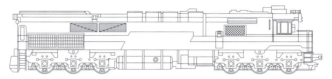

Last remnants of a legendary train.

Launched in 1930, the Taurus Express was intended to extend the route of the equally legendary Orient Express – which actually wasn't an express and didn't technically travel to the Orient – from Istanbul to Damascus and Baghdad. At the time, there was another train that linked the Iraqi capital to Basra. Suspended in stages between 2003 and 2010, then relaunched in 2012, it now serves merely to connect the magnificent Turkish cities of Eskişehir, Konya and Adana.

Opposite page: The Taurus Mountains, a limestone range bordering the Anatolian Plateau.

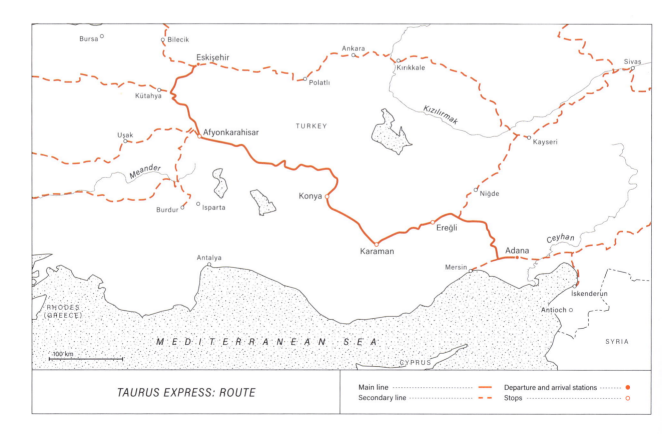

TAURUS EXPRESS: ROUTE

OPERATING SINCE
1930, 2012

JOURNEY LENGTH
9 to 10 hours

DISTANCE
541km

COUNTRIES VISITED
Turkey

🚂 THE FORGOTTEN TRAINS OF TURKEY AND IRAQ

The conflicts in Iraq and then Syria were what put paid to the original route of the Taurus Express. The remnants of this legendary train still exist in these two countries, which are grappling with humanitarian crises and dire political situations to this day. The rusty old carriages, some of which have suffered bomb damage, remind those familiar with this line that the region hasn't always been quite so isolated from the rest of the world...

• Castle in Sazova Park, Eskisehir.

THE VENICE OF TURKEY

Eskişehir certainly doesn't top the list of most famous cities in Turkey. Nevertheless, this city, often referred to as 'Little Venice' and situated 300km south-east of Istanbul, is one of the country's lesser-known gems. Eskişehir's charms mainly centre on the water due to its location on the banks of the Porsuk, where boats resembling a cross between a gondola and a dugout canoe glide down the river, laden with home-grown, and sometimes even international, tourists. On the river's flower-carpeted banks, the voices of the town's vibrant student population are a constant accompaniment, from café terraces to the city's many green spaces, echoing off the walls of the colourful houses.

As we move on, we are in no doubt that Anatolia, the Asian part of Turkey, contains any number of forgotten treasures – and the remainder of our journey will prove us correct. Back on board, this time on a standard Turkish train, Mother Nature picks up the baton. Beyond the confines of the train, huge fields glow in the Anatolian sunlight. In the distance, massive grey mountains define the horizon. In their foothills, a scattering of shimmering white towns break up their dark mass. Soaring high above the peaks, a cascade of towering, fluffy clouds destined never to float down to Earth.

• Konya, 1,017m above sea level.

RUMI'S HOMELAND

When the Taurus Express reaches Konya, a whole new world opens up before us. Although it now only rules the Anatolian steppe, this city, at an altitude of 1,017m, was once one of the Orient's greatest intellectual and spiritual centres. This was where the legendary Jalāl al-Dīn Muḥammad Rūmī, better known simply as Rumi, spent some of his life. Philosopher and Sufi mystic, author of astoundingly beautiful verse and founder of the Mevlevi Order, with its famous whirling dervishes, he is now laid to rest in an elegant mausoleum. Following this moving experience for those who are familiar with the poet's work, we set off for Alaeddin Hill to have tea on its verdant slopes. This hill takes the name of the Seljuk ruler who made Konya his capital and is crowned by the city's oldest mosque, built between the 12th and 13th centuries.

• Central Anatolia, a green and pleasant land.

OUTLIVING THE ANCIENT GODS

Now it's time to return to our train and head for Adana. Our route passes by the Taurus Mountains, after which our train is named, their imposing presence quite something. The mountains themselves take their name from the bull, symbol of the pre-Islamic storm and fertility god, Adad. Caring little for mere human concerns and naming conventions, they assume the form of a 600-km-long mountain range with a number of peaks over 3,000m.

These rock behemoths dominate the landscape, reminiscent of a fantasy film set. They certainly look as though they own the place, having outlived the ancient Gods; no wonder they are imperturbable in the face of anything else that might come their way. At a distance befitting their rank, they accompany us until we reach our terminus, Adana. This is the fifth largest city in Turkey by population, but it is also the birthplace of the well-known kebab that bears its name and the setting for the Sabanci Central Mosque with its six soaring minarets.

• Taurus Mountains, a 600-km-long mountain range.

ESKIŞEHIR → KONYA → ADANA

• *Adana Viaduct, built in 1916.*

Bandar-e Torkaman → Bandar-e Emam Khomeyni

From the Caspian Sea to the Persian Gulf

on the
TRANS-IRANIAN RAILWAY

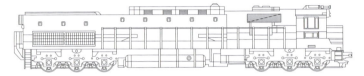

Across four climate zones by train.

Iran has been governed by a ruthless religious dictatorship since the Islamic Revolution of 1979 and is therefore particularly difficult for travellers to access. Yet it is still a bewitchingly beautiful country for all that. One of the best ways to admire it is from a UNESCO World Heritage railway line that passes through four different climate zones and some of the nation's most iconic sites.

Opposite page: A UNESCO World Heritage-listed railway line.

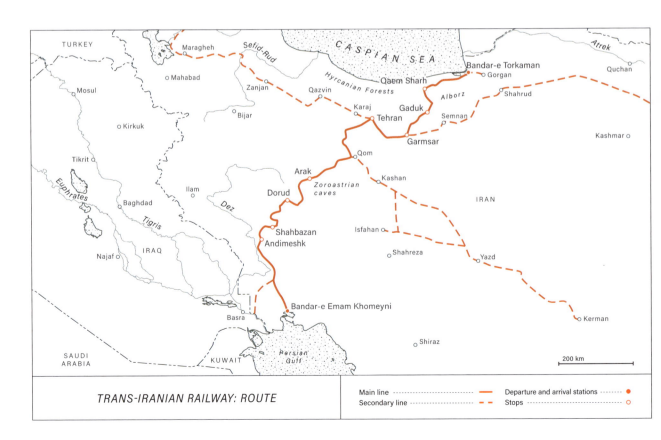

TRANS-IRANIAN RAILWAY: ROUTE

① **BANDAR-E TORKAMAN** ② **QAEM SHARH** ③ **GADUK** ④ **GARMSAR** ⑤ **TEHRAN** ⑥ **QOM**

CONSTRUCTED
1925–1939

JOURNEY LENGTH
2 days, 1 night

DISTANCE
1,394km

COUNTRIES VISITED
Iran

HEIGHT OF VERESK VIADUCT
110m

NUMBER OF LARGE BRIDGES
174

NUMBER OF MINOR BRIDGES
186

NUMBER OF TUNNELS
224

• *A 1,394km rail journey.*

FORESTS ALONG THE CASPIAN SEA

We are in Bandar-e Torkaman. In the heart of this eco-region made up of Hyrcanian forests, a belt of deciduous trees dating back 50 million years, this little harbour town on the shores of the Caspian Sea is the starting point for our journey through Iran, from north to south. Our train awaits us on the platform in front of a small, light-coloured building with clean lines. As part of the preparations for departure, the train crew beat attractive coloured rugs before laying them in the individual compartments. Only then are the passengers allowed to board. Men in short-sleeved shirts, boys in shorts, women covered from head to toe in black robes, alongside others, more numerous, wearing coloured headscarves, carefully arranged to defy the intolerable rules imposed upon them by the mullahs' strict regime. Virtually all social strata can be found on this historic line. The roads in Iran have a dangerous reputation, unlike trains, which are usually considered a safe form of transport.

• *Mount Damavand, the highest volcano in Iran.*

• *Tehran, at the foot of the Alborz Mountains.*

ON THE SLOPES OF THE ALBORZ MOUNTAINS

In our comfortable seats upholstered in a green checked fabric, we draw back the embroidered curtains to better admire the scenery in the Alborz mountain range, sometimes spelled Elborz, where the highest peak, Mount Damavand, is 5,610m above sea level. This lofty summit is the source of many ancient legends, not least those telling of a mythological bird and a three-headed dragon. With no particular sense of urgency, the train makes its way through these rocky fortresses via the many engineering structures along its route, including the impressive Veresk Viaduct, 110m above the valley it spans. All around us, our fellow passengers have their smartphones out, snapping picture after picture.

Before long, we arrive in Tehran. With a population of over 9 million, Iran's sprawling capital city reaches as far as the foothills of the Alborz mountains, so extensive is the area it covers: more than 700km². The city's altitude varies from 1,700m in the north to 1,100m in the south. The city has been in existence for nearly 6,000 years, over which time it has been influenced by so many cultures that it's impossible to list them all; some have left behind undoubted architectural treasures, however. The 12th-century Mausoleum of Imamzadeh Saleh in all its flamboyant glory, the 16th-century Golestan Palace, where you just want time to stand still, the Museum of Contemporary Art with its Brutalist lines, the incredible Shahr Theatre and the gargantuan Azadi Tower.

BANDAR-E TORKAMAN → BANDAR-E EMAM KHOMEYNI

HOLY CITY

The scenery undergoes a radical change between Tehran and Qom. Now we're in the Iranian desert, which takes the form of a long arid line on the horizon, interrupted only by hostile rocky outcrops. Despite the heat we can sense outside, the efficient air-conditioning system inside our compartment keeps us pleasantly cool. We can barely take our eyes off the desolate beauty of this landscape, but eventually we arrive at Qom station.

Regarded as one of the holiest cities and one of the most important spiritual centres of Shi'a Islam, Qom welcomes over 20 million pilgrims from across the world every year. Some come to study under the teachers based here, while others pray or pay homage to the many holy figures who have passed this way over the course of history. Like us, they wander from the Shrine of Fatima Masumeh to mosques such as Jamkaran or Imam Hasan al-Askari, close to the Grand Bazaar. Nature lovers may also consider making a trip to Namak Lake, a saltwater lake 100km or so to the east of the city.

• Qom, Shi'ite spiritual centre.

• Namak, a saltwater lake to the east of Qom.

📣 ONE TRAIN, 43 CONSTRUCTION COMPANIES

The vast array of landscapes encountered on the Trans-Iranian Railway line meant that its designers had to use every last inch of ingenuity at their disposal. In total, 70,000 workers built 174 large bridges, 186 minor bridges and 224 tunnels, including 11 spiral tunnels. To avoid interference, the project involved 43 foreign companies rather than one single contractor.

• The River Dez in Andimeshk.

ONWARDS TO THE PERSIAN GULF

After a night lulled by the murmuring of prayers, we return to the train and head southwards. En route, we pass a number of little-known towns with an extraordinarily rich cultural heritage. Arak, with its splendid ochre and blue mosque and the sacred caves of the Zoroastrians, located in the environs of the city. Andimeshk, from where it's possible to visit the ruined water mills, some 1,700 years old, built on the River Dez during the reign of the Sasanian Empire. Ahvaz, also known by the Iranians as the 'City of Bridges' for reasons that will become only too evident.

The natural environment between these towns isn't too shabby either. When our train begins to cross the Zagros Mountains, another mountain range on our route, we're rendered speechless all over again. The Dez valley forces us to wend our way between massive rock buttresses, almost as if it's toying with us. It's hard to know where to look with all those buttresses and jagged rocks commanding our attention. By the time we reach our terminus, Bandar-e Emam Khomeyni, we are worn out with this feast of rugged beauty. The Persian Gulf is just metres away. We have succeeded in crossing Iran.

• The Zagros Mountains, to the east of the country.

183

RUSSIA & THE MIDDLE EAST

Mecca → Medina

From one holy city to another

on board the
HARAMAIN

An ultramodern train linking two holy cities.

Around 450km is the distance separating Mecca and Medina, Islam's two holiest cities. Since 2018, they have been linked by a brand-new high-speed train. Thanks to this train, millions of pilgrims are able to travel between these two cities in just over two hours, compared to the five hours or so it would take by car or 10 by bus. A significant change for believers across the world.

Opposite page: Kaaba, at the centre of the Great Mosque of Mecca.

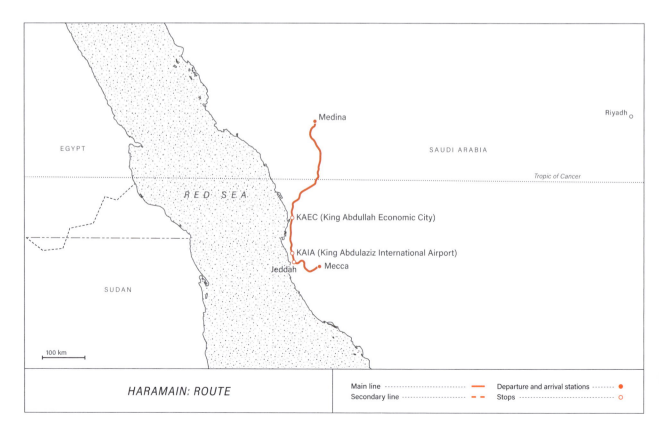

HARAMAIN: ROUTE

OPERATING SINCE
2018

JOURNEY LENGTH
2 hours, 20 mins

DISTANCE
450km

COUNTRIES VISITED
Saudi Arabia

📢 **ONE TRAIN, TWO HOLY CITIES**

The cities of Mecca and Medina are regarded as being entirely and exclusively dedicated to the practice of the Muslim faith. Mecca and most of Medina are therefore strictly off-limits to non-Muslims.

- *Jabal Thawr, mountain in Mecca.*

FROM MECCA TO MEDINA

Regardless of our faith and our attitude towards religion, we're all familiar with images of the hajj. This is the compulsory pilgrimage that all Muslims are expected to make at least once in their lifetime if they are physically fit enough and can afford to do so. It is also one of the Five Pillars of Islam and is completed by over two million pilgrims each year, although there was a significant slowdown in the years immediately after the Covid-19 pandemic. Most believers then go on to Medina, where the Prophet Muhammad sought exile. To make it easier to travel between the two holy cities, a journey that takes anything from five to ten hours by road, Saudi Arabia launched an exceptional high-speed rail service in 2018.

This journey begins on a platform in Mecca station under huge arches shielding passengers from the blistering heat. Sitting proudly on the track, a long white train with green doors awaits its passengers, uniformed attendants standing smartly to attention at the front end. Dozens of men sporting white robes take their places on the generous beige seats, each equipped with a small screen. Some also wear red-and-white-checked keffiyehs, secured in place by an agal, a black cord traditionally used with this headdress. Their faces reveal a variety of ages and very different backgrounds.

- *Haramain station in Jeddah.*

- *Bab Makkah, the 'Gateway to Mecca', in Jeddah.*

- *Balad, Jeddah's historic district.*

- *The mountainous Hejaz region – the word is Arabic for 'barrier'.*

A TRAIN IN THE HEJAZ

In order to tackle the Saudi landscape, the Haramain trains are specially designed to withstand the 50°C temperatures that the thermometer can reach in this part of the world. On board, passengers chat among themselves, turn their thoughts to prayer, or simply admire the views. The panoramic windows show off the splendours of the surrounding scenery, which seems to stretch on and on to infinity. The train is currently passing through the Hejaz region – which means 'barrier' and includes the Hijaz mountain range that runs alongside the Red Sea from north to south.

The train, which isn't solely reserved for use by pilgrims, stops at Jeddah. The Kingdom's economic capital, this former fishing village first came into being 2,500 years ago, but has long since thrown off its village vibe and transformed itself into a prosperous city, awarded UNESCO World Heritage status in 2014. On its streets and busy seafront, tall, modern tower blocks stand side-by-side with charming old buildings. Jeddah's principal claim to fame, however, is that it is home to the Bab Makkah, the 'Gateway to Mecca', a large structure with three arches and two turrets, intended to guide believers in the right direction.

The train then whisks its passengers on towards Medina through the stunning desert landscape of Saudi Arabia. On arrival, yet another list of holy places to visit, including the Prophet's Mosque, which can accommodate a million believers, or Quba Mosque, said to be the first mosque in the history of Islam.

• Jeddah, modern city and the country's financial hub.

Asia

17 TRAIN JOURNEYS
11 countries
A kaleidoscope of mystical rail adventures
FROM BENGALARU TO YOGYAKARTA

① **Bengalaru → Goa**
🇮🇳 GOLDEN CHARIOT
p. 190

② **Siliguri → Darjeeling**
🇮🇳 DARJEELING HIMALAYAN RAILWAY
p. 194

③ **Chennai → Rameswaram**
🇮🇳 SETHU EXPRESS
p. 198

④ **Mettupalayam → Ooty**
🇮🇳 NILGIRI MOUNTAIN RAILWAY
p. 202

⑤ **Kandy → Badulla**
🇱🇰 HILL COUNTRY TRAIN
p. 208

⑥ **Beijing → Ulaanbaatar**
🇨🇳 TRANS-MONGOLIAN RAILWAY
p. 212

⑦ **Nyingchi → Lhasa**
🇨🇳 FUXING HAO
p. 216

⑧ **Hefei → Fuzhou**
🇨🇳 HEFEI-FUZHOU
p. 220

⑨ **Xi'an → Lanzhou → Urumqi**
🇨🇳 XI'AN-URUMQI
p. 224

⑩ **Unazuki → Keyakidaira**
🇯🇵 KUROBE GORGE RAILWAY
p. 228

⑪ **Tokyo → Hakodate**
🇯🇵 TOHOKU SHINKANSEN
p. 232

⑫ **Tokyo → Kagoshima**
🇯🇵 KYUSHU SHINKANSEN
p. 236

⑬ **Aomori → Akita**
🇯🇵 RESORT SHIRAKAMI
p. 242

⑭ **Bangkok → Singapore**
🇹🇭 EASTERN AND ORIENTAL EXPRESS
p. 246

⑮ **Bangkok → Pa Sak Jolasid Dam**
🇹🇭 ROT FAI LOI NAM
p. 250

⑯ **Hanoi → Ho Chi Minh City**
🇻🇳 REUNIFICATION EXPRESS
p. 254

⑰ **Bandung → Yogyakarta**
🇮🇩 INDONESIAN RAILWAY
p. 258

Bengalaru → Goa

The pride of Karnataka

on board the
GOLDEN CHARIOT

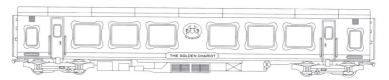

A train through the lesser-known parts of India.

Of the many trains that criss-cross India's 3,287 million km², there is one that stands out from the crowd. Known as the Golden Chariot, this long purple and gold train snakes its way between some of the most iconic places in the state of Karnataka, an adventure covering nearly 2,600km at the heart of one the most exotic regions on the planet.

Opposite page: View over the rooftops of Badami.

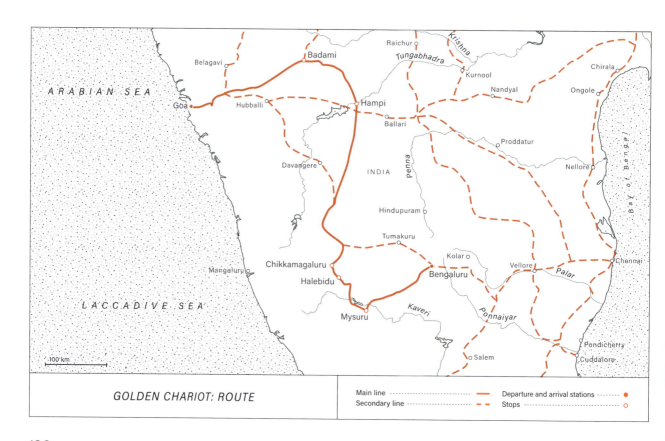

ASIA

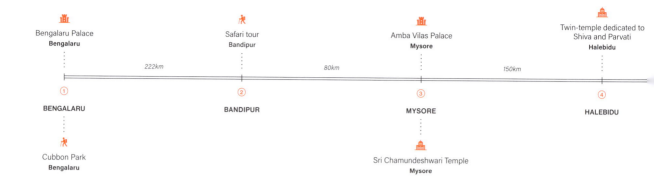

① BENGALARU	Bengalaru Palace — Bengalaru · Cubbon Park — Bengalaru
② BANDIPUR	Safari tour — Bandipur
③ MYSORE	Amba Vilas Palace — Mysore · Sri Chamundeshwari Temple — Mysore
④ HALEBIDU	Twin-temple dedicated to Shiva and Parvati — Halebidu

222km · 80km · 150km

OPERATING SINCE
2008

JOURNEY LENGTH
7 days, 6 nights

DISTANCE
2,588km

COUNTRIES VISITED
India

NUMBER OF CABINS
44

NUMBER OF RESTAURANT CARS
2

NUMBER OF SPAS
1

MUSICAL ENTRÉE

Bengalaru station is anything but peaceful this morning. As we arrive on the platform, we're greeted by a troupe of musicians playing long trumpets and drums, alongside sari-clad women draping garlands of marigolds around our necks and placing a *tilaka* on our foreheads. Staff members, their hands behind their backs, line up along the train, ready to relieve us of our luggage. The Golden Chariot's reputation is well-deserved and passengers really are treated like royalty.

We are then taken on board this magnificent purple chariot, so flamboyantly opulent that it is reminiscent of the world's grandest hotels. Its carriages are named after former Indian dynasties, with 44 richly decorated cabins – one of which is equipped for disabled passengers – two restaurant cars – Ruchi and Nalapaka – serving Indian, Chinese and international cuisine prepared on board, a bar offering a range of spirits, wines and cocktails, a spa providing Ayurvedic treatments, a fully equipped gym and even a business centre with guaranteed internet access.

▪ *Golden Chariot, in its purple and gold livery.*

▪ *The skyscrapers of Bengalaru.*

▪ *Elephant in Bandipur National Park.*

FAREWELL TO THE GARDEN CITY

These are the sumptuous surroundings in which we leave Bengalaru, formerly known as Bangalore, a city of some 8 million inhabitants, after lunch on board. Yet the Garden City has stolen our hearts, the bustle of its wide shopping streets contrasting with the tranquillity of its narrow tree-lined alleyways. The surreal architecture of the Iskcon Temple also challenges our aesthetic sensibilities. Its royal palace bears witness to men's folly, while Cubbon Park is a showcase for the wisdom of trees. But these pleasures are all behind us as we pull into Nanjangud, our departure point for Bandipur and a safari in a national park featuring tigers and Asian elephants.

The following morning, we wake up in Mysore, cultural capital of the Indian state of Karnataka and spiritual home of yoga. This city is a wonderful blend of peace, harmony and quiet streets, quite an unusual attribute in most large Indian cities. We seize the opportunity to wander slowly though the colourful jumble of thoroughfares. Across the street, a horse-drawn carriage holds its own with the cars. In one of the squares, women in bright orange saris squat on steps, chatting away. But then the real treasures unfold: the staggering scale of Mysore Palace, also known as Amba Vilas Palace, with its columns and red domes; the vertiginous beauty of Sri Chamundeshwari Temple; or the immaculately ordered planting in Brindavan Gardens.

▪ *Amba Vilas Palace, Mysore.*

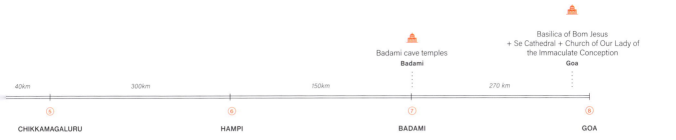

A STROLL AMONG THE RUINS

On the third day of our journey we leave the train at Halebidu, site of a 12th-century twin-temple dedicated to the Hindu god Shiva and his goddess Parvati. Renowned for the exquisite sculptures adorning its walls, this shrine was never completed, for reasons now lost in the mists of time. We then climb back on board the Golden Chariot for a hearty lunch, during which the train continues on to Chikkamagaluru and its spectacular coffee plantations.

On day 4, the atmosphere changes again. After being in the realms of trees, we re-enter man's domain. We visit a monumental collection of ruins in Hampi, former capital of the Hindu Vijayanagara Empire. Fifteenth-century chronicles describe it as a powerful and extremely wealthy merchant city, on a similar scale to Peking (as Beijing was known in those days). A stroll among the ruins is an education in itself. Greatness doesn't always endure. This thought lingers in our minds as we return to our luxury train to be treated to the heady delights of an Indian-themed evening.

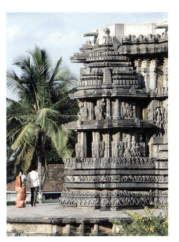

• *Shiva and Parvati Temple, Halebidu.*

🔊 A MODERN LUXURY TRAIN

Many present-day deluxe trains are made up of old carriages that used to belong to their most illustrious predecessors. However, the Golden Chariot came about as a result of a wholesale revamp of a standard train. Led by architect Kusum Pendse, the project required skilled craftsmen, including 200 carpenters working flat-out for four months.

• *Badami, former capital of the Chalukya Dynasty.*

• *Church of Our Lady of the Immaculate Conception, Goa.*

AMID THE TEMPLES

After another night on board and a morning spent travelling through the lush landscapes of Southern India, the train stops in Badami, formerly known as Vatapi and capital of the Chalukya Dynasty between the 6th to 8th centuries. This town is home to wondrous temples carved out of the red rock of this region. The façades of these monuments, worthy of a Hollywood film set, conceal long passages sculpted from floor to ceiling and walls covered with reliefs and statues. A stunning example of the tons of rock that faith can move when combined with power. Our exploration of Hindu architecture continues at Aihole and Pattadakal, where over a hundred magnificent temples rub shoulders with one another.

Eventually, on our last day, we arrive in Goa, host to any number of wonderful sights, stories and flavours of this part of India. Here, Hindu temples stand side-by-side with the Basilica of Bom Jesus, Se Cathedral and the light-filled Church of Our Lady of the Immaculate Conception. But while the faithful pay homage to their gods or meditate at the tomb of St Francis Xavier, others practise yoga or shake their heads to the beat of electronic music reverberating across idyllic beaches. In Goa, everyone has their own niche. You just need to find the right one.

193

ASIA

Siliguri → Darjeeling
On top of the world

on the
DARJEELING HIMALAYAN RAILWAY

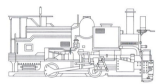

Otherwise known as the 'Toy Train'.

Made famous by the black tea that bears its name, the Indian city of Darjeeling is served by one of the world's most picturesque railway lines. Built without the need for a single tunnel, the line winds its way between mist-capped mountains bedecked with tea plantations. The train itself is a miniature blue ensemble with proportions so modest and so endearing that it's hard to believe it has the strength to climb up to 2,073m.

Opposite page: A miniature blue locomotive and carriages on the Darjeeling Himalayan Railway.

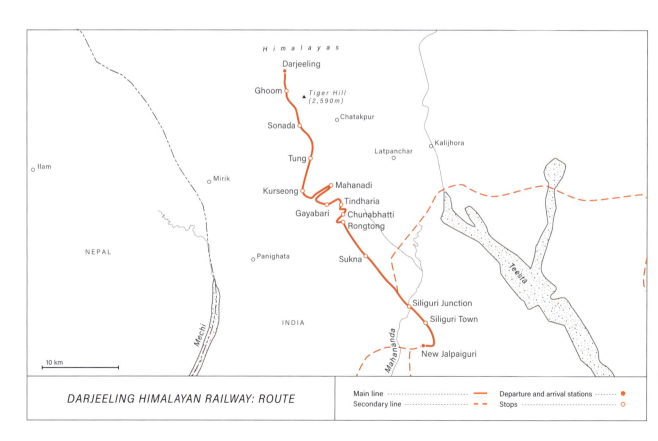

DARJEELING HIMALAYAN RAILWAY: ROUTE

Main line — Departure and arrival stations ●
Secondary line --- Stops ○

ASIA

CONSTRUCTED
1879–1881

JOURNEY LENGTH
5 to 6 hours

DISTANCE
82km

COUNTRIES VISITED
India

• *A train the size of a toy.*

SUCH A PRETTY LITTLE TRAIN

We are at New Jalpaiguri station in Siliguri, in the Indian state of West Bengal. The atmosphere is oppressive, the sky hazy. All around us is green as far as the eye can see. If it weren't for this small station and the rail tracks, we might as well be in the middle of nowhere. All of a sudden, a little train arrives, blue from top to tail, covered in marigolds, those orange or yellow flowers commonly used as a decoration in India. Smartphones and cameras emerge as soon as the train appears, snapping images of the spectacle. After all, the *Toy Train*, as it's nicknamed by the Indians, is the real star of the show.

• *Verdant landscape in West Bengal.*

Soon, the small crowd gathered on the platform are on board and our journey can commence: 82km over five to six hours. Sitting in comfortable seats with panoramic views, we travel alongside railway lines where other trains, enormous compared to ours, operate at more regular rail speeds. As we start to climb, the Toy Train runs parallel to the road, scooters and cars passing within two metres of us. On each side, a vast and luxuriant forest covers the slopes of the mountains, caressing the roof of the train as it passes.

SO NEAR AND YET SO FAR

From time to time we veer away from the road and plunge into the forest completely. Then there's nothing but ourselves and those tiny little tracks to guide us. As we approach a diminutive station, the driver sounds his horn and waves a flag out of the cab window. On the platform, a man responds silently, waving another flag, red this time. Along the tracks, Indian people take pictures as if they've never seen the Toy Train before. Are they tourists, soaking up the sights of their own country? Or simply locals who never tire of its beauty? We'll never know.

This time, we've gained height. All around us, mighty peaks leave sheer drops in their wake. Only the thick mist that has followed us throughout our journey prevents us seeing their full extent. The green of the surrounding vegetation is so intense, almost luminous, that it almost looks unreal. Suddenly, the train slows down. A couple of branches have fallen down, obstructing the way forward. A lucky escape, as we could have encountered one of the landslips that regularly shut down the Darjeeling Himalayan Railway until workers have had time to clear away the debris. On this occasion, a member of the train's crew simply jumps down and removes the obstacles.

• *A tricky climb up to Darjeeling.*

SILIGURI → DARJEELING

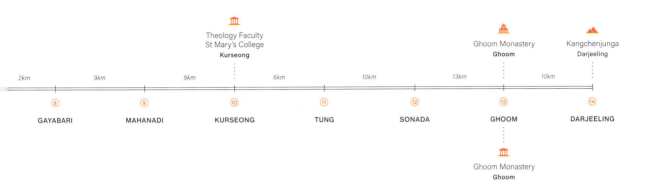

IN THE HIMALAYAN FOOTHILLS

- *Full steam ahead to Kurseong.*

- *Kurseong, 1,458m above sea level.*

We arrive in Kurseong, more or less halfway to our final destination. The track passes right through the middle of this small town, which seems to have been built around it. We pass houses with a mix of different architectural styles as we cross the town, assisted by an employee who slows down the traffic to ensure we can pass through safely. Some shops are so close to the train that we can almost grab an item from their stalls and leave a few rupees in exchange.

Out of nowhere, just as the mountains are starting to look even more beautiful, more exuberantly smothered with greenery, even more verdant than we'd thought possible, rain starts to fall. A heavy, intense downpour. At the next station, the driver takes his time before setting off again, almost as if he's waiting for the worst of the weather to abate. It's an all-encompassing experience. After all, it's said that the name Darjeeling means 'Land of the Thunderbolt'.

📢 STEAM VERSUS DIESEL

After decades of good and loyal service, the Darjeeling Himalayan Railway's steam locomotives were replaced by diesel engines. In response to demand from locals and tourists alike, the Indian authorities have now reintroduced a number of steam locomotives on part of the route.

- *Kangchenjunga (8,586m).*

THE WORLD'S GIANTS

A few kilometres beyond Ghoom, where there is a stunning and brightly coloured little monastery, we stop at the Batasia Loop. As its name suggests, this part of our route takes the form of a loop allowing the train to gain height while spiralling around itself. At an altitude of over 2,000m, this loop also provides an ideal viewpoint over the surrounding mountains, especially Kangchenjunga, the third-highest mountain in the world at 8,586m.

Eventually, we arrive in Darjeeling. We have climbed from 114m to 2,073m over the course of our journey. Former summer retreat for British colonists who sought to escape the heat of the big cities, this timeless spot is a hotch-potch of influences. Colonial buildings consort with monasteries and traditional houses, all linked by streets decorated with multicoloured prayer flags. But the city's main attraction is, of course, its view of the Himalayas, particularly the spectacular panoramic outlook from Tiger Hill, overlooking both Everest and Kangchenjunga.

- *Terminus in Darjeeling, at an altitude of 2,073m.*

197

ASIA

Chennai → Rameswaram
The best way to reach an island

on board the
SETHU EXPRESS

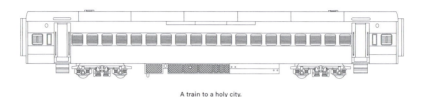

A train to a holy city.

In the southernmost Indian state of Tamil Nadu, the Sethu Express, an unprepossessing little train, links the cities of Chennai and Rameswaram. This route is the ideal way to explore any number of Hindu wonders and cross one of the world's most amazing railway bridges. Spanning the sea, the latter leads to one of India's holiest cities.

Opposite page: Pamban railway bridge, 2.07km long.

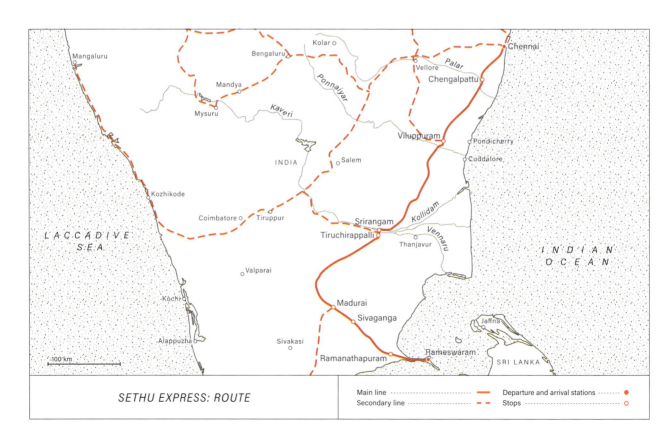

SETHU EXPRESS: ROUTE

ASIA

CONSTRUCTED
End of the 19th–
early 20th century

JOURNEY LENGTH
10 hours, 50 mins

DISTANCE
602km

COUNTRIES VISITED
India

LENGTH OF PAMBAN BRIDGE
2.07km

🔊 **A UNIQUE PILGRIMAGE DESTINATION**
Often compared to Varanasi, which is located in the state of Uttar Pradesh and regarded by Hindus as the holiest place in India, Rameswaram is a favourite destination for pilgrims. Ramanathaswamy Temple, renowned for its thousand-pillar corridor, is said to have been built on the site where Rama, the seventh avatar of the god Vishnu, prayed to Shiva to absolve any sins he may have committed during his war against the demon king Ravana.

• *The Hindu Kapaleeshwarar Temple, Chennai.*

TAMIL COUNTRY

We are in Chennai, formerly known as Madras, the capital of the Indian state of Tamil Nadu. Founded in the 17th century by British colonists on the site of a small fishing village, this city, which now has a population of over 6 million – mainly made up of Tamils, who are for the most part based in South-East India – covers an area in excess of 426km^2 along the Coromandel coast. Despite its colossal size, Chennai tends to have a more relaxed atmosphere than most large Indian megacities. Along its tree-lined streets, thronged with two-wheelers, little shrines and stalls selling brightly coloured fruit, we pass any number of treasures: Fort St George with its imposing stone walls, the chiselled lines of St Thomas Cathedral Basilica, and the eccentrically multicoloured Kapaleeshwarar Temple.

• *St Thomas Cathedral Basilica, constructed in 1896.*

• *Chennai railway station.*

• *Chennai, a city with around 6.6 million inhabitants.*

INDIA IN ALL ITS GLORY

We head for the station to hop on the Sethu Express, a modest yellow train with a slightly dated feel. There are no other tourists on board, though admittedly this commuter train doesn't set out to attract any. As dusk starts to fall across the skyline, we make our way through the outskirts of the city. Some houses look to be on the verge of collapse, while others are resplendent. The tiniest space between buildings is filled with vegetation battling to survive, be it a few blades of grass, or gangly trees. The weather conditions here are so favourable that any seed falling to the ground is liable to germinate and form a new plant. A calm atmosphere reigns all around – allowing us to enjoy India in all its glory. Other passengers have already settled into their berths. Whether seated cross-legged or stretched out barefoot, they chat quietly or tuck into the food they've brought along in sizeable bags. A lady in an orange and fuchsia-pink sari reads her book as her husband taps away on his smartphone. Whenever the train stops, a number of people get out to have a smoke or stretch their legs. We decide to order food from a little kiosk on the platform: tender meat, pancakes and spiced rice, all wrapped up in paper and designed to be eaten with the fingers.

• *Road bridge to Pamban Island.*

FLOATING ON THE RAILS

During the night, some passengers get off, while others join the train. Srirangam is where people leave to visit Sri Ranganathaswamy, one of the most important Hindu temples, regarded as the largest functioning religious complex in the world. At Sivaganga, they disembark to pray in one of the many places of worship to be found here. Or to admire the fabulous birds that nest and strut their stuff in the Vettangudi Bird Sanctuary not far from the city. Spirituality takes many forms, especially in a country as mystical as India.

Finally, we approach our terminus on Pamban Island, opposite Sri Lanka. But first we have to cross the 2.07-km-long rail bridge that seems to float above the turquoise sea. From the train, the view is almost like a mirage. As if we're riding a huge sea monster, we soar over the waves until we reach Rameswaram, holy Hindu city, where we can dwell on all the beauty we have seen.

• *Sethu Express on the rail bridge to Pamban Island.*

200

Sri Ranganathaswamy Hindu Temple, Srirangam.

Mettupalayam → Ooty
The Blue Mountains

on the
NILGIRI MOUNTAIN RAILWAY

A little train but a steep climb.

Awarded UNESCO World Heritage status in 2005, Nilgiri Mountain Railway is one of the most spectacular rail routes in the world. Not only does it pass through the most stunning scenery, it also tackles a gradient of as much as 8.3 per cent with rolling stock that looks as though it would be more at home in a museum.

Opposite page: Nilgiri Mountain Railway and its little blue carriages.

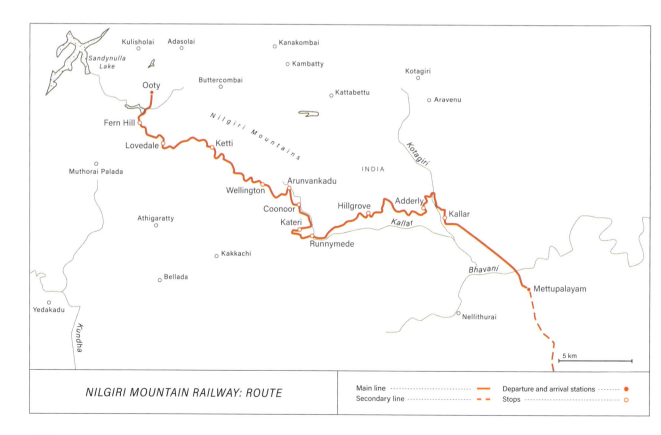

NILGIRI MOUNTAIN RAILWAY: ROUTE

ASIA

①	②	③	④	⑤	⑥	⑦
METTUPALAYAM	KALLAR	ADDERLY	HILLGROVE	RUNNYMEDE	KATTERI	COONOOR

CONSTRUCTED
1899

JOURNEY LENGTH
5 hours

DISTANCE
46km

COUNTRIES VISITED
India

GRADIENT (PER CENT)
8.3

NUMBER OF BRIDGES
250

NUMBER OF TUNNELS
16

- *The Blue Mountains, shrouded in clouds.*

- *The delightful Art Deco interior of the Nilgiri Mountain Railway.*

THE BLUE MOUNTAINS IN THE DISTANCE

It's 7 o'clock in the morning, but the atmosphere at Mettupalayam station is already oppressive. Before us stands a small blue train, or *toy train* to use its local nickname. Above our heads, the sky is pearly white. In the distance we can see the Nilgiris, or Blue Mountains, although from here they rather resemble a hulking brown mass shrouded in clouds. As the train gets ready to depart, a silver-haired woman draped in a turquoise sari hands a bag of food to a young man in a T-shirt. She rather looks as though she won't take no for an answer. After all, he might get hungry; the journey lasts all of five hours. Eventually the train leaves as we settle into one of the plush first-class seats upholstered in colourful patterned fabric. The track runs alongside small gardens with ornate, yet rickety fences, beyond which lie houses cobbled together from whatever their owners could lay their hands on or afford. Behind a level crossing, a gaggle of two-wheeled vehicles are impatiently waiting for the train to pass. After this, houses start to become thin on the ground, giving way to a natural landscape pulsing with vitality. Just a few metres from some palm trees, a woman in a tiny signal box waves a green flag in our direction. Beyond this point, our train will use a rack-and-pinion system to climb the steep gradients. To the rear of the train, in the steam engine that has pushed us thus far (rather than pulling us, as is usually the case), the driver has to respond with his own flag. Or perhaps that's the job of the man crouching on the tiny deck at the very front of the train?

MONKEYS AND PHOTO OPPORTUNITIES

The surrounding landscape becomes more and more mountainous, with bridges and tunnels galore. To be more specific, the route has a total of 250 bridges, large and small, and 16 tunnels. At Adderly station, we stop again for the tender to fill up with water. In the meantime, all the passengers head for the viewpoint to take pictures of the mountains fringed with clouds. They fire off shot after shot – beauty captured in digital memory cards. Then suddenly, as the gradient gets steeper, a vast panorama opens up to the left. Rows and rows of mountains overlapping towards the horizon, the landscape stretching out as far as the eye can see. Gasps of awe can be heard echoing through the carriages.

At Hillgrove station, somewhere in the depths of the jungle, some curious visitors daringly come right up to the train: mischievous monkeys, circling around us. One even jumps on top of a carriage before departing without so much as a by-your-leave. Others follow us for a few metres or simply sit alongside the track, watching as we disappear.

- *Hillgrove, in the depths of the jungle, with its colony of monkeys.*

METTUPALAYAM → OOTY

Cultural heritage of the Toda people
Ooty

| 3km | 5km | 9km | 5km | 3km | 4km |

⑧ ARUVANKADU   ⑨ WELLINGTON   ⑩ KETTI   ⑪ LOVEDALE   ⑫ FERN HILL   ⑬ OOTY

• *Coonoor, 1,850m above sea level.*

THE GODS HAVE SPOKEN

Eventually, they recede into the distance as we resume our ascent. The higher we climb, the more insubstantial the bridges seem – not a barrier in sight! – and the more spellbinding the surrounding scenery. Those tree-studded mountainsides feel kind of reassuring, like a mother hugging us to her bosom. They speak of the ancient gods of nature protecting our planet despite the harm we humans inflict on a daily basis. Even though we know this isn't true, this luxuriant wilderness encourages us to believe, just for a few seconds.

As we approach Coonoor, at an altitude of 1,850m, the colours of urban life once again start to filter through: blues, oranges and violets provide relief from the vast expanses of green all around. As we breakfast on dosas – delicious, crispy little pancakes commonly found in Southern India – the crew uncouple the steam locomotive and replace it with a diesel engine. Less picturesque, to be sure, but more suited to the final stage of our journey.

• *Tea plantation near Coonoor.*

PRECIPITOUS GRADIENTS

With an average gradient of 4.1 per cent and one section with an incline of 8.3 per cent, the Nilgiri Mountain Railway is one of the steepest railway lines in the world. This is why the engine is placed behind the carriages when travelling uphill. On the downward leg, the carriages are attached behind the locomotive so they can't roll downhill unimpeded if they become uncoupled.

THE LAND OF THE TODA

We carry on climbing through the breathtaking scenery of the Nilgiri Mountains. Now, our ascent is only interrupted by pretty little sky-blue stations and shorter stops to allow passengers to embark or disembark. On one stretch of track, a little quieter than the rest, the driver does his best to push the engine to its maximum speed, somewhere between 25 and 30km/h. From this point on, we are travelling beneath the canopy held aloft by vast, gnarled tree trunks. We can't see it, but we know it's there. And then this tropical illusion disappears, once more revealing the mountains in all their glory. At their feet, clusters of tiny houses reflect the whiteness of the overcast sky. At last, after passing through the sixteenth tunnel on our itinerary, we arrive in Ooty. Short for Udagamandalam, this town lies 2,240m above sea level. Founded by British colonists from the city formerly known as Madras, this was where the settlers came to cool off during the sweltering heat of summer. The area around the town was originally occupied only by the mysterious Toda, a pastoral tribe. Only a few thousand of these people are left nowadays, but, you never know, we might be lucky enough to come across some of them.

• *Tea bushes near Ooty.*

• *Ooty, after a five-hour climb.*

205

• Incredible shades of green and tea plantations alongside the Nilgiri Mountain Railway.

ASIA

Kandy → Badulla
Steam and tea

on board the
HILL COUNTRY TRAIN

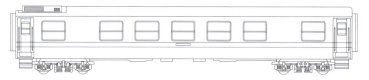

A blue train taking us back in time.

Built in a number of stages during the time of British colonial rule, the main line of the Sri Lankan rail network links Colombo, the country's capital, with the city of Badulla, in the centre of the island. Between these two places, a little blue train follows a breathtaking route through hills, jungle and tea plantations.

Opposite page: Nine Arch Bridge, just before Ella.

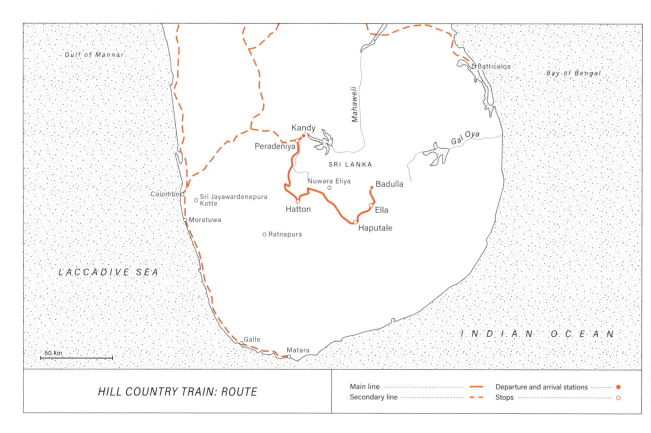

| HILL COUNTRY TRAIN: ROUTE | Main line ——— Departure and arrival stations ● |
| | Secondary line - - - Stops ○ |

208

ASIA

CONSTRUCTED
1864–1924

JOURNEY LENGTH
approx. 7 hours

DISTANCE
163km

COUNTRIES VISITED
Sri Lanka

📢 **A-HUNTING WE WILL GO…**

Reserving a seat on this train may prove to be more complicated than you'd expect. The best way of getting a seat is by turning up at the ticket office in person to buy a ticket without a reservation in the hope that you'll find one as you wander up and down the train – otherwise, just sit in the doorways, as so many others do…

IN THE HEART OF HILL COUNTRY

Crowds on the platform. Not much better on board. Not a free seat to be found, and the majority of Sri Lankans are leaning against the carriage walls. Despite its slow progress and unreliable reputation, the little blue steam train we've just boarded is an extremely popular way of getting around this area.

• *The modest station in Kandy.*

We are currently in Kandy, right in the middle of the island, where the most spectacular part of the route begins. Several groups of Western backpackers wearing sleeveless T-shirts and weighed down by huge rucksacks have managed to worm their way in between the locals. Still no seats, so some of the Sri Lankan youths are sitting in the carriage doorways; given the speed of the train, it doesn't look too hazardous a compromise. Plus the air there is a lot fresher than in the crammed carriage.

FROM PADDY FIELDS TO TEA PLANTATIONS

After passing through Kandy's run-down outskirts, the train starts to wind its way between paddy fields. The brownish, muddy waters of the Mahaweli Ganga (literally 'Great River of Sand') slice abruptly through the luminous green of these crops, followed by a deeper, more intense shade of green. This is the jungle in this region, known as the Hill Country. Not the most imaginative of names given that this area is defined by its undulating landscape, the horizon ever changing as it follows the rounded curves of the terrain. The only time we can tear our gaze away from the surrounding views is when the train stops at one of the tiny, pale-coloured stations. Each time we stop, hawkers arrive down the tracks as if from nowhere, selling water and wade, fritters made from lentils. Tourists, both local and international, take this opportunity to get on or off as they see fit. Some are returning to their families, others are on the lookout for a backpackers' hostel or about to join a hiking trail.

• *Tea plantation, Nuwara Eliya.*

IN SEARCH OF COOLER CLIMES

By this stage, our views are of hills and tea plantations in equal measure. These attractive little shrubs were one of the reasons why the British had this railway line built in the first place. The colonists were keen to find a better way of transporting tea from Ceylon – as they called this territory – to the port of Colombo, or to Galle, further south. Even nowadays, the way tea is cultivated and harvested seems quite tortuous. While those images of women crouched over their work may look like picture postcards, they also serve to remind us that, even in paradise, the poorest always work their fingers to the bone. Misery is no less painful when the sun is shining, but it always looks better seen from a train. Nevertheless, the view is just staggering. Beneath the infinite blue sky, there are layers upon layers of hills, their colours changing the further away they are – from a brilliant green to the darkest of browns. The natural environment isn't the only thing that's changed. As the journey unfolds, the number of Buddhist temples decreases in inverse proportion to their Hindu counterparts. An indication, albeit a barely perceptible one, of the subtle spiritual differences that abound on this island that bears the marks of many and varied influences. The very air we breathe seems to have changed too. Without realizing, we have gained height, well over 1,000m between Kandy (at 500m) and Nuwara Eliya (at 1,868m), our next stop. In their quest for cooler climes, the British transformed this town into a hill station, a green lung when the temperatures by the coast became unbearable. They may have long since gone, but Nuwara Eliya is often referred to as 'Little England' on account of its colonial-style architecture.

UP AMONG THE CLOUDS

While many tourists get off at this point, we stay on board. Our ultimate destination isn't much further, but we have to wait until our train is ready. Unsurprisingly, the old steam locomotive has overheated. The driver and a couple of station attendants bring large buckets of water in an attempt to cool it down. These old mechanical engines are indestructible, but creativity is often required to keep them going – never in short supply in the Sri Lankan countryside! After 20 minutes or so, we're off again. The higher we climb, the more stunning the scenery. What was jungle has now become forest and the hills are turning into mountains. Above all, we can appreciate the clouds, shrouding the rounded forms of the landscape. Almost within touching distance, yet ethereal at the same time, they are reminiscent of jolly giants about to take a snooze in a rocky hollow. Just like the paddy fields, the jungle and the tea plantations, they eventually disappear as we drop down towards Ella, only 1,000m or so above sea level. This is where our journey ends, overlooking the unforgettable valley below us.

- Hill Country Train, a charming blue steam train.

ASIA

Beijing → Ulaanbaatar
Travelling the Tea Road

on the
TRANS-MONGOLIAN RAILWAY

A train fit for the challenges of the Gobi Desert.

Since time immemorial, cultivating and trading tea have played a fundamental role in the respective economies of Asia and Europe, defining exchanges between these two continents. Extending from Beijing (formerly Peking) to Ulaanbaatar, the Trans-Mongolian Railway follows one of the main routes used by traders carrying this valuable commodity. The unparalleled beauty of this journey reaches its zenith as the line crosses the Gobi Desert.

Opposite page: The line runs alongside the Great Wall of China for a 20-km stretch.

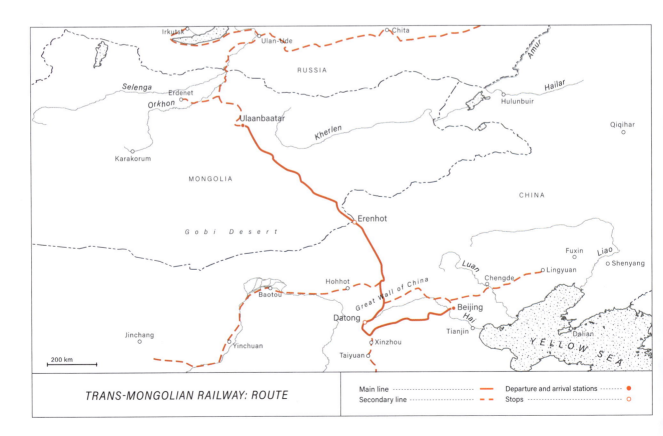

212

ASIA

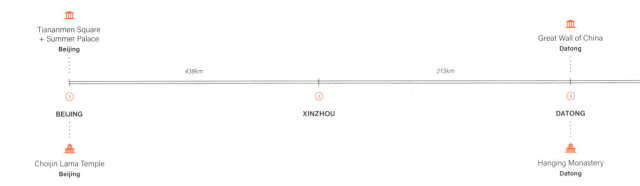

CONSTRUCTED
1949–1961

JOURNEY LENGTH
2 days, 1 night
(28 hours,
30 mins)

DISTANCE
2,080km

COUNTRIES VISITED
Mongolia
China
Russia

- *Beijing – where tradition meets modernity.*

THE CITY WHERE SPRING REIGNS ETERNAL

Beijing is one of those cities that are hard to pin down in just a few words. From its narrow hutongs, tiny alleyways lined by higgledy-piggledy dwellings, to its towering skyscrapers, from the Forbidden City – built to accommodate gods rather than mere mortals – to the extensive parks where families enjoy some fresh air, street food in their hands, the Chinese capital refuses to be neatly pigeonholed. Tiananmen Square, notorious for all the wrong reasons, the enchanting Summer Palace and the magical Choijin Lama Temple are just some of the treasures the city has in store for us. This city is so ancient, so sprawling and so complex that it undoubtedly harbours the ghosts of millions of unknown souls, dramas, hopes and glories, conquests and authoritarian powers. After exploring this fascinating capital, a treat on so many levels, we leave Beijing to discover one of the world's most underrated rail routes, the Trans-Mongolian Railway.

- *The green carriages of the Trans-Mongolian train.*

THE LONGEST WALL OF ALL

It's nearly 7.30am when our train finally leaves Beijing. Our cabin, nice and roomy, has seats that convert into beds, pretty bright-pink curtains and panoramic windows for taking in the views. As soon as we leave the city limits, those views start to work their magic. First of all, we pass huge rock formations in jagged, tortured shapes. Then, what joy to follow the Great Wall of China for 20 or so kilometres as it twists its way through the mountains to protect the country from onslaughts by invaders from the north. Shortly before we cross the Wall, we stop in Datong. This mining city is renowned for its caves, its statues of Buddha carved into the rocks and its incredible Hanging Temple, which looks as though it might come crashing down from its cliffside perch at any minute.

At the Chinese-Mongolian border, where Inner Mongolia, an autonomous Chinese region, adjoins the separate country of Mongolia, our train stops for several hours. The rail gauge in each country is different, so the train bogies have to be changed over before we can continue on our way. On the platform, after going through the usual customs checks, other passengers seek out shady spots to shelter from the sun. We are in the heart of the Gobi Desert, where it can be freezing cold, but on this particular day we experience scorching heat. Renowned for its hostile temperatures, fluctuating between 42°C and 38°C below zero, this vast expanse covering 1.3 million km² is as capable of freezing travellers to death as it is of frying them to a crisp.

- *Hanging Temple of Buddha, Datong.*

BEIJING → ULAANBAATAR

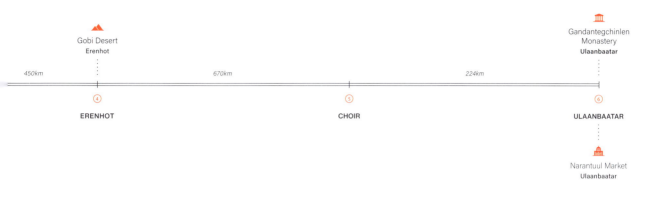

- *The Trans-Mongolian as it crosses the Gobi desert.*

THE OUTER REACHES OF THE GOBI

The very dangers of the Gobi Desert do have their compensations: the magnificence of this arid landscape is our reward, extending over hundreds and hundreds of kilometres. Sparse vegetation, sand and views stretching on and on to infinity. It's a bewitching place where life seems impossible and where wandering at random seems the only conceivable option. Safely inside our cabin, we can feel the unbearable dryness, picture little creatures constantly on a quest for food and imagine the galloping hooves of the steeds of bygone horsemen. Legend has it that Mongolian riders never got off their horses – which we can quite readily believe. In this desert environment, setting foot on the ground would be tantamount to a certain death. Suddenly, in the middle of the desert, a town comes into view: Choir – not a name we've ever heard of before. It seems to be an oasis, despite the singular lack of palm trees, mirages or life-saving bodies of water. On the platform, diminutive women with burnished skin, wearing hats and dayglo green aprons, sell drinks and provisions piled up in shopping trolleys. Like many of our fellow passengers, we can't resist the tiny meat-filled buns and pot noodles, by far the most popular ready meal on trains in this part of the world. Just add boiling water and hey presto!

- *The Gobi: deserts can be cold too.*

📢 AS FAR AS LAKE BAIKAL

The Mongolian capital is not the end of the line for the Trans-Mongolian Railway. It continues to Ulan-Ude, on the shores of the renowned Lake Baikal in Russia. Travellers with time and inclination may wish to remain on board until the furthest point and then – why not? – jump straight onto one of the Trans-Siberian trains that also end up back in Ulaanbaatar.

- *Bogd Khan Palace, Ulaanbaatar.*

GALLOPING ACROSS THE STEPPES

After the desert, we enter the steppe. Mongolia is known for this kind of terrain and finally we get to experience it. This time, our surroundings are green, sometimes becoming slightly rounded as the land starts to undulate. Yet again, the sound of hooves echoes through our heads. Anyone who has ever had a good gallop on horseback cannot fail to understand why generations of Mongols felt the urge to ride their mounts hell for leather through this endless terrain.

Our train finally reaches its terminus in Ulaanbaatar, the country's capital. A far cry from the idealized images we might have in our heads, this city shot from a population of 700,000 to nearly 1.7 million in the space of 20 years and is now home to more than half of Mongolia's population. This rural exodus forced the city to undergo a drastic transformation, turning it into one of the most polluted in the world. Despite these ongoing changes, a number of treasures have remained intact: the opulent Winter Palace, Sukhbaatar Square (once known as Genghis Khan Square), surrounded by glass tower blocks, the immensely spiritual Gandantegchinlen Monastery and the unmissable delights of Narantuul Market. Above all, Ulaanbaatar teaches us to forget our preconceptions: one person's end of the world might be the centre of the universe to someone else. And things are never quite how we expect them to be...

- *Herd of horses galloping across the Mongolian steppe.*

215

Nyingchi → Lhasa
Last train for Lhasa

on board the
FUXING HAO

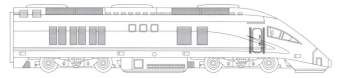

The very latest in Chinese rail technology.

On 25 June 2021, China launched an incredible new high-speed train. Designed to withstand high-altitude weather conditions, it links the city of Nyingchi with Lhasa, in Tibet, in less than three and a half hours compared with the previous travel time of five hours. This extraordinary line has an average altitude in excess of 3,000m and climbs to the roof the world via a series of 121 bridges and 47 tunnels.

Opposite page: Milha Pass, in the Tibetan Mountains.

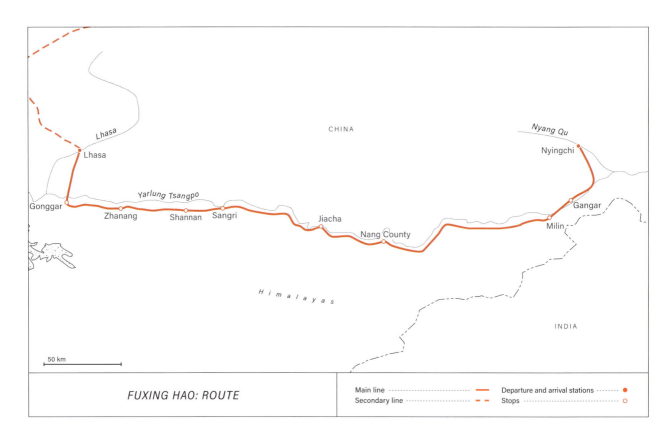

ASIA

OPERATING SINCE
2021

JOURNEY LENGTH
3 hours, 30 mins

DISTANCE
435km

COUNTRIES VISITED
China

NUMBER OF TUNNELS
47

NUMBER OF BRIDGES
121

WAY, WAY ABOVE SEA LEVEL

The sun is already high in the sky as we arrive at Nyingchi station, a substantial white building with a distinctive red roof. Also known as Linzhi, this prefecture-level city in the autonomous region of Tibet – one of five such regions in China – lies at an altitude of 3,040m. Surrounded by the towering summits of the Himalayas, this is the departure point for our journey to the legendary city of Lhasa. Right at the heart of the sacred mountains.

With its long green body, comfortable red seats and tapered nose, our train doesn't look vastly dissimilar to the rest of the Fuxing Hao series at first glance. These are the Chinese high-speed trains that hurtle across the plains of the Middle Kingdom at average speeds of up to 350km/h. However, this train also includes some special technological wizardry: first of all, it has an oxygen supply system that keeps oxygen levels at 23.6 per cent – as compared to 21 per cent at sea level – to make sure passengers don't struggle to breathe. The windows also incorporate a filter to provide protection from UV radiation; at these altitudes, this can be 30 per cent higher due to the sun's rays reflecting off the snow.

▪ Nyingchi, at 3,040m.

▪ Jiacha station, Tibet.

📢 A FIERCELY CONTESTED REGION

Mountainous plain, autonomous Chinese region or territory claimed by a government in exile? The word 'Tibet' covers a multitude of possibilities. Although it has been effectively controlled by the all-powerful Chinese government since the invasion in 1950, it remains the focus of international controversy, with the historical subtleties of the dispute hotly contested by specialists on both sides.

▪ The Tsangpo river, better known as the Brahmaputra river.

HEADING FOR THE TOP OF THE WORLD

Enough of the technical stuff, it's time to begin our journey to the roof of the world. It's not long before the windows are once again filled with the sheer beauty of the surrounding landscape. Huge mountains make up almost the entire skyline. Smothered in dense vegetation, they occasionally reveal glimpses of a dazzling white sky. From time to time, these titans part, leaving way for a substantial river, or permit the occasional village to cling precariously to their steep sides. At random intervals, one of the seven towns served by the Nyingchi-Lhasa line comes into view, each encompassed by lofty peaks with their summits in the clouds. On their outskirts are broad green fields, reminding us that humans can still grow things even at this elevation, albeit with the help of technology.

As our train racks up the kilometres, the mystical charms of Tibet's natural beauty just keep on coming. We pass over bridges, through tunnels, right in the very heart of it all. Whether penetrating the very rock itself, circumnavigating huge masses or great divides, we cross peaks standing over 8,000m high without even needing to climb them – all thanks to the wonders of engineering. Of these man-made structures, one in particular captures our attention: the Zangmu Railway Bridge. Some 525m long, it offers spectacular views over the canyon carved out by the Tsangpo river, perhaps better known as the Brahmaputra river.

▪ Lhasa's futuristic station.

THE SOUL OF TIBETAN BUDDHISM

After this stunning journey through the Himalayas, we eventually arrive at Lhasa station, an architectural tour de force that looks more like the headquarters of an arch-villain in a Hollywood movie than a Buddhist temple. Either way, we are here, in one of the world's most mystical places. The sun is shining, the air is cold and rather rarefied. But most of all, the legendary Potala Palace, former residence of the Dalai Lama, rises up before us in all its glory, against a backdrop of the Himalayan mountain range. To say nothing of Jokhang Temple, spiritual heart of Tibetan Buddhism. It's quite a climb to get there through the lively streets of this unique city, but well worth the effort.

• *Potala Palace, the Dalai Lama's former residence in Lhasa.*

Hefei → Fuzhou
It's raining mountains...
on board the
HEFEI-FUZHOU

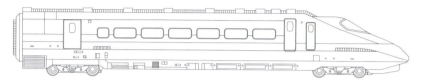

All aboard for the UNESCO World Heritage Sites.

Opened in 2015, the high-speed line connecting Fuzhou, in the province of Fujian, to Hefei, in the province of Anhui, introduces its passengers to the splendours of a little-known part of China. These include three sites awarded UNESCO World Heritage status: the Yellow Mountains, Mount Wuyi and Mount Sanqingshan.

Opposite page: *Mount Huangshan, in the Yellow Mountains.*

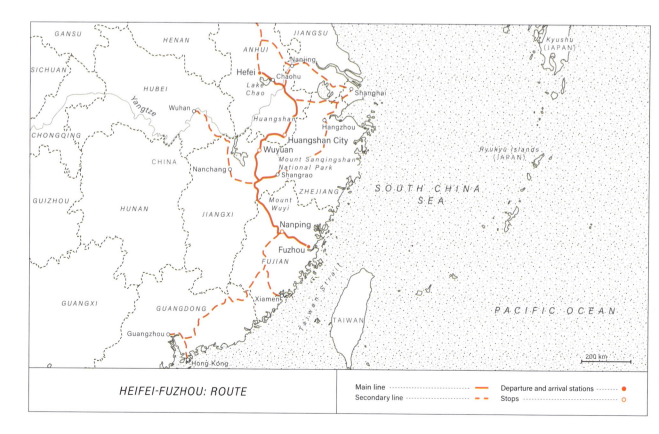

HEIFEI-FUZHOU: ROUTE

① HEFEI — 330 km — ② HUANGSHAN — 90 km — ③ WUYUAN

Bao Zheng's tomb — Hefei
Yellow Mountains — Huangshan

OPERATING SINCE
2015

JOURNEY LENGTH
4 to 5 hours

DISTANCE
850km

COUNTRIES VISITED
China

THE FLAVOURS OF ANHUI

You've probably never heard of Hefei. Capital of the province of Anhui in eastern China, this city with a population of nearly 8 million is one of those giant metropolises that rarely come to the attention of people outside the Middle Kingdom. As with all Chinese cities, you have to know where to look if you're to track down the mysteries it conceals. Which is precisely what we do, visiting the house and tomb of Bao Zheng, an 11th-century judge renowned in popular Chinese history as a stickler for doing the right thing, and now a character in literary and dramatic productions.

Our next stop is Hefei-South station, where we join our high-speed train for Fuzhou. Having found our seats, we allow our thoughts to wander, drifting back to the wonderful food we've enjoyed in Anhui, which boasts one of China's eight great regional cuisines. The names of the dishes often have rather quirky and whimsical English translations: shrimp love nest, fatty kingfish in milk, fried fish masquerading as a bunch of grapes...

We look out on the passing countryside, but before too long, after wide expanses of vegetation, the station of Chaohu-East comes into sight. From here, it's but a hop, skip and a jump to Lake Chao, a heart-shaped freshwater lake (when viewed from above) famed for the diverse and beautiful scenery in the surrounding area but also notorious for serious pollution issues due to overexploitation.

• *Chao, a heart-shaped lake.*

• *A high-speed bullet train on the Hefei-Fuzhou railway.*

• *The Yellow Mountains, peak after vertiginous peak.*

THE HEART AND SOUL OF FOREVER CHINA

Our first actual stop is at Huangshan station, where we leave the train to explore the Yellow Mountains. These enchantingly beautiful mountains are quite ethereal – they resemble a jumble of craggy peaks and improbably contorted pines, all floating in a sea of cloud. Painted, described and photographed many millions of times, they form perhaps the purest image of Forever China you could imagine. Within half an hour of climbing back on board our train, we arrive in Wuyuan. This region was for many years cut off from the rest of the country due to its geographical isolation and it still feels out of touch with modern times. So we slow right down as we wander through the streets of perfectly preserved villages, where the China of the first millennium seems tantalizingly close. If we're lucky and happen to be visiting in springtime, we may just hit the jackpot and see the crimson azaleas in full bloom across the mountainsides, along with the bright-yellow rapeseed cultivated alongside tea plantations.

• *Wuyuan, encircled by fields of rapeseed.*

HEFEI → FUZHOU

FOREST OF ROCK

The wonders of the Chinese hinterland are never-ending, each unique in its own way. Mount Sanqingshan National Park can be accessed from Shangrao, for example. Another UNESCO World Heritage Site on account of its outstanding natural beauty, this 22,950-hectare area includes 48 granite peaks and 89 granite pillars. Yet you only have to look beyond the physical landscape to understand that these are much more than rocks. As we make our way through the park, they sometimes seem to magically evolve into gigantic human beings, colossal animals or even the fabled monsters of Chinese mythology. Only if you are completely lacking in imagination will these rock formations remain lifeless.

As our train sets off again, a question comes to mind: how many bridges and tunnels have we negotiated? Have we actually been on Chinese soil at all? We certainly can't be sure... Hardly surprising, as 86.1 per cent of our route passes through and over structures that are so improbable, they span several highways that already criss-cross over one another in a spaghetti-like jumble of roads.

• *Mount Sanqingshan National Park and its granite peaks.*

🔊 A HOAX IN VILLAGE FORM

Just over two hours from Fuzhou by road, a funny little village in the xian (county) of Xiapu has made the international headlines for all the wrong reasons. An investigation by *The New York Times* has revealed that the bucolic scenes photographed by hordes of visiting tourists were in fact staged by local villagers, most of them transformed into actors...

• *Traditional dwelling in Nanping.*

• *Tea plantation at the foot of Mount Wuyi.*

THE NINE BENDS OF THE RIVER

These thoughts whirling through our mind, we arrive at Nanping station, where we disembark and head for Mount Wuyi, the third UNESCO World Heritage Site on this treasure-filled route. Despite the beauty we've become accustomed to since the beginning of our journey, our marvelometer ticks up to a whole new level. Words aren't enough to describe the tranquil gorges of the Nine-Bend River. Hidden away in the rock formations are temples and monasteries, taunting us with philosophical musings. Some appear so inaccessible that surely only the gods could have put them there in the first place. Others go out of their way to welcome us, providing the ideal spot for a quiet moment of contemplation to the tune of the gentle rumble of the nearby waterfalls.

At last we arrive in Fuzhou, our terminus. Despite being as unfamiliar to us as our starting point, the capital of the province of Fujian also has a number of secrets up its sleeve, beneath the radar of the major international ranking bodies. Its cuisine is the first thing that springs to mind, of course: another of China's eight great culinary traditions. This time, it takes the form of succulent street food that we gorge on before we begin our ascent of Mount Gushan. Some 870m high, this little hill embodies everything you might expect, with temples where people meditate, caves where you can linger for a while, and viewpoints from which you can gaze on the city below. Yet another treasure, tiny in the grand scheme of things, yet so few people know of its existence. Or at least, they didn't until now...

223

Xi'an → Lanzhou → Urumqi
On the Silk Road

on board the
XI'AN-URUMQI

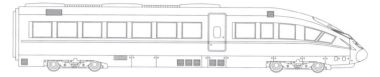

By train on the old Silk Road.

For centuries, the Silk Road, which linked Xi'an and Antioch (now known as Antakya, in Turkey), was the main trade route between the greatest civilizations known to mankind. Although this 'road' was actually made up of a network of many land and sea-based routes, it was a conduit for religions and cultures as well as commodities. Nowadays, there is a railway line that operates on part of this route between mighty Xi'an and Urumqi, capital of the Uyghur people.

Opposite page: Mountainous terrain near Lanzhou.

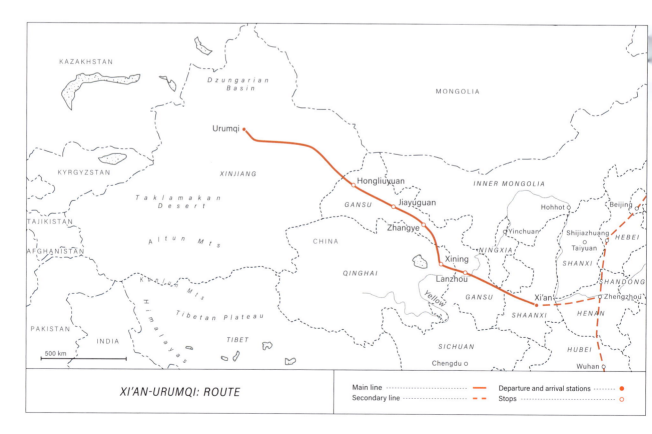

ASIA

①	②	③
XI'AN	LANZHOU	XINING

OPERATING SINCE
1966

JOURNEY LENGTH
25 hours, 58 mins

DISTANCE
2,894km

COUNTRIES VISITED
China

• Xi'an – Urumqi, the start of the Silk Road.

THE UNDERGROUND ARMY

Eight thousand Chinese soldiers are lined up in front of us. Their faces implacable, determined, their armour made up of hundreds of small plates hammered together; no doubt whatsoever that they are ready go into battle for the first Emperor of China. Fortunately, he died in 210 BC, but his troops are here to stay. They are made of terracotta and were buried with their master near Xi'an, in the Chinese province of Shaanxi.

With a population of over 8 million, this city, which dates back more than 3,000 years, is our starting point. After exploring the walls, the Bell and Drum Towers and, perhaps most importantly, savouring the delicious Xi'an dumpling soup, we climb the few steps leading to the station concourse. Just enough time to fill our bags with bottled water and the inevitable pot noodles (to sustain us on yet another long journey in a Chinese train) before we jump on board. The train is packed with travellers hurrying to find their seats or compartments.

• Terracotta army, Xi'an (3rd century BC), discovered in 1974.

• Huang He, or Yellow River.

• Bingling Temple Grottoes.

UNDER THE GAZE OF BUDDHA

We are sharing our compartment with a couple and their young son, who soon dashes into the corridor to play with other children. The woman holds out Tupperware dishes, inviting us to share the contents: tiny morsels stuffed with vegetables. Outside, the landscape looks like an etching: a patchwork of pretty fields extending to the foot of small hills, murky rivers winding between craggy cliffs. If we'd been asked to paint a picture of the Chinese countryside, this is exactly what we'd have come up with.

Soon, we reach our first destination, Lanzhou, capital of the province of Gansu. Known as the Golden City back in the glory days of the Silk Road, this metropolis was founded over 2,000 years ago under the Han dynasty. Nowadays, it is as famous for its pollution levels as for the splendour of the Bingling Temple Grottoes some 70km from the city centre. Located along the former silk roads, these were constructed on the banks of the Yellow River (Huang He in Chinese) in the 3rd century. Visiting this huge site is an absolute must, including highlights such as the enormous statue of Buddha that stands over 27m tall, carved out of the rock wall made from the characteristic yellow earth, or loess, of this region.

• Tower at Jiayuguan Fort (14th century).

MONSTERS IN THE GOBI

Afterwards, we make our way through the vast Gobi Desert. This rugged landscape consists of more rock than sand, and its deadly beauty continues for miles on end. Ensconced in our berths, a pot of steaming noodles in one hand, chopsticks in the other, we are almost hypnotized by the emptiness of this desolate land. It feels like a gigantic monster, spreading its tentacles over 1.3 million km². An insatiable gargantua devouring almost everything that tries to eke out its existence in this place. Only certain species, smarter than the ogre that is the Gobi itself, are able to survive in the desert. In our case, it is the railway that guarantees us free passage.

Another stop: Jiayuguan this time. There's certainly plenty to see here. Its magnificent 14th-century fort, awarded UNESCO World Heritage status in 1987, represents the western limit of the Great Wall of China. This strategic position was said to have been held by outcasts exiled from China by the emperor of that time. Surely the similarity with the wall in *Game of Thrones* isn't just a coincidence?

📢 POTENTIAL CRIMES AGAINST HUMANITY

In 2022, a United Nations report suggested that the Chinese government may have committed human rights abuses against the Uyghur minority. This document also provided credible evidence of torture and sexual violence. It came about in response to several international NGOs condemning these actions.

URUMQI, IN UYGHUR COUNTRY

At last we reach Urumqi, capital of the Xinjiang Uyghur Autonomous Region. We should perhaps start by pointing out that this official title is rather controversial, both locally and internationally. The majority of the population are Uyghurs, a Muslim minority who some believe to be descendants of the original Turkish inhabitants. The region is also referred to as East Turkestan by opponents of the Chinese regime.

Much to ponder as we explore this wonderful city and its surrounding area. From the hustle and bustle of its Grand Bazaar to Shaanxi Mosque with its distinctive East Asian style, from the Flaming Mountains to the Caves of the Thousand Buddhas, Urumqi is the perfect symbol of its unique standing at the crossroads of cultures. This exceptional cultural status becomes more and more apparent in the many thousands of restaurants in the city. With countless different kinds of bread, hearty soups, braised meat and chunky noodle dishes with a range of unique flavours, Uyghur cuisine is like no other. Or perhaps there are some similarities? It all depends on your point of view. One thing is for sure: it's an absolutely unforgettable culinary experience.

• Urumqi, Uyghur capital of Xinjiang.

Unazuki → Keyakidaira

An autumn rail trip

on the
KUROBE GORGE RAILWAY

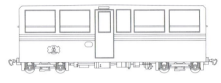

Train ride to happiness.

Constructed between 1927 and 1936 to transport materials and workers to and from the Kurobe Dam, the Kurobe Gorge Railway opened a passenger service in 1953. Ever since, travellers on this line have been able to admire one of the most unspoiled and impressive landscapes in the entire Japanese archipelago. The peak time to visit is undoubtedly in autumn, when the trees turn stunning shades of orange and gold.

Opposite page: One of the 121 metal bridges over the Kurobe gorges.

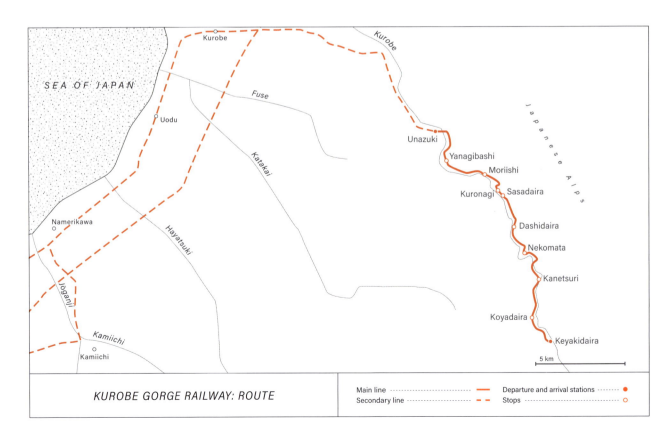

ASIA

OPERATING SINCE
1953

JOURNEY LENGTH
1 hour, 20 mins

DISTANCE
20km

COUNTRIES VISITED
Japan

NUMBER OF TUNNELS
47

NUMBER OF BRIDGES
121

LENGTH OF SHIN YAMABIKO BRIDGE
166m

📣 **A BRIGHT RED BRIDGE**

Overall, there are 40 tunnels and 20 bridges strung along the Kurobe Gorge railway line. The most impressive of them all is the 166-m-long Shin Yamabiko Bridge spanning the river. Its flamboyant red colour contrasts subtly with the complex hues of the forest in its autumn garb, leading to photographs celebrated across the globe.

- Panoramic views from the open-sided carriages.

SMALL TRAIN, MAXIMUM OOH-AAH FACTOR

With its compact orange locomotive and tiny open-sided carriages, the train awaiting us at Unazuki station, in the Japanese prefecture of Toyama, almost looks like a model railway. Despite this, we climb on board.

It looks to be a narrow-gauge line too. And given that it's no more than 20km long, we've probably got nothing to lose by giving this oversized toy a try.

NATURE'S WORK OF ART

It doesn't take long to conclude that we've definitely made the right choice as, on both sides of the train, an amazing spectacle beckons. Steep gorges, the deepest in Japan, open up before us. The mountains are clothed in a dense forest featuring thousands of shades of orange and green, all so pleasing to the eye that the scene could have been painted by a skilled artist. If you peer closely through the branches of the trees as they prepare for the winter season, you can almost see the faces of the *kodama*, tiny woodland spirits now famous the world over thanks to Hayao Miyazaki's film, *Princess Mononoke*.

On our right, there's a huge lake in an incredible shade of turquoise with an unusual medieval castle perched on its banks. The closer we get, the more we realize it's not old at all. Our guide explains that it's a hydroelectric power station designed to be in keeping with the surrounding landscape. Discombobulating proof of that well-known Japanese sense of aesthetics.

- Unazuki Lake with its dam-cum-fortress.

- Onsen, a hot spring.

GETTING INTO HOT WATER IN AN ONSEN

We alight at Kuronagi station. After a rather challenging climb up a staircase carved in the rock, we follow a cliffside path made up of wooden boards with rope barriers at the side. Suddenly we spot a small building and large plumes of steam emerging from the onsen, a hot spring on the riverbank. Impossible to resist such a temptation, so we plunge into the steaming water to soothe our tired joints. Beneath the canopy of the mighty trees, our bodies completely immersed, soothed by the babbling sound of the nearby river, everlasting life seems eminently possible.

A MOMENT OF CONTEMPLATION

After crossing more of the magnificent metal bridges and tunnels excavated through the rock, we stop at another station, Kanetsuri. Still surrounded by towering mountains that look as though they've been smothered in greenery since the dawn of time, we climb up to a little shrine hidden beneath the trees. You don't have to be a Buddhist or a Shintoist to worship here. The beauty of the natural world is a constant reminder of a kind of spirituality that transcends all divisions and debates gripping mankind. Our last stop is also our terminus: Keyakidaira. But the Kurobe Gorge haven't finished with us yet, not by a long chalk. Here there's an extraordinary 360° viewpoint from a high metal footbridge painted red. We soak up this incredible scenery with all our senses for one last time. Resinous scents through our nose and mouth. Our eyes take in the astounding colour palette of greens, oranges and golds. Our ears are filled with the sounds of the river, animals, *yokai* – supernatural beings in Japanese folklore – hidden out of sight, and, of course, the train as it sets off again. Silently, we murmur our thanks to Mother Nature – such a gift, one we'll never forget.

- Steep track overlooking the Kurobe Gorge.

- Red bridge above the Kurobe Gorge.

• Alpine landscape in the Kurobe Gorge region.

Tokyo → Hakodate
Sunset over Hokkaido

on board the
TOHOKU SHINKANSEN

A high-speed train over land and beneath the sea.

Commissioned in 1964, the famous Shinkansen bullet trains are so much more than just a train. Efficient, fast, clean and punctual, they have become a symbol of high-quality Japanese engineering and embody the archipelago's determination to become, and indeed remain, a technological force to be reckoned with. It's on one of these that we head towards the north of Japan.

Opposite page: Tokyo, a megacity with a population of 14 million.

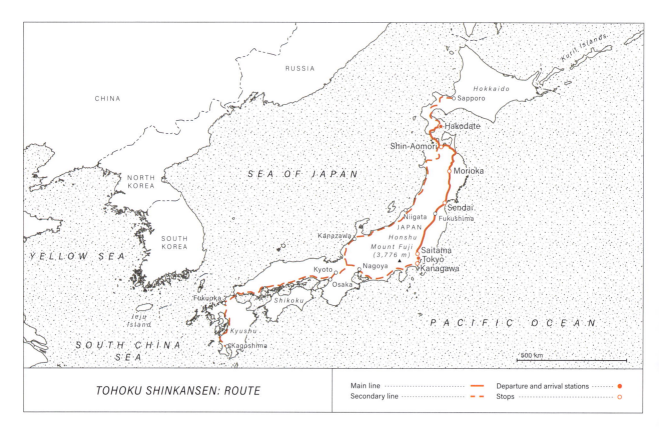

TOHOKU SHINKANSEN: ROUTE

OPERATING SINCE
1964

JOURNEY LENGTH
4 hours, 50 mins

DISTANCE
822km

COUNTRIES VISITED
Japan

📢 **ONE BULLET TRAIN, TWO DIFFERENT LINES**

This route uses two lines, the Tohoku Shinkansen and the Hokkaido Shinkansen. The former is the longest such line in the archipelago and links Tokyo with Shin-Aomori. The second starts at Shin-Aomori and goes as far as Shin-Hakodate-Hokuto station. Work on this line only started in 2005. There are also new maintenance workshops for the Shinkansen trains at the end of the Hokkaido line.

A HUGE GREEN DRAGON

Our bullet train goes by the name of Hokkaido, a fitting reference to Japan's most northerly island and the Shinkansen's ultimate destination. Its jade-green colour and long pointed nose, so typical of Japanese high-speed trains, are reminiscent of a long and snake-like dragon about to carry us off on its back. But rather than sitting astride the beast like celestial knight riders, we are relieved to slip inside and take our places in the comfortable grey seats of the Green Car, as the first-class carriages on Japan Railways are known.

Inside the carriage, all is calm, as the Tokyo skyline flashes past the windows. There's something rather unworldly about the silence that surrounds us in contrast to the external urban hustle and bustle, almost as if we are watching from inside a goldfish bowl. Fortunately, the sensation fades as soon as the city gives way to the Japanese countryside. This takes the form of dense green forests that look like they could be full of game, gently rounded hills, and small, quiet-looking towns. Above them all, a brilliant blue sky makes for a picture-perfect scene.

- *Automatic Shinkansen ticket machines at Tokyo station.*

- *Culinary treats at Fukushima.*

THE EPICUREAN DELIGHTS OF EKIBEN

As we approach the city of Fukushima, now sadly synonymous with the nuclear disaster that took place here in 2011, we start to feel a little peckish. The ideal time to treat ourselves to an *ekiben*, which actually stands for *eki uri bento* and means 'tray of food sold in a station'. Unlike the food found on trains in most other countries, what you get in Japan is usually a selection of delicacies, often based on regional specialities.

We continue on to Sendai, on the Pacific coast. Established in 1601 by Samurai lord Date Masamune, who was known as the 'One-Eyed Dragon', the city is now renowned for its grilled beef tongue, something very different from the dishes usually associated with Japanese cuisine. In a bid to understand why Sendai is often called the 'City of Trees', we take a detour via Jozenji-dori, a magnificent boulevard lined with Japanese Zelkova trees before rounding off our day in the lively Kokubunchô district for a rousing karaoke session.

- *Sendai, City of Trees, with a population of over 1 million.*

- *Takamatsu Pond, surrounded by cherry blossom, in Morioka.*

DUSK IN THE LAND OF THE RISING SUN

The following day, after spending the night in a traditional inn, or *ryokan*, we rejoin the bullet train and continue northwards. When we reach Morioka, there's a branch line that veers off towards Akita. After another long section through the delights of the Japanese countryside, we suddenly plunge into the depths of the ocean, as our train heads into the Seikan Tunnel, an exceptional feat of engineering measuring 53.85km from start to finish, 23.3km of which lie beneath the seabed of the Tsugaru Strait.

On emerging, we find ourselves on the island of Hokkaido. There is just enough time to enjoy the spectacular scenery, forged by the island's many volcanoes, before we arrive in Hakodate. Back on dry land, we have lots to explore, including Goryokaku Fort and its star-shaped park, designed to reduce the number of blind spots that could be targeted by potential invaders. Then there's Our Lady of the Angels Abbey, and of course we need to watch the sunset from Mount Hakodate. Even in the Land of the Rising Sun, this is still a moving spectacle.

- *Morioka, at the foot of Mount Iwate.*

• *Noboribetsu, spa resort famed for its hot springs.*

Tokyo → Kagoshima
Off to the south of the archipelago

on board the
KYUSHU SHINKANSEN

A long metal dragon heading southwards.

Millions of people scurry like ants around the base of Tokyo's towering skyscrapers, making for Shibuya and Shinjuku if shopping is in their sights, or Akihabara to lay their hands on the latest electronic gizmos sold in dedicated hi-tech outlets. Others may prefer to visit the Shinto shrine of Meiji Jingu, with its huge *torii*, an impressive gate carved from 1,500-year-old wood. Then there are those, like us, who are intent on catching the Kyushu Shinkansen to the south of the country.

Opposite page: Japan, a modern country devoted to its traditions.

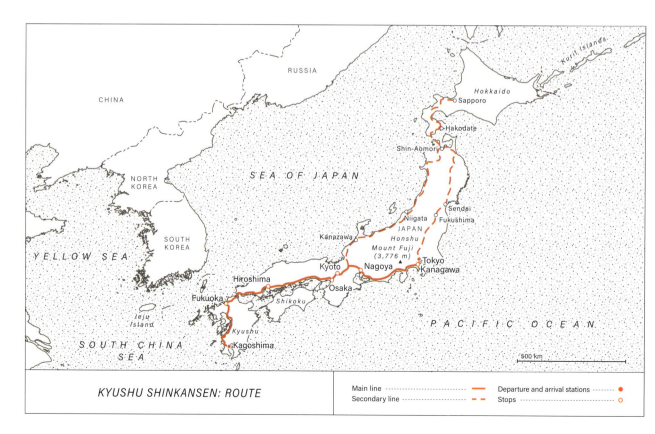

KYUSHU SHINKANSEN: ROUTE

CONSTRUCTED
2004–2011

JOURNEY LENGTH
6 hours, 46 mins

DISTANCE
962km

COUNTRIES VISITED
Japan

🔊 **TRAINS LARGE AND SMALL**

Anyone keen to prolong their railway experience on the island of Kyushu can hop on board a splendid little train from Kagoshima to Ibusuki. With its wood panelling, comfortable seats and large panoramic windows, it's a great way to admire the spectacularly beautiful coastline with a glowering volcano smoking away in the background.

THE REIGN OF FUJI-SAN

Stretched out along the track, its long, pointed nose facing the direction of travel, our bullet train looks like a large crouching animal. A hollow dragon crammed with seats upholstered in a brownish fabric. When the train sets off, it almost feels as though the city is moving, those famous Tokyo skyscrapers upping sticks and setting off to explore the islands. But when the Shinkansen accelerates, it becomes only too clear that we are the ones in motion, not the other way round. Tall buildings, districts, crowds, soon they're all behind us.

We've made sure we're sitting on the right-hand side of the train so as not to miss the view of the main event, Fuji-San (or Fuji-Yama), as Japan's highest mountain is known in Japanese. Around an hour later, it appears in the distance – lucky us to be travelling on such a clear day. For several minutes we enjoy stupendous views of this mighty mountain in all its 3,776-m-high glory. The unmistakeable aura that surrounds it is what draws hundreds of thousands of visitors every year, be they Shintoist or Buddhist pilgrims, hikers or ordinary tourists. To explore it at closer quarters, simply get off at Mishima, then take the train to Fujinomiya on the lower slopes of Mount Fuji.

• Fuji-San, lord of all it surveys.

• The streamlined front end of the Shinkansen.

• Street scene in Nagoya.

THE WORLD IN A CITY

Now we're arriving in Nagoya, where the first sight we see is the station itself. It is regarded as one of the largest railway stations in the world by floor area (410,000m²). The two ultra-modern towers on either side offer outstanding views across the entire city. From these vantage points, we can see all the other treasures in store for us before we leave: Nagoya Castle and its many roofs, the shrine of Atsuta-jingu, some 1,900 years old, resting place of the sacred Kusanagi sword, the temple of Osu Kannon, where worshippers can write their dearest hopes and prayers on scraps of paper and attach them to wires hanging beneath a huge lantern, and, last but not least, the Great Green Buddha at Togan-ji Temple.

For miles on end, the scenery seems to constantly switch between town and country, almost as if it can't make up its mind. Neither has the upper hand. Rather like the board game Go, each house and each green space preventing the other from asserting its dominance. Then suddenly we are in Kyoto, Japan's former capital, a city unlike any other. To visit Kyoto is to take a step back into the Japan of long ago. We could lose ourselves in one of its 1,600 temples or 400 Shinto shrines. Or wander through Nishiki Market to grab some kebabs to nibble on as we walk. Ending up in Gion, in the hope of coming across one of the country's last remaining geishas.

Next stop: Osaka. This city may boast a 16th-century castle, temples and shrines, but that isn't why we're here. Food is what has drawn us to this vibrant urban centre. Known as Japan's foodie hub, Osaka is the best place to sample the sheer variety of Japanese street food: takoyaki, little octopus fritters, perfect for nibbling or squished between slices of bread; ikayaki, a kind of thick squid pancake, or kebabs of anything you can think of, including scallops. The other reason for stopping at Osaka is the punk culture that lingers on behind the doors of certain bars and clubs in the city; you'll need to delve deep though, as these places don't feature in the regular tourist guides.

ON ARRIVAL IN KYUSHU

Our heads still spinning just a little, we set off again at high speed for the south of the archipelago, gobbling up the kilometres as we go. Towns with light-coloured buildings, rectangular towers, squat mountains draped in fairytale forests. Then Hiroshima, victim of the American atomic bomb dropped in 1945, with its peace memorial and the enchanting Shukkei-en Garden, where you can forget the horrors of war for a while.

And finally, after traversing a good part of the splendid island of Kyushu, we arrive in Kagoshima. In days gone by, this city was known as the 'Naples of the East' due to the imposing presence of the Sakurajima volcano. Nowadays, it offers a very different vision of Japan. In a more southerly location, with a more maritime climate and a slower pace of life, this is Japan as you've rarely seen it before. From here, at the southernmost tip of the archipelago, Tokyo has never felt so remote.

• Hiroshima, victim of the US atomic bomb in 1945.

• Osaka, foodie hub of Japan.

Osaka, major port city and commercial centre of Honshu Island.

Aomori → Akita
The opposite of a bullet train

on board the
RESORT SHIRAKAMI

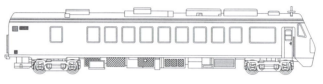

The joyful train.

Running alongside the Sea of Japan in the Tohoku region in the north-east of the country, the Gono line offers a radically different experience to the legendary bullet trains. The Resort Shirakami shares this line with standard commuter trains, travelling at a slower pace so that passengers can appreciate the scenic coastal views.

Opposite page: Mototaki Falls, Akita.

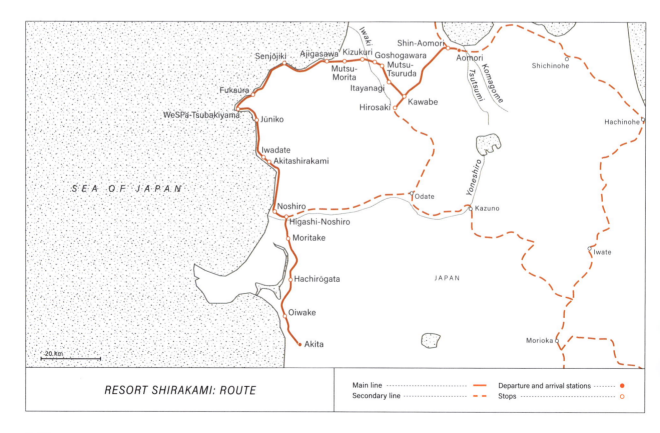

ASIA

CONSTRUCTED
1908–1936

JOURNEY LENGTH
approx. 5 hours

DISTANCE
147.2km

COUNTRIES VISITED
Japan

- *Spacious, light-filled carriages.*

TRAIN-HOPPING

On the platform at Aomori station, where we begin our journey, all is calm. There are just a few Japanese people wearing lightweight clothes and masks, tapping away on their phones or munching snacks as they wait. Unlike them, as soon as our train arrives and we hop on board, we are impatient to get going. This modest commuter service is merely one essential link to today's real objective: the Resort Shirakami, waiting for us at Kawabe station.

This little blue train, sometimes referred to as the 'joyful train', has a rather more relaxed ambience. In our spacious, light-filled carriage, a young man is playing the *shamisen*, a traditional Japanese long-necked lute, while a young woman sings along melodiously. All around, passengers clap in time or video the proceedings on their phones. The Resort Shirakami is not your everyday train. It's an opportunity to sit back and relax without any sense of urgency, suspended in a bubble where time no longer exists.

- *Aomori, a large industrial city in Japan.*

- *Squid fishing boats.*

A THOUSAND TATAMI MATS BY THE WATER

You may be surprised to hear that, on some sections of the route, the Resort Shirakami reduces its speed to as little as 10km/h. Thanks to this slow pace, we are able to appreciate the vast green expanses of the countryside. Somewhere between Kizukuri and Ajigasawa, the pleasant fertile fields give way to the coast of the Sea of Japan. Then, sticking to the coastline, the train launches itself into dense vegetation separated only by the tracks themselves. At Senjojiki, which translates as 'a thousand tatami mats', we disembark to walk out to the sea, where a huge rock plateau makes it clear why it got its name. It has been sculpted into irregular yet appealing shapes by the constant action of the waves and an earthquake back in 1792. According to legend, this geological phenomenon was the scene of banquets held by the local feudal lord. Each to their own. All we can say is that it's a great place for a paddle in the sea.

- *Coastline of the Sea of Japan.*

244

AOMORI → AKITA

- *A tourist train, taking it nice and slow.*

OCEAN LULLABY

Truth be told, our feet are still a little damp when we return to the train. It continues its unhurried pace along this magnificent coast without ever deviating. On our left, substantial rugged hills are just crying out to be walked. On our right, the deep-blue Sea of Japan sparkles in the sunshine. Suddenly, huge jagged rock formations soar out of the water, followed by discreet man-made structures to enable visitors to indulge their passion for bathing.

We stop again at WeSPa-Tsubakiyama, our minds set on taking a dip – but not in the sea. We are drawn to an onsen, a hot spring. This particular one has two special features that make it unique: first of all, the unusual ochre colour of its iron-oxide-laden water, hence its name, Furofushi, which means 'hot spring of eternal youth'. Then there's the position of the two baths, just metres away from the sea. The perfect place for a spot of relaxation, lulled by the soothing rhythms of the ocean.

- *Rocky coastline at Senjojiki.*

🔊 A TRAIN IN WINTER

Although the area is best known for its seaside towns, it's also possible to travel the route of the Resort Shirakami in the depths of winter. In fact, it's almost as popular in this season as in balmier weather. Indeed, when the green mantle of the forests and the breathtaking beach scenes have given way to a snow-capped winter wonderland, this is very much a paradise on Earth…

- *Beech trees, home to numerous bird species.*

- *Beech forest in Shirakami-Sanchi.*

THE 33 JUNIKO LAKES

All good things must come to an end, much to our regret, despite the promise of eternal life after our dip in the onsen. Fortunately, the line still has other delights in store. Not least a UNESCO World Heritage Site known as Shirakami-Sanchi, readily accessible from Akitashirakami station. This area is a wild, forested landscape covering one-third of the Shirakami mountain range. There are very few paths through the beech forests, home to many species of birds, black bears and serows, a goat-like mammal native to these parts. One of its star attractions is the fabulous collection of lakes and ponds that make up the Juniko Lakes (33 in total). The finest of them all, Aoike, is so incredibly blue, its colour constantly changing, that it almost makes you believe in magic.

Finally, after our brief visit to one of the most unspoiled parts of Japan, we resume our trip to Akita. On the train, the atmosphere is if anything even more chilled than when we set out. This abundance of beauty, purity and harmony has undoubtedly had a subtle but profound effect on all the passengers. Certainly enough to guarantee we finish our journey rather more at peace with the world than before.

Bangkok → Singapore
Journey back in time

on board the
EASTERN AND ORIENTAL EXPRESS

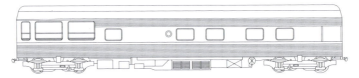

A luxury voyage through the Orient – and through time.

With its opulent wood-panelled cabins, gourmet cuisine, impeccable service and the routes it travels through the splendours of the Malay Peninsula, the Eastern and Oriental Express has been offering a unique railway experience since 1993. It offers a unique dive into the beauty of colonial Asia – open to all, but especially those with deep pockets.

Opposite page: Gardens by the Bay, a 101-hectare green lung in the heart of Singapore.

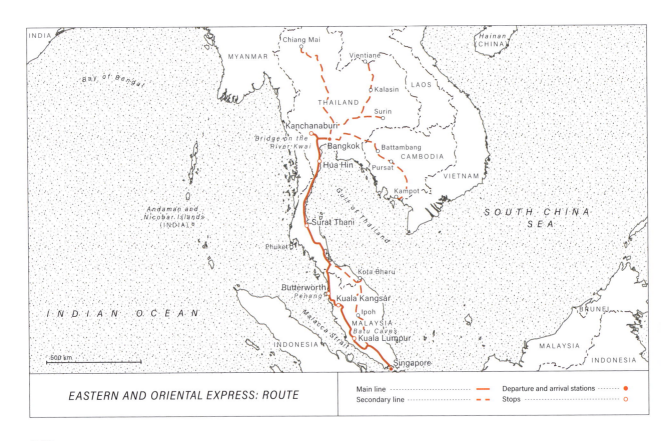

EASTERN AND ORIENTAL EXPRESS: ROUTE

ASIA

OPERATING SINCE
1993

JOURNEY LENGTH
4 days, 3 nights

DISTANCE
2,000km

COUNTRIES VISITED
Thailand
Malaysia
Singapore

CABIN AREA:
25m²

LENGTH OF
WANG PHO VIADUCT
400m

- *Buddhist temple of Wat Arun.*

- *Bangkok, capital of many contrasts.*

ONE NIGHT IN BANGKOK

Vast green parks surrounded by glittering skyscrapers. Architect-designed houses on the banks of the Chao Phraya River. Millions of people thronging the streets, avenues and Metro lines, tiny cafés with low tables and mega-shopping malls. So many temples, so ornate – it's impossible to view them all. Bars, nightclubs and red-light districts where entire generations of tourists have lost their way… A palace belonging to one of the most powerful ruling families in the world. Have you guessed where we are yet? Yes, our next journey begins in the indescribably beautiful city of Bangkok.

However, the sprawling capital of the Kingdom of Thailand is merely the starting point for our voyage of discovery. The atmosphere changes dramatically as soon as we reach the dedicated platform of the Eastern and Oriental Express. In a flash, the staff in their silk uniforms and the train's smart green and cream livery give us a glimpse of a whole new world of luxury and extravagance. This sensation becomes even more pronounced on board, where we are bowled over by the splendour of the carriages: the restaurant car with its immaculate white tablecloths, the bar car where a talented pianist tickles the ivories, and the observation car from which Bangkok can be seen receding into the distance. Not forgetting the individual cabins, ours measuring 25m², with sofas converting into comfortable beds at night, private bathroom and decor worthy of a palace.

- *The River Kwai, in western Thailand.*

BRIDGE ON THE RIVER KWAI

It doesn't take us long to become accustomed to this level of luxury. After an aperitif, a gourmet dinner and a pleasant chat with the other passengers, we drift off to sleep feeling right at home. On drawing back the curtains in our cabin the next morning, we see that the train is running alongside a cliff, over the impressive Wang Pho Viaduct, made from wooden trestles. Although our final destination is south of Bangkok, we have made a brief detour via Kanchanaburi, to the west of the capital, to view the famous Bridge on the River Kwai from a raft with the expert guidance of a historian. We go on to the Don Rak War Cemetery (also known as the Kanchanaburi War Cemetery), containing the graves of those who died during construction of the Siam-Burma Railway, known as the 'Death Railway', at the height of the Japanese invasion. After which it's back to our hotel on rails.

- *The infamous Bridge on the River Kwai, immortalized by the film of the same name.*

248

BANGKOK → SINGAPORE

• The cosy interior of the cabins.

PADDY FIELDS AND PLANTATIONS

On the second morning of our journey, we only wake up after the train has crossed the border between Thailand and Malaysia. As the magnificent Malaysian countryside streams past, we enjoy a delightful breakfast in bed delivered by the on-board staff. So cosy are we that we decide to stay in our cabin until the train arrives at Kuala Kangsar. Located at the confluence of the Kangsar and Perek rivers, this modest town is the starting point for one of the two excursions organized by the Eastern and Oriental Express.

The first is a visit to a so-called 'traditional' village with folk dancing, martial arts, local beverages and regional crafts galore. As we've said before, the route followed by this train, which is owned by the Belmond Group, harks back to the colonialism that prevailed in much of Southeast Asia for so long. This is followed by a walk through the paddy fields and plantations where rubber, bananas and even durians are grown. The second option entails a long hike through the amazing hills of the surrounding area where vegetables and the crops mentioned above are also cultivated. Do note that in bad weather these excursions will be replaced by a tour of Kuala Kangsar, renowned for its Ubudiah Mosque and Sultan Azlan Shah Gallery, before carrying on to Kuala Lumpur.

• Sultan Azlan Shah Gallery, Kuala Kangsar.

🕪 A JOURNEY BOTH EXCLUSIVE AND EXCLUSIONARY

A trip on board the Eastern and Oriental Express is not a cheap affair. The most affordable accommodation starts at 3,325 dollars per person, while the Presidential Suite comes in at 7,575 dollars per passenger. All-inclusive, of course, at these prices.

• Gardens by the Bay, Singapore's park.

SINGAPORE, THE GARDEN CITY

Amazingly, it's already time to enjoy our last evening on board the Eastern and Oriental Express. On this particular occasion, the atmosphere is even more celebratory than usual, the food more delectable and the wines even more exquisite. Conversation flows more readily as we passengers have got to know each other over the course of the past few days. There are Europeans and Americans, of course, but also a sprinkling of Australians, as well as Japanese, Thai and Chinese travellers. It goes without saying that English is our lingua franca as we exchange anecdotes of previous trips. After all, tomorrow we'll be saying our farewells at Singapore station. We'll all go our separate ways as we explore this particularly vibrant city. Some of us will saunter through the Gardens by the Bay, where flora and fauna jostle with huge art installations, while others will be tempted to take the plunge in the oh-so-instagrammable infinity pool at the top of the Marina Bay Sands, while the rest will hit the shops in the Malay neighbourhood of Kampong Glam, or admire the fabulous houses in the Katong district.

249

Bangkok → Pa Sak Jolasid Dam
Rails over the water

on board the
ROT FAI LOI NAM

A train that appears to float on water.

Every year, from November to January, a rather magical train travels from Bangkok, the Thai capital, to Pa Sak Jolasid Dam in the province of Lopburi. Unlike most of its peers, it is reputed to be able to float on water.

Opposite page: Rot Fai Loi Nam crossing the Pa Sak Jolasid Dam.

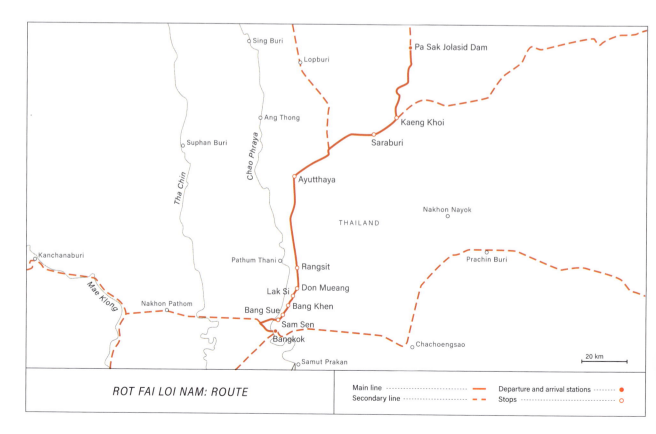

OPERATING SINCE
1998

JOURNEY LENGTH
6-hour return trip

DISTANCE
165km

COUNTRIES VISITED
Thailand

🔊 A POPULAR SEASONAL EVENT

Thailand's floating train doesn't run on a regular basis, which only adds to its popularity. During the brief season it operates, it offers just a dozen or so trips, so you need to book as soon as possible. In 2022, all tickets sold out in barely one week.

▪ Hua Lamphong station, Bangkok.

▪ Bangkok, Thailand's capital.

BANGKOK AWAKENS

It's six o'clock in the morning in Bangkok. Early or not, we are already at Hua Lamphong station, its corridors, concourses and platforms packed with milling crowds made up of Thai people and tourists. The former, along with uniformed police officers, monks in saffron-yellow habits and civilians with a purposeful look about them, give the impression of knowing where they're going. The rest are searching high and low in their tourist guides or scouring the internet to find out where they need to be. We know exactly where we're heading: the platform where the Rot Fai Loi Nam, or 'floating train', is waiting.

By the time we leave the station, the sun is already beating down on the multifaceted architecture of the Thai capital. After passing through kilometres of suburban neighbourhoods, ranging from affluent districts with their swanky condominiums to near-slums, the landscape suddenly opens out into verdant countryside. Little towns are interspersed with agricultural areas where water buffaloes wallow in semi-submerged fields. Low houses line the tracks or the road running alongside. Tiny guesthouses and restaurants with equally minuscule terraces shaded from the sun's rays by umbrellas in the distinctive colours of well-known soft-drinks manufacturers eagerly await their first customers.

▪ Buddha in the ancient city of Ayutthaya.

THE SPLENDOURS OF AYUTTHAYA

Inside the train, the passengers, almost all tourists wearing sun hats, smothered from head to toe in sun cream, and eagerly clutching their smartphones, snap away at everything in sight: children watching as the train trundles past, women working the fields, little temples. Nothing escapes these digital eyes. They seem determined to record every single moment of this trip in their phone memory. And who can blame them? This train, which only runs between November and January, was designed for them – for us, in fact.

One of the places we pass through catches our eye: Ayutthaya. Now it is the administrative centre of the province that bears its name, but from 1350 to 1767 it was the capital of the Kingdom of Siam. These days it covers an area of some 289 hectares, has UNESCO World Heritage status and is full of ancient Buddhist monasteries, temples and ruined towers. Later, when the train makes its return journey to Bangkok, we will stop here to explore these spectacular ruins, looking out for the iconic Buddha's head embedded in the roots of a tree.

▪ Ruins in Ayutthaya, former capital of Siam.

▪ Full speed ahead on the floating train.

FLYING OR FLOATING? A TRAIN EXTRAORDINAIRE

Eventually we arrive at the Pa Sak Jolasid Dam, which holds an incredible 785 million cubic metres of water. Just as it seems as if we're going to crash headlong into the waves, the train carries straight on, regardless. On board, we can't see the tracks, so it feels as though we're floating above the surface of the water, flying at full speed over the magnificent expanse of blue. And then the train stops, giving us 20 minutes to hop off and take as many photos as we like. Whoever came up with the idea of this tourist train really understood their target market. Once again, phone cameras are out in force. We'll have the opportunity to stop again later to buy a selection of local products and dishes and have a quick walk around the local area before returning to Bangkok.

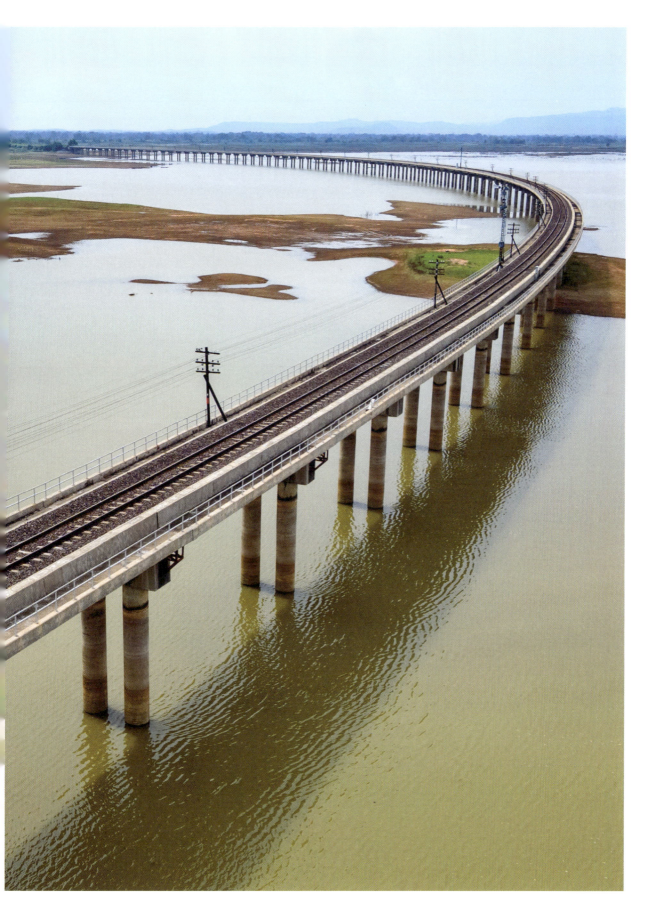

• Aerial view of the Pa Sak Jolasid Viaduct.

Hanoi → Ho Chi Minh City
The road to freedom

on board the
REUNIFICATION EXPRESS

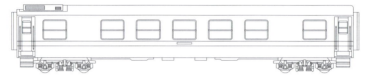

Symbol of the reunification of Vietnam – in the form of a train.

Constructed by French settlers in the 1930s, the railway line that runs from the north of Vietnam to the south links the country's two main cities: the capital, Hanoi, and Ho Chi Minh City, formerly known as Saigon. Although it used to go by the name of the 'Transindochinois', the train using this line these days is now called the Reunification Express. Quite some symbol.

Opposite page: Ho Chi Minh City, formerly Saigon, a pulsating city with a population of 8 million.

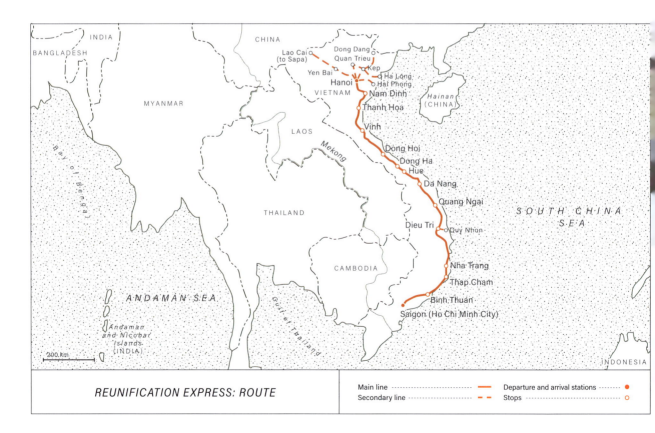

REUNIFICATION EXPRESS: ROUTE

ASIA

①	②	③	④	⑤	⑥	⑦
HANOI	NAM DINH	THANH HOA	VINH	DONG HOI	DONG HA	HUE

OPERATING SINCE
1936

JOURNEY LENGTH
2 days, 1 night

DISTANCE
1,736km

COUNTRIES VISITED
Vietnam

• *Hanoi, chaotic city with a crazy charm all of its own.*

THE ONE AND ONLY HANOI

Hanoi is quite unlike any other city. Whatever time of day or night you visit, it has its own very special buzz. As we explore this vibrant, bustling metropolis, there's something about it that touches us to the core, an infectious *je ne sais quoi* that makes us feel we could live a thousand different lives here. One life in the Temple of Literature, another quaffing a few beers and sampling Vietnamese rice rolls as we perch on the low stools of a nearby terrace, yet another revelling in the beauty of Hoan Kiem Lake. No wonder our hearts are heavy when it's time to head for Hanoi station where a rather chaotic atmosphere, incredibly laid-back yet tremendously effective in its own way, reigns supreme – as in the rest of this wonderful city. This time, as we board the train, we are greeted by music, which we eventually identify as the sound of a local radio station. Our four-berth compartments are simple, clean and fit for purpose. As our train starts to get underway, we are still making ourselves comfortable.

A LEGEND BEHIND EVERY TREE

Our beloved Hanoi slips past the windows. Swarms of two-wheeled vehicles ebb and flow on a road running alongside the rail tracks, swerving then re-forming around cars and pedestrians. In the aptly named Train Street, we pass so close to the buildings that we could easily shake hands with their occupants if we felt so inclined. As we emerge, the varied architectural forms of the city open out before us. Temples, stadiums, green spaces and tiny coloured shop fronts, all tightly packed together. Then comes the Vietnamese back country. The rain of the past few days has left the countryside glistening, washed clean and super verdant. Beautiful light-coloured buildings, a little dated perhaps, but from their size we assume they must be secondary schools or local government buildings. From time to time, a large church appears, reminding us that seven to eight per cent of Vietnam's citizens are Christian, compared to 12 per cent Buddhists. Over 45 per cent practise the traditional religion of these parts, worshipping a broad pantheon of gods, including their ancestors. The remainder are not affiliated to any particular faith.

Groups of tourists disembark in Ninh Binh, intent not only on visiting the ruins of Vietnam's first capital city, but also going up river to explore the Trang An Grottoes. They take flat paddleboats operated by boatwomen who use their feet rather than their hands to row, passing between impressive densely forested hills dotted with temples and shrines. Sometimes referred to as Terrestrial Halong Bay, this place is so incredible, you can hardly believe it's real; it feels as though there's a legend hidden behind every tree, stone and bend in the river.

• *The Trang An Landscape Complex near Ninh Binh, with its limestone karst peaks.*

256

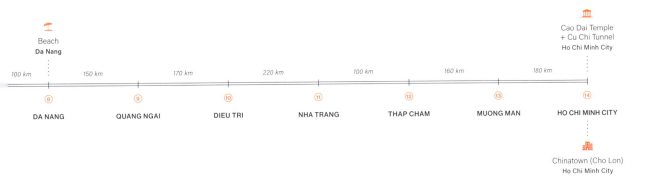

THE FOLLY OF EMPERORS

Thanh Hoa, Vinh, Dong Hoi, Dong Ha. We pass town after town of low houses and brightly coloured stalls. From our vantage point on the train, they look like subtle variations on the same theme. Some a little brighter or less hectic than their predecessors. Interspersed by palm trees, paddy fields, rough-hewn rocky formations, a modest yet colourful shrine, or hills polished to within an inch of their life by the painstaking handiwork of a bygone giant. The dichotomy between the urban hubbub and the absolute tranquillity of the countryside is omnipresent yet paradoxical. Vietnam is irrepressible in some respects, yet set in its ways in others.

There's certainly no shortage of reasons to get off the train and explore. Our first stop is at Hue, famed for its royal citadel, Imperial City and perhaps most of all for the mind-blowing tombs of the emperors of the Nguyen Dynasty. A little further south, the mood changes completely when we stop at Da Nang with its picture-postcard beaches to die for. Those with even more time to spare might like to push on to Hoi An and stroll beneath the lanterns of this UNESCO World Heritage-listed old town. A cornucopia of magical options, each very different, but no less stunning for all that.

• *Vietnam, major rice-producing country.*

• *Da Nang, coastal city in central Vietnam.*

A SYMBOLIC BAPTISM

Formerly known as Saigon, in honour of the river on which it stands, Ho Chi Minh City was renamed in 1975, when the American troops withdrew at the end of the Vietnam War, to commemorate the leader of the anti-colonial resistance movement. The country's first leader, Ho Chi Minh, has his final resting place in a huge mausoleum in Hanoi.

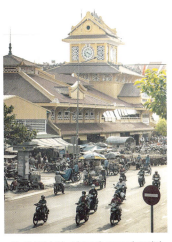

• *Ho Chi Minh City, Vietnam's economic capital: vast, teeming and buzzing.*

SUPERCHARGED HO CHI MINH CITY

Eventually, after a rail journey of just over 1,700km, we arrive in Ho Chi Minh City. Vast, teeming and completely buzzing, Vietnam's economic capital and largest city offers a very different take on the country to Hanoi. In fact, it's hard to know where to start. To get ourselves in the mood, we hire a small scooter, then set off to explore the grand boulevards lined with skyscrapers and spectacular colonial buildings. They in turn conceal some absolute gems: Chinatown (Cho Lon), temples so intricately decorated that they make your head spin, and the exclusive rooftop bars from which the whole city takes on a magical glow.

• *The blue carriages of the Reunification Express.*

Bandung → Yogyakarta
The many faces of Java

on the
INDONESIAN RAILWAY

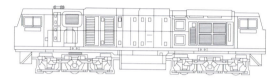

Silver train through the heart of Java.

The elongated shape of the Indonesian island of Java lends itself perfectly to the construction of a railway. The country, regarded as the world's largest Muslim democracy, made the most of this geographical attribute and went on to develop an efficient rail network. One of its premier routes is the line that runs from Jakarta, the capital, to the important spiritual centre of Yogyakarta via Bandung.

Opposite page: A green backdrop for the Buddhist temple of Borobudur (9th century).

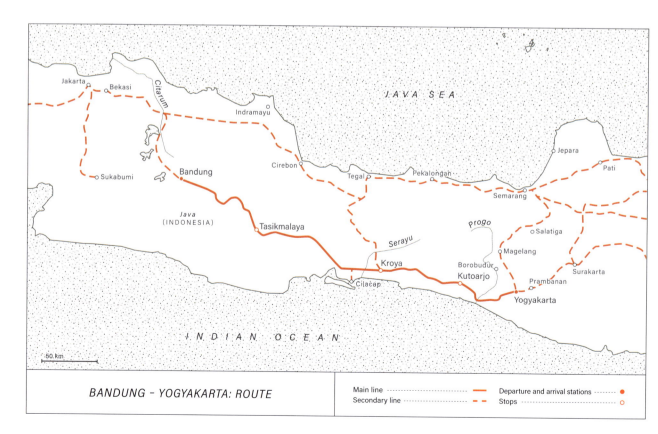

BANDUNG – YOGYAKARTA: ROUTE

Main line ———— Departure and arrival stations ●
Secondary line ‑‑‑‑ Stops ○

OPERATING SINCE
1945

JOURNEY LENGTH
7 hours

DISTANCE
319km

COUNTRIES VISITED
Indonesia

- *Bandung, known as Little Paris, probably due to its many cafés.*

LITTLE PARIS – OR NOT?

As we stroll along the streets of Bandung, just over 150km east of Jakarta, it's hard to understand why it's known as the Little Paris of Indonesia. Although magnificent, its architecture has a rather more colonial feel about it than the Haussmann-inspired original. Perhaps it's simply down to the many pleasant cafés to be found in the attractive city centre? Or its vibrant atmosphere come nightfall, when families and young people alike come out to frequent the street food stalls. Then again, that's hardly what you'd expect in the French capital… Whatever. Bandung is a lovely place to stroll around and people-watch. Perhaps that in itself is the biggest thing these two cities, separated by thousands of kilometres, have in common? Enough pondering. Time to head for the station this fine morning and set off on a new journey. A long silver train awaits us on the quiet platform, the air already hot even at this early hour. It's nothing special, but the seats are comfortable and some classes have working power sockets. Since we're going to be on board for nearly seven hours, information is key. Whether we decide to take notes, message our nearest and dearest at the other side of the world, or simply charge our phones, these sockets will be extremely handy.

- *Paddy fields at the foot of Mount Merapi, an active volcano.*

PADDY FIELDS BENEATH THE PALM TREES

It's not long before the city of Bandung disappears from view. Instead, we're now passing through a vast expanse of paddy fields, overhung by lofty palm trees. The gentle curve of their trunks makes them look like lanky teenagers, too weary to support the weight of their own heads. Much of this farmland is partially underwater, but tiny family houses raised above the fields are just about visible from the train. Occasionally, they are clustered together in modest hamlets of several dwellings with sloping roofs. Despite the sunshine bathing the landscape today, the rains here must be brutal. It's an international rule: the steeper the pitch of the roofs, the heavier the precipitation they have to contend with.

- *Java, the Land of Volcanoes: Mount Bromo.*

Nasi goreng, a rice-based dish.

A TASTE FOR *NASI GORENG*

The train makes a number of stops as we continue on through this captivating landscape. Some are scheduled halts, but there seems no rhyme or reason for the others. Rail companies often operate in mysterious ways, no matter where in the world they are… It's now a few hours since we left Bandung, so we work our way down the many carriages to find the restaurant car. Behind the counter stands a man in a chef's hat, white jacket and dark apron, stirring nasi goreng, an Indonesian fried rice dish, cooked in a massive wok, ready for decanting into small cardboard boxes. This isn't the first time we've had this delicious concoction, so ubiquitous is it in Indonesia, but it always goes down well.

The beauty of Java's scenery is matched by the taste of its cuisine, but whereas the latter explodes on the palate, the landscape changes more subtly. The paddy fields, tiny houses and tall but slender trees are still there, but further away. The horizon has now widened, with more depth of field, its limits defined by sizeable, gently rounded hills. But just as we are succumbing to their hypnotic outline, the rice fields turn into terraces with a pleasing sense of harmony. Then suddenly we are upon a large metal viaduct, crossing a muddy river, which marks the start of a palm forest so beautiful you just want to curl up beneath the trees.

Exuberant nature here we come.

📢 A MULTI-DENOMINATIONAL NATION

Although most Indonesians are Muslims (around 85 per cent), the country also recognizes five other religions: Catholicism, Protestantism, Hinduism, Buddhism and Confucianism. As a result, Indonesia is an exceptionally multi-denominational society, albeit a fragile mix at times, where mutual respect is paramount.

Museum of Independence, Yogyakarta.

JAVA'S HEART AND SOUL

Sadly, we don't have time for a siesta, as we are already approaching Yogyakarta. Regarded as the heart and soul of the island of Java, this city has one foot in the past and one in the future. To truly comprehend all its subtle nuances, we go from modern cybercafés in the new town to local markets overflowing with the traditional batik fabrics of Indonesia. This textile printing method was added to UNESCO's Intangible Cultural Heritage of Humanity list in 2009. Then there are the mosques in the Kraton Palace, the residence of the Sultans of Yogyakarta, little restaurants, or maybe a *wayang kulit* show, a typically Javanese form of shadow puppetry.

Finally, we can't miss Borobudur and Prambanan, two 9th-century sites that have also been awarded UNESCO World Heritage status. The former is one of the most spectacular Buddhist temples on Earth and draws pilgrims from around the world, especially at sunrise. The latter is a collection of exceptionally well-preserved Hindu temples. In both of these, hearing the call of the muezzin from one of the nearby mosques is a spine-tingling spiritual experience you will never forget. Despite the many different faiths and how they have evolved, it makes us realize that we can live in harmony and still protect the heritage of those who have different spiritual beliefs to our own.

North America

11 TRAIN JOURNEYS
3 countries
Extraordinary adventures on the titans of the tracks
FROM ANCHORAGE TO LOS MOCHIS

① **Anchorage → Fairbanks**
🇺🇸 *DENALI STAR*
p. 264

② **Vancouver → Kamloops → Banff**
🇨🇦 *ROCKY MOUNTAINEER*
p. 268

③ **Toronto → Jasper → Vancouver**
🇨🇦 *THE CANADIAN*
p. 272

④ **Halifax → Montreal**
🇨🇦 *OCEAN*
p. 276

⑤ **Cochrane → Moosonee**
🇨🇦 *POLAR BEAR EXPRESS*
p. 280

⑥ **New York → Miami**
🇺🇸 *SILVER METEOR*
p. 284

⑦ **Chicago → San Francisco**
🇺🇸 *CALIFORNIA ZEPHYR*
p. 290

⑧ **Seattle → Los Angeles**
🇺🇸 *COAST STARLIGHT*
p. 294

⑨ **Seattle → Chicago**
🇺🇸 *EMPIRE BUILDER*
p. 298

⑩ **New Orleans → Los Angeles**
🇺🇸 *SUNSET LIMITED*
p. 304

⑪ **Creel → Los Mochis**
🇲🇽 *CHEPE EXPRESS*
p. 308

Anchorage → Fairbanks
Alaska's heart of gold

on board the
DENALI STAR

A panoramic train through the heart of Alaska.

From mid-May to mid-September, the Denali Star travels through the magnificent scenery of Alaska, connecting Anchorage, the state's largest city, and Fairbanks, in the very centre of the territory. It is a genuine lifeline, helping residents in the most far-flung corners of the state to go about their daily lives. The fact that it's also an extraordinary rail journey in its own right is an undisputed bonus.

Opposite page: Autumn colours in Alaska.

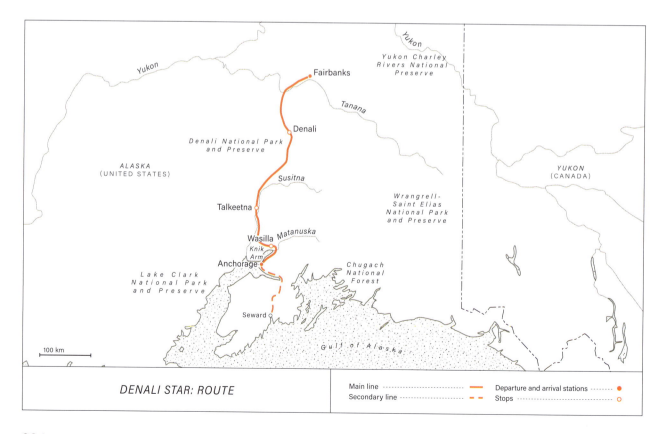

DENALI STAR: ROUTE

Main line — Departure and arrival stations ●
Secondary line --- Stops ○

NORTH AMERICA

① ANCHORAGE — 69km — ② WASILLA

Knik Arm + Matanuska — Anchorage
Denali National Park — Wasilla

CONSTRUCTED
1903–1923

JOURNEY LENGTH
12 hours

DISTANCE
573km

COUNTRIES VISITED
United States

LENGTH OF HURRICANE
GULCH BRIDGE
280m

• Anchorage, Alaska's largest city.

GLACIER COUNTRY

The sun is high in an azure sky and it's summertime. Yet even on a day like this, the temperature barely climbs above 15°C. We're in Anchorage, Alaska, the northernmost state in the USA. For many years, this city really was just a 'port of anchorage' (hence its name). Here, distances and proportions don't mean quite the same as they do elsewhere. It only has around 300,000 inhabitants but is less than 80km from over 60 glaciers. There are 100,000 or so in the state as a whole, all threatened by climate change in the medium to long term.

FROM THE BACK OF BEYOND TO THE MIDDLE OF NOWHERE

Some people might call Anchorage the back of beyond. All very well, but that's precisely what makes it so special: its isolation, its very solitude and the feeling of solidarity that unites its residents. And yet here we are, leaving this back of beyond to head for the middle of nowhere, even further north, as we clamber aboard the Denali Star, Alaska Railroad's flagship train. Its destination? Fairbanks. With its midnight blue livery offset by yellow stripes, this train offers simple, yet perfectly serviceable accommodation.

Its passengers know the drill and are clad for all weathers in coats, fleeces and sturdy footwear. Cold, mud, snow? You just never know...

One thing we do know is that you're never very far from nature in Anchorage. We've barely covered a few kilometres before it reveals itself in all its glory in the shape of Knik Arm, a broad waterway leading deep inland from the Gulf of Alaska. On board, we make our way to the dome car with its panoramic roof, perfect for gazing at the splendiferous views as we travel though the vast boreal forests. These are our constant companions as we cross the Knik and Matanuska rivers at the foot of mountains that, confusingly, feel both so near and yet so far.

• The Denali Star, running alongside Turnagain Arm.

• Cabins on the mountainside, Hatcher Pass.

THE CHAMELEON HUES OF LATE SUMMER

After Wasilla, our first stop, the light suddenly changes. It's the tail end of summer and the foliage is already starting to turn. The green of the forest is subtly mottled with oranges and browns. The Denali Star passes so close to the statuesque trees that their branches brush the top of the large picture windows in the dining car, their shadows dancing on the tables where passengers are enjoying a welcome cup of coffee.

ANCHORAGE → FAIRBANKS

③ FAIRBANKS

A TRAIN WITH A VIEW

Over the PA system, there's an announcement, one of many throughout the trip: if we look out of the windows, we should be able to see Mount Denali. Some 6,190m high, our train's namesake mountain is also the highest point in North America. Its summit bleached white by glaciers, the peak soars skywards, way above the horizon. We watch it for miles, unable to resist the clarion call of its imposing presence. Or is it the other way around? Is this mountain at the back of beyond actually watching over our train and making sure it reaches its destination? This is a part of the world where stranger things have happened... Our surroundings are too vast, too impenetrable not to have some other divine purpose.

We run alongside the Susitna River for a while, eventually parting ways. Now the landscape is dominated by the Talkeetna Mountains, their wooded valleys undoubtedly full of game. The peaks themselves almost feel like a barrier, forcing us to continue alongside; woe betide anyone who dares to try and cut across. It's as if there's nothing worthwhile beyond them. And yet the most spectacular view on this journey still lies before us, just a few kilometres away, when we cross Hurricane Gulch Bridge. This metal viaduct was built in 1921, is 280m long and straddles the eponymous valley at a height of 90m, towering conifer forests on either side.

• *Denali, the highest peak in North America.*

• *Caribou: the true natives of Denali Park.*

AN ESSENTIAL LIFELINE

In addition to its regular stops, the Denali Star also often drops supplies off at various locations along its route, as agreed in advance with the grateful recipients. A great way for Alaska's most isolated inhabitants to access food, equipment and other essential items.

• *Cabin in the Alaskan mountains.*

THE ENDURING BEAUTY OF THE MOUNTAINS

There's no respite from the haunting beauty of Alaska. It goes on and on, right to the end of our journey, in all its technicolour magnificence: the tawny shades of the plains in the foreground, then ever-changing clusters of majestic green trees, dusky mountains on the horizon and, above them all, that vast deep blue sky. Civilization seems so far away; perhaps this is what the planet was like before humans came on the scene with their roads, towns and grid patterns? Only the railway bears witness to man's presence here. Yet back in the days when gold was discovered near Fairbanks, our final destination, many a would-be gold miner descended on these parts to try their luck in the rivers and on their banks. No sign of them now, though – only the mountains remain.

• *Talkeetna village – where time seems to have stood still.*

267

Vancouver → Kamloops → Banff
First passage to the west

on board the
ROCKY MOUNTAINEER

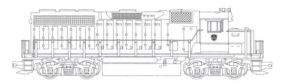

A panoramic train to the ends of the earth.

With its huge picture windows and impeccable service, the Rocky Mountaineer offers a unique contemporary rail travel experience in the lap of luxury. Passengers will also have the opportunity to follow the route of the railway promised to British Columbia in return for them joining the fledgling Canadian Confederation.

Opposite page: Canada, where lakes abound: this one is near Banff.

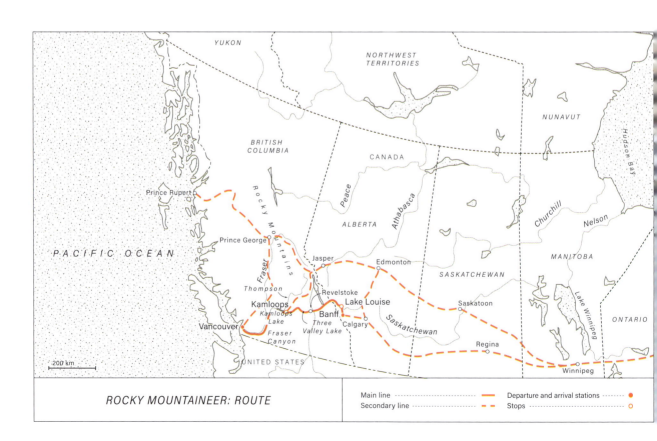

ROCKY MOUNTAINEER: ROUTE

NORTH AMERICA

Fraser Canyon
+ Thompson River
Vancouver

Kamloops Lake
+ Three Valley Lake
+ Rocky Mountains
Kamloops

430km

① VANCOUVER

② KAMPLOOPS

OPERATING SINCE
1990

JOURNEY LENGTH
2 days, 1 night

DISTANCE
957km

COUNTRIES VISITED
Canada

A TRAIN LIKE NO OTHER

Wisps of steam emerge from small metal tubes, playing an intriguing little tune, a cross between Pan pipes and a train whistle blowing before departure. But it's only Vancouver's iconic steam clock in Gastown, the city's Victorian district. We were keen to pay our respects to this impressive example of retro technology before leaving this endearing city, with its vibrant downtown areas, cafés, beaches and the fabulous natural environment all around. Just in time, as we have another outstanding railway adventure ahead of us: a ride on the Rocky Mountaineer.

Unusually, our trip doesn't start in a conventional station. Instead, we go to a private station owned by the company that bears the same name as the train. It's a large red-brick building with wide rectangular windows, and the train awaiting us has much the same feel of understated utilitarian luxury. It has huge blue and gold carriages over two levels, the upper deck being fully glazed to ensure optimum enjoyment of those stunning views. A member of the train staff shows us to our spacious and comfortable seats, with plenty of room for even the longest of legs and a range of reclining options. Coffee is served as we wait patiently for our breakfast sitting.

- The steam clock in Vancouver's Gastown district.

- The Rocky Mountaineer at Banff station.

THE CRISP AIR OF BRITISH COLUMBIA

This train ticks even more boxes thanks to its outdoor viewing platform, where you can be out in the fresh air as you soak up the breathtaking scenery of vast forests, powerful rivers and lakes of the clearest blue while the train travels smoothly on. Yet one of the most thrilling experiences is when we come up alongside another train, especially a freight train, with its heavily laden wagons within touching distance. Admittedly, stretching out a hand to achieve such a feat would be an incredibly dangerous thing to do – but the mere possibility gives us a tingle of anticipatory pleasure.

The viewing platform also gives the train a much more human dimension. Passengers are encouraged to leave their seats at regular intervals to visit this amazing observation deck and of course conversations always flow more freely in the open air. Who better to share our amazement at the jaw-dropping scenery of the Fraser Canyon with than our newfound friends? The river of the same name flows through steep gorges that change direction so abruptly that we pass through tunnel after tunnel. Nature on this scale cannot be tamed; free passage is all we can hope for. It merely tolerates our presence; no more, no less.

- Forests, rivers and lakes – a stunning landscape.

VANCOUVER → KAMLOOPS → BANFF

Banff National Park
Banff

512km

③
BANFF

- *Train passing a church, Kamloops.*

THE TRIP THAT KEEPS ON GIVING

After this initial section, the landscape becomes softer, more welcoming, The terrain is less rugged, the waters calmer. This is particularly noticeable as we follow the Thompson River and then travel for some 30km along the shores of tranquil Kamloops Lake, a continuation, though wider, of this waterway. The semi-arid mountains in this region are to be our last memorable sight of the day, as we will shortly be arriving in Kamloops, where we'll spend the night in a hotel. Keys are issued while we're still on board the Rocky Mountaineer, which only operates in daylight hours.

The next morning, when we arrive back on board, the train staff, attentive as ever, are ready for us with a splendid breakfast of fried eggs, generous portions of bacon and succulent potatoes. We tuck in with gusto as we admire the views: a return to a greener landscape with water popping up when we least expect it, and any number of little wooden houses, painted a cheery blue and black. Fluffy white clouds hover around the mountaintops, like annoying flies on a heavyweight giant. Given their colossal size, the engineering masterpieces we use to forge our way across them – not least some spectacular spiral tunnels – seem minute in comparison.

At last we arrive in Banff, at the heart of the national park of the same name, in the province of Alberta. There's just time to swim in the calm waters of a lake with our eyes still drawn to the summits of the Rockies all around; even now, they seem to be looking down on us, in both senses of the expression. And who can blame them? We are mere mortals playing at life compared to their eternal presence.

red. Shortly after passing Three Valley Lake, we come to the town of Revelstoke, where we start our climb up into the Rocky Mountains.

- *Downtown Revelstoke, where the ascent of the Rocky Mountains begins.*

📢 **TWO HUGE SPIRALS**

Two spiral tunnels were opened in 1909 to make crossing the Rocky Mountains a much safer endeavour. The lower of the two passes through Mount Ogden, enabling trains to cover a distance of 891m and emerge 15m higher. The second runs through Cathedral Mountain, climbing by 17m over a distance of 991m.

- *Wild sheep in the Rocky Mountains.*

IN THE ROCKIES

Despite the chill in the air, we head for the outdoor viewing platform. After all, this legendary mountain range isn't just the name of our train; it's also the real reason why many of us are here. The mountains rise up before our very eyes, powerful and forbidding, almost fierce, against a sky with conflicting shades of

- *Banff National Park – mountains and lakes.*

271

Toronto → Jasper → Vancouver
Across Canada's heartland

on board
THE CANADIAN

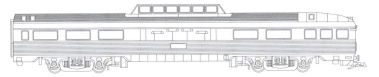

A train through the scenic heartland of Canada at its wildest.

Canada covers an area of some 9,984,670 km² and spans 5,514km, east to west, at its widest point. Over the course of its history, it has developed a significant rail network. At 4,466km long, with a journey length of four days, the stretch between Toronto and Vancouver is its most impressive section.

Opposite page: In the background, the CN Tower represents the heart of downtown Toronto.

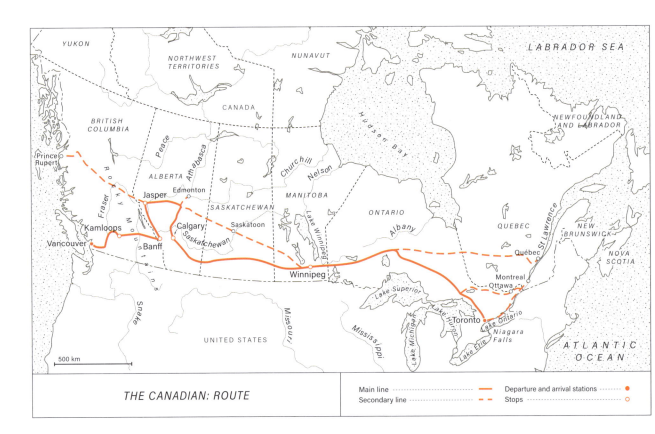

THE CANADIAN: ROUTE

Main line — Departure and arrival stations ●
Secondary line --- Stops ○

OPERATING SINCE
1955

JOURNEY LENGTH
4 days, 4 nights

DISTANCE
4,466km

COUNTRIES VISITED
Canada

STAYING THE DISTANCE

The Canadian only passes through the towns and cities on its itinerary once every three days, no matter which direction you're travelling. When buying tickets, you can't simply get off and on again a few days later; you have to schedule your stopovers in advance and book accordingly.

• Toronto, Canada's largest city.

A VERY CANADIAN TRAIN

Our journey across Canada begins when we board a historic train: the Canadian. Why this name? For the simple reason that it spans the country, linking two of the most iconic Canadian cities: Toronto, the capital of Ontario, and Vancouver, in British Columbia, some 4,466km away. The train itself is a fairly simple service, efficient and comfortable; its only real luxuries take the form of an elegant dining car and three panoramic observation cars.

A BEAUTIFUL FRONT LINE

We spend much of our time in one of these observation cars, hunkering down in the roomy leather seats and watching the eternal combat between the dazzling white of the snow and the deep green of the trees, between the bitter cold that slows life right down and the lifeforms that have adapted to these extreme temperatures. This kind of confrontation is not an isolated skirmish but rather an ongoing front line stretching right across this vast country. The mirror-like surfaces of frozen lakes, row upon row of conifers clad in their evergreen regalia and the streets of the towns we pass through over the next few days and nights are the battlegrounds for this war of the elements. Sioux Lookout, in Ontario, Winnipeg, the capital of Manitoba, Saskatoon, in the heart of the province of Saskatchewan, Edmonton, the capital of Alberta – snow is no stranger to any of these Canadian towns and cities.

• The Canadian: well equipped for the extreme cold.

• A journey of 4,466km in a frozen world.

THE MANY FACES OF CANADA

Although these place names may not be immediately recognizable as typical Canadian tourist destinations, they are all well worth a visit. Each in their own way, they represent the varied faces of this country. It has a history that parallels that of its close neighbour, the United States, in so many respects, yet is radically different in so many others. There, as here, the country was colonized by settlers originally from Europe. There, as here, there were gold rushes, great swathes of trees were felled and the territories of indigenous peoples were unceremoniously invaded. There, as here, local populations were oppressed and suffered unimaginable abuse. But here there was also a burning ambition to create a different kind of nation. Somewhere more contemporary, more multicultural and more united. This mission, as difficult and imperfect as it may seem, is reflected in all these places, be it in their names, their museums or their local cultural identities.

Another particular feature of this train is the journey length. Spending four days and four nights on board a long metal tube, no matter how comfortable, verges on meditation after a while. A marathon of thought processes and rhetorical questions: how tiny are humans compared with the planet on which we live? Just how many kinds of snow are there? And how do animals manage to work with the white stuff to make it their friend, rather than their enemy? Quite mind-blowing.

EVERLASTING YET TRANSIENT AT THE SAME TIME

These musings punctuate our days, as do the meals on board, where the limited number of seats in the dining car dictates, in line with custom, that we share our table with strangers. Over the course of the journey, some are bound to become more than travelling companions. They feel like genuine friends, although in most cases they will vanish without trace from our lives once we reach our destination. Just another quirky aspect of this transcontinental crossing, so fleeting in some respects, yet it feels like it goes on forever in others. It leaves its mark on us as subtly as the delicate patterns of the snowflakes that land on the magnificent windows of the observation car, then disappear in a trice.

We arrive in Jasper, in the Rocky Mountains. Located in the eponymous national park, the largest in Canada, this town is the perfect base from which to explore the glaciers of the Columbia Icefield, along with countless hot springs, lakes and waterfalls. From here, the Canadian continues on to Vancouver, or, in our case, to Banff. There's a different train that goes to Vancouver from there. But that's a whole other adventure – one that also features in this book.

• To the east, Vancouver, the train's final destination after four days on board.

Coastal road, near Vancouver.

Halifax → Montreal
From the Atlantic to La Belle Province

on board
THE OCEAN

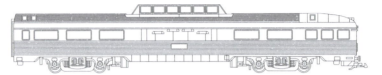

Travel in comfort to La Belle Province of Quebec.

Linking Halifax and Montreal, the Ocean is a superb introduction to rail travel on Canadian territory. From the rocky bays of the Atlantic coastline to the pulsating hub that is Quebec, this poetically named train takes us through a relatively unknown part of this country, otherwise so beloved of tourists.

Opposite page: The port of Halifax, on the Atlantic coast.

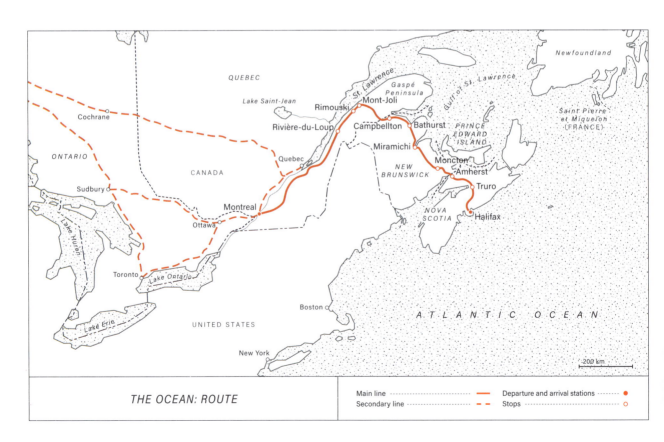

THE OCEAN: ROUTE

OPERATING SINCE
1904

JOURNEY LENGTH
1 day, 1 night

DISTANCE
1,346km

COUNTRIES VISITED
Canada

THE CHARMS OF NOVA SCOTIA

Halifax, the capital of the province of Nova Scotia, isn't necessarily the first place that comes to mind when you think of Canada. Nevertheless, this delightful port city, first established in 1749, with a population of over 400,000, has an interesting back story. After visiting the charming local fishing villages of Peggy's Cove and Fisherman's Cove, we stroll through the city on a bright but cold day. The 4-km-long waterfront boardwalk and a trip to the historic Citadel, built at the same time as the city itself, were at the top of our agenda, as was Pier 21, where entire generations of immigrants first set foot on Canadian soil.

- *Wild nature at its best: Peggy's Cove.*

THE CANADIAN PACIFIC RAILWAY

It may seem a straightforward task to get from one side of Canada to the other these days, but it's all down to the Canadian Pacific Railway. Constructed between 1881 and 1885 under the most incredible conditions, this line originally linked Montreal to Vancouver and became the backbone for the rail network across the whole country.

- *Ocean, a comfortable and functional train.*

A TRAIN CALLED OCEAN

Then it's off to the station to catch our train for Montreal: the aptly named Ocean. Such a romantic name for a train – and despite lacking the requisite white sails and waves under its bow of any self-respecting seafaring vessel, it has all the other attributes you might expect to handle the 22-hour journey that lies ahead. Our two-berth cabin is comfortable, practical and functional. It has everything we need: bunk beds, a large window, mirror, power sockets, individual heating, ventilation and air-conditioning controls, and an optional private shower. Other configurations are available for parties of three or four. Meals on board are taken in the elegant dining car, which offers various options according to the time of day.

By the time the Ocean leaves Halifax station, at 1pm, we are already nicely settled in. We soon have a first-class view of the city's massive port area, the insect-like forms of gigantic metal structures standing out starkly against the blue of the sky. Cruise ships as tall as skyscrapers are preparing to make the return journey across the Atlantic to the old continent, in the opposite direction to that travelled by so many European immigrants in the past. The whole area has a rugged beauty all of its own – industrial and metallic to be sure, but lovely nonetheless. Quite the contrast with the views we can expect over much of the forthcoming journey.

THE ESSENCE OF CANADA

What we can see through the train windows has to be the essence of Canada in its purest distillation: a landscape of vast green expanses, mighty trees, crops and towns with wide streets and low houses. Travelling can be tiring on the back, so we stretch to give ourselves a break, raising our eyes to the sky. Not a thing to be seen, no signs of life – just an infinite blue canvas that a master painter might feel inspired to adorn with a flourish of statuesque white clouds. The sky reflects how we feel about Canada on this particular day: a country that never stands still, somewhere with immutable rules, where our train is the only thing that's moving.

We pass stations, towns and provinces on our route: Truro and Amherst, in Nova Scotia, Moncton, Miramichi, Bathurst and Campbellton, in New Brunswick, Matapédia, Mont-Joli, Rimouski, Rivière-du-Loup and Sainte-Foy, in Quebec province. This last station, which we reach at around 6am, is our access point to Quebec City, with its incredible fortified old town, its ancient streets that date back further than anywhere else on the American continent, and Montmorency Falls Park. But then it's time to head off for Montreal, just over 200km away.

- *Fundy Park, New Brunswick.*

ON THE STREETS OF MONTREAL

This truly unique city needs no introduction. Historically, it is where American and European cultures have collided and the laidback atmosphere of the old city centre, with its cobbled streets, cosy bars and ramparts, offers plenty of scope for sightseeing. Its extraordinary energy then draws us to the modern side of town, especially the hippest neighbourhoods with their buzzing nightlife and concerts a-plenty. Then, when the cold really starts to bite, where better to take cover than the famous Underground City? Montreal is a city like no other – not unlike our own trip across the world's second largest country.

- *The one and only Montreal.*

Fisherman's cottage at Peggy's Cove.

Cochrane → Moosonee
Journey through bear country

on board the
POLAR BEAR EXPRESS

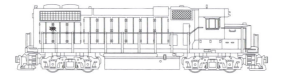

By train to the town with no roads.

If you travel on the Ontario-based train known as the Polar Bear Express, there are no guarantees that you'll see the great white icons of the Canadian Far North. However, it's a sure way to admire the desert-like splendours that extend to the furthest reaches of human territory.

Opposite page: Polar Bear Express, a train with the wherewithal to handle extreme cold.

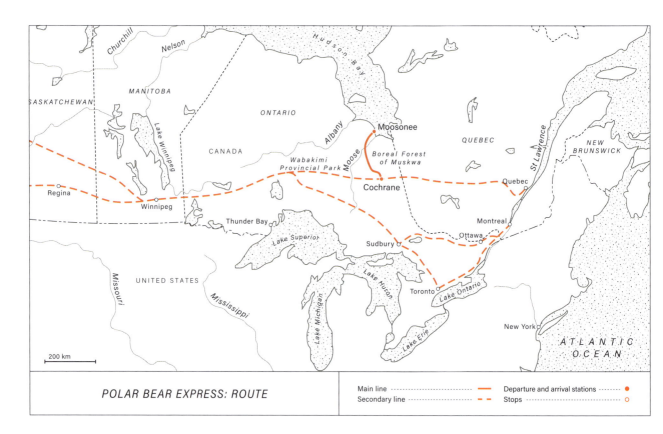

POLAR BEAR EXPRESS: ROUTE

Main line — Departure and arrival stations ●
Secondary line --- Stops ○

OPERATING SINCE
1964

JOURNEY LENGTH
5 hours

DISTANCE
300km

COUNTRIES VISITED
Canada

📢 *NO THROUGH ROAD*

There are no roads that go to Moosonee. The nearest is some 148km away, in Otter Rapids, an *unincorporated place* that isn't governed by any particular municipal council. As well as the Polar Bear Express, Moosonee is also served by barges delivering goods along the Moose River.

FAR, FAR AWAY IN ONTARIO

Even getting to Cochrane is a mission in itself. From Ottawa, Canada's capital city, it takes just under nine hours of non-stop driving to reach this remote township. It's a far cry from what most of the planet's inhabitants would consider to be a town, however. With its low-rise housing, for the most part built of painted timber, its vast skies, enormous statue of a polar bear and the dedicated 7-hectare Polar Bear Habitat, home to three actual polar bears, it's a cross between the Wild West towns portrayed by Hollywood movies and settlements in Northern Scandinavia.

Given its surroundings, the town's station is a real tourist attraction. It's the starting point for our next train, the Polar Bear Express. With its powerful tank-like locomotive and long blue carriages, this no-nonsense train looks ready for whatever the weather can throw at it. Which is just as well, when you see the thick blanket of snow covering the entire area. The engine powers up at 9am on the dot. The crew had loaded the designated wagons, known as boxcars, with equipment, goods, vehicles, trucks and snowmobiles the night before. It makes no sense for trains in these remote regions to travel without a full load.

• *The powerful locomotive of the Polar Bear Express.*

• *Big deer territory.*

IN THE GRIP OF THE COLD

Despite the polar cold prevailing outdoors, it's nice and warm inside the train. In this part of the world, a working heating system is a must. The other passengers on board, all locals, have started making themselves comfortable. Some have rolled up items of clothing to act as pillows under their head so they can continue their night's sleep. Others have descended on the restaurant car to grab a hot drink or chat with other travellers. They are well used to this landscape, whereas for us it's a magical new world. Routine and wonder rarely go hand in hand. Yet here, the sights really are worth seeing.

Under our gaze, the train powers through 300km of boreal forests and *muskeg* – an Algonquin word that translates as grassy bog. Thousands, if not millions of spruce and larch trees stand proudly to attention along our route. Stalwart guardians of this desolate land, they look on stoically as our train glides past. Any number of animals may well be sheltering under their sturdy boughs, hidden from the naked eye. Moose, caribou or elk, even. The largest members of the deer family are very much at home in these parts.

• *The Moose, a coastal river that flows into James Bay.*

BRIDGE OVER MOOSE RIVER

The Moose River is our constant companion throughout this journey. We follow it to its mouth in Hudson Bay. Yet we don't realize quite how impressive it is until we come to cross it via a bridge that we'd definitely think twice about tackling on foot. We're not in any real danger, but it certainly feels as though we might be. This is the price we have to pay to reach Moosonee, our terminus, where the river joins the sea. Still no polar bears to be seen, just the staggering beauty of James Bay and Hudson Bay beyond.

• Herd of elk, some of the largest members of the deer family, in Eastern Canada.

New York → Miami
En route for the Old South

on board the
SILVER METEOR

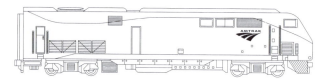

Riding the east coast by train.

The Silver Meteor has been operating between the cities of New York and Miami, in Florida, since 1939. In doing so, it runs down a sizeable part of the east coast, passing cities such as Washington, Richmond, Charleston, Savannah and Orlando. A deep dive into this most famous, yet underexplored part of the United States.

Opposite page: New York's renowned Brooklyn Bridge.

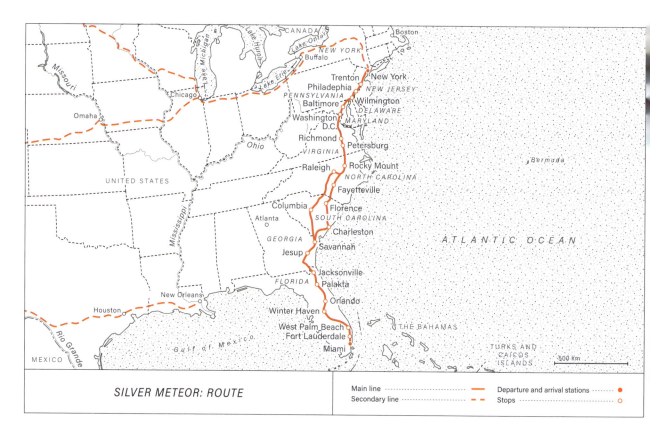

SILVER METEOR: ROUTE

1	2	3	4	5	6	7	8	9
NEW YORK	NEWARK	PHILADELPHIA	BALTIMORE	WASHINGTON	ALEXANDRIA	RICHMOND	FAYETTEVILLE	KINGSTREE

OPERATING SINCE
1939

JOURNEY LENGTH
2 days, 1 night
(27 hours, 54 mins)

DISTANCE
2,235km

COUNTRIES VISITED
United States

• *New York, otherwise known as the Big Apple.*

A BITE OUT OF THE BIG APPLE

New York City needs no introduction. Every last one of New York's neighbourhoods, its residents' tiniest foibles and all the latest food fads or fashion trends, no matter how fleeting, are famous the world over thanks to movies, TV series and the media in general. It goes without saying that just because you think you know the city from these rather fantasized images, you almost inevitably do not: this is a complex, yet subtle megalopolis, with an incredibly multicultural population. Before we join our southbound train, we take time to explore this beautiful city to find out whether our screen-based knowledge chimes with reality. Let's make our own memories of those place names that trip off the tongue as if we've known them forever: Manhattan, the Bronx, Central Park, Greenwich Village, Brooklyn, Williamsburg and so many more.

ONE TRAIN, ONE ROOMETTE

This city needs several days to do it justice, but once we've had our fill we head for Moynihan Train Hall, directly opposite Penn Station, to board our train, the poetically named Silver Meteor. Inaugurated in 1939 by the Seaboard Air Line Railroad but now operated by Amtrak, this legendary train has seen a number of changes over its illustrious history. The one standing before us is silver with red, white and blue stripes. Once on board, we take our seats in what's known as a roomette. At first glance, it looks rather like a mini compartment with two armchairs facing one another. But in reality this roomette also includes a mirror, beneath which there's a dinky washbasin, power sockets, controls for the air-conditioning system, thermostat and lighting, and the option to sleep two passengers by converting the existing seats into one berth and bringing another bed down from the ceiling.

• *Clock in Moynihan Train Hall.*

• *Philadelphia, founded in 1682 on the Delaware River.*

FROM PHILLY TO WASHINGTON

As we're discovering the delights of our roomette, our train pulls out of the station. From the lower row of windows we can see the New York skyline, not least the streamlined shape of the One World Trade Center. Snow is falling as we depart, covering the suburbs of the Big Apple and the forests beyond. Then it's just one legendary name after the other: Philadelphia with its Liberty Bell, said to have tolled to celebrate the independence of the United States in 1776; Baltimore and its enormous harbour, packed to the gunwales with famous ships; not forgetting Washington, the US capital, home of the White House and the Capitol Building, seat of the US Congress. This is also where our electric locomotive is replaced with a diesel, as the line onwards to Miami isn't electrified.

NEW YORK → MIAMI

⑩ CHARLESTON — 213km — ⑪ SAVANNAH — 500km — ⑫ JACKSONVILLE — 100km — ⑬ ORLANDO — 100km — ⑭ WINTER HAVEN — 10km — ⑮ TAMPA — 30km — ⑯ FORT LAUDERDALE — 235km — ⑰ HOLLYWOOD (City of Hollywood) — 15km — ⑱ MIAMI (City of Miami) — 30km

• *Sturdy metal carriages for a two-day journey.*

DINING ON THE SILVER METEOR

While the scenery along the east coast route alternates between residential areas, business parks and a variety of natural landscapes, we decide to take a trip down to the dining car, which feels rather like an American diner. All meals are included in the ticket price. It would certainly be a pity to miss out on a delicious plate of beef ribs cooked in a wine sauce and served with carrots, green beans and mashed potato. Or perhaps grilled salmon and stir-fried prawns, a red curry or marinated chicken with fettuccine. It's certainly no secret that Americans don't believe in half-measures when it comes to food – and the chefs on board this train have definitely got the message.

📢 A METEOR AND A STAR

Another train, the Silver Star, also runs between New York and Miami. They operate different routes between Selma-Smithfield station and Savannah, in Georgia, where they converge again. During their time apart, the Silver Star also stops at Raleigh, the state capital of North Carolina. There's also a branch line that goes as far as Tampa in Florida.

THE GHOSTS OF THE OLD SOUTH

It's the same story the next morning: the menu offers three different breakfast choices – continental, pancakes with sausages, and a three-egg omelette with tomato and mozzarella. We can even press the attendant button to have breakfast delivered to our roomette. We enjoy ours in peace and quiet, our eyes trained on the forests that precede our arrival in Jacksonville, our first stop in Florida. The previous stop, Savannah in the state of Georgia, saw passengers leaving the train to explore the city's magnificent Victorian district, the historic street of Factor's Walk, and the stately Bonaventure cemetery, on a scenic bluff of the Wilmington River. There are many ghosts in the Old South, but the place has an undeniable beauty.

IT CAN ONLY BE FLORIDA...

Outside, the scenery has changed. There's no denying that we're in Florida now. From our comfortable seats (the attendant having kindly put away the beds), we can see modest single-storey houses surrounded by gardens laid to lawn and edged with tropical trees. We almost expect an alligator to emerge from the undergrowth at any moment. As in New York, our collective imagination takes over. But here, the hipsters hanging out in coffee shops are replaced by scary, slow-moving reptiles lurking beneath the waters of the St. Johns River, which runs beneath the track for a short while.

Florida unfurls outside the windows, although it doesn't always match up to what we expect from the movies. The Silver Meteor's route also shows us the unglamorous parts of the state, things we never see from our sofa in front of the small screen: built-up areas, warehouses, long lines of monster trucks gearing up to launch themselves on the American highways. And therein lies the beauty of this kind of trip: it also offers an insight into the not-so-picturesque side of life behind those idealized images. Talking of which, here we are in Miami – time to go and explore. Let's form our own impressions.

• *Miami – beaches in the sunshine.*

287

- *Philadelphia, the sixth most populous city in the United States.*

Chicago → San Francisco
From Illinois to California

on board the
CALIFORNIA ZEPHYR

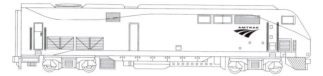

From the Windy City to the Golden State.

The California Zephyr is a very special kind of train. It travels nearly 4,000 kilometres across no fewer than seven American states: Illinois, Iowa, Nebraska, Colorado, Utah, Nevada and California. It also wends its way through some of the most stunning parts of the country, not least the Rocky Mountains and the Sierra Nevada. A truly American adventure – a trip out west by train.

Opposite page: The characteristic red rock formations of Nevada.

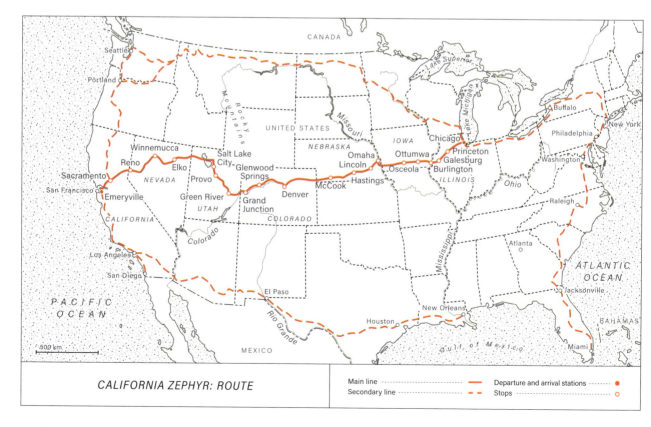

NORTH AMERICA

①	②	③	④	⑤	⑥	⑦	⑧	⑨	⑩
CHICAGO	PRINCETON	BURLINGTON	MOUNT PLEASANT	CRESTON	OMAHA	LINCOLN	HASTINGS	FORT MORGAN	DENVER

50km · 100km · 40km · 80km · 170km · 100km · 155km · 90km · 130km

Start of the Rockies
Denver

OPERATING SINCE
1949, 1983

JOURNEY LENGTH
3 days, 2 nights

DISTANCE
3,924km

COUNTRIES VISITED
United States

• Well-equipped cabins in substantial carriages.

AN EXPERIENCE TO REMEMBER

There's nothing remotely ordinary about travelling on a train like the California Zephyr. It feels rather like an endurance test – both physically and mentally. So before we board, we make sure to pack a few books, crisp new notebooks, pens and plenty of snacks. We may even download the odd film (legally, of course) and videos of a couple of stretching exercises to keep us moving. We may well need them by the time we reach the end of this journey, a veritable rail marathon, no matter how delightful the scenery.

After dropping into the lounge reserved for passengers travelling on Amtrak trains, the California Zephyr being one of their fleet, we finally climb on board and get settled into our roomette. This cute name is a perfect description for the compartments in the sleeper trains operated by this American rail company. They have two seats, face-to-face, two beds, a washbasin, mirror, power sockets, controls for the lighting, thermostat and air-conditioning, and a call button to summon the on-board attendant.

• Westward bound.

• Leaving Chicago, gateway to the Great Lakes.

AMERICA: LAND OF THE PRAIRIES

Chicago slips past our windows as the train gets underway. The skyscrapers of the Windy City – Willis Tower, Vista Tower (now known as St Regis Chicago), the John Hancock Center (now known as 875 North Michigan Avenue, which offers a superb 360° view of the city) – have their heads in swirling grey clouds. Under the rain-laden sky, our thoughts turn to the places we have seen – from the shores of Lake Michigan to Millennium Park, from the unmissable Doughnut Vault to the white galleries of the Art Institute. It's hard to leave this place without a wistful second glance, but we can't remain sad for long. After all, we're about to fulfil a childhood dream: crossing America by train.

The first day is taken up with a long haul through Illinois and Iowa. This may not be the most spectacular scenery on our route, but it certainly shows America at its most authentic. There are miles upon miles of cultivated fields, stretching on and on to the horizon. Farms large and small, with the occasional dark shape of an agricultural vehicle devouring the crops like a gigantic insect. Small towns with individual clapboard houses, often painted in a variety of colours, just the setting for age-old family feuds and hidden secrets that go back generations. Or maybe we've just been watching too much television? As we turn in for the night, we are passing Omaha, in Nebraska.

• Omaha, in the central plains of the Midwest.

292

CHICAGO → SAN FRANCISCO

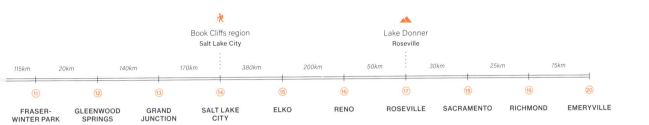

IN THE HEART OF THE ROCKIES

When we open our eyes the next morning, we're in Colorado. After passing through Denver, the state capital, we begin our ascent of the Rockies, a 3,000-kilometre-long mountain range along western Canada and the United States. The California Zephyr makes short work of the inclines thanks to its powerful locomotive and a series of bends. Between Denver and the highest point on the line, the Moffat Tunnel, some 10km long, climbs from an altitude of 1,610m to 2,800m. Not that these figures mean anything compared to the spectacular mountain views. They start off as rolling grassy slopes with a few trees dotted here and there, but the well-named Rockies gradually make their presence felt, turning into mountains proper with vast expanses of evergreen forests. This is an unforgiving landscape and, just for a moment, we spare a thought for our hard-working train as it climbs ever upwards. Then our thoughts turn to the people who roamed these rocky heights before the colonial settlers looking for a new life in the Great West arrived on the scene with their European garments and their dreams of owning a home of their own.

🔊 *MOON RIVER*

Along the canyons of the Colorado river, an area beloved of campers, hikers, anglers and water-sports enthusiasts, a rather bizarre tradition started some years ago and persists to this day. It's called 'mooning the Amtrak' and yes, it really does involve people flaunting their bare behinds at the passing Amtrak trains. It's as well to be prepared – you may see rather a lot of them on this route!

• *Great Sand Dunes National Park, Colorado.*

• *The contrasting landscapes of Colorado.*

FROM CANYONS TO BOOK CLIFFS

After the mountains, we plunge into Colorado's famous canyons. This feels like the kind of terrain you'd expect to find hidden beneath the surface of the planet, yet here we are, exploring its deepest crevices and darkest nooks. As we continue westwards, the rugged rocks around us become even redder, wilder than ever. The landscape changes yet again as we cross into Utah, becoming more desert-like with great arid plains from which rise the daunting Book Cliffs, a mountain range carved into such unusual formations, it might just as well have been sculpted by a divine hand. When we wake up on the second morning, the train is travelling through Nevada. After passing the city of Reno, we embark on another mountain crossing, this time the great Sierra Nevada. Although it starts off as a scene of magnificent desolation, it becomes more craggy and thickly forested as we progress. In winter, as its name suggests (Sierra Nevada means snow-covered mountain range), the peaks are cloaked in a deep white

• *The sandstone rocks of Red Rock Canyon.*

mantle of snow. Those old Westerns certainly captured the essence of this place, but it turns out they sold us short: this area is even more beautiful than we'd thought possible. Finally, we reach California, famed for its trees and its bears, Donner Lake and Sacramento Valley, which shares its name with the state capital. We follow this valley along San Francisco Bay until we get to Emeryville, just a stone's throw from Frisco itself.

293

Seattle → Los Angeles
Sunshine after the rain

on board the
COAST STARLIGHT

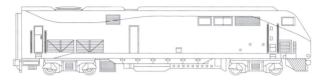

An Amtrak train along the West Coast.

Linking Seattle, just 150km from the Canadian border, with Los Angeles, some 200km from the Mexican frontier, the Coast Starlight covers practically the full length of the West Coast of the United States. This legendary train carries its passengers from a rainy city to the land of sunshine.

Opposite page: Skyscrapers in the sprawling city of Los Angeles.

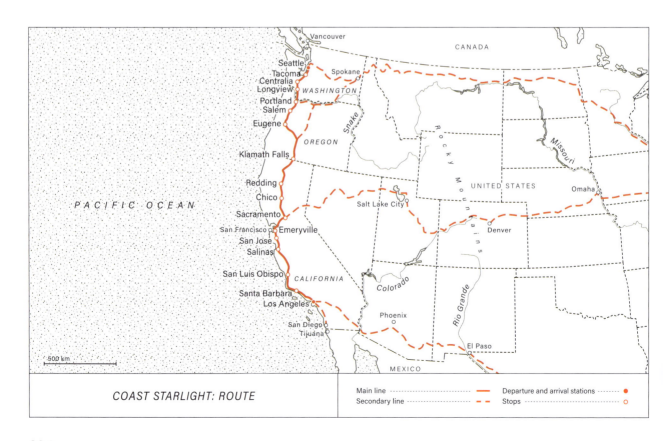

COAST STARLIGHT: ROUTE

NORTH AMERICA

OPERATING SINCE	JOURNEY LENGTH	DISTANCE	COUNTRIES VISITED
1971	2 days, 1 night	2,216km	United States

• *Seattle, on Lake Washington.*

A GREY DAY IN THE EMERALD CITY

It's raining in Seattle the morning we leave. Huge raindrops pour out of thick black clouds. They hammer down on the futuristic lines of the Needle Tower, soaking the piers on the waterfront, drenching Public Market Center, filling up Lake Washington and virtually obscuring the fine clock tower at Seattle's King Street station. In the station itself, passengers' damp footprints are the only indication of the downpour reigning outside. We're only too happy to shelter from the elements as we board our train, the Coast Starlight, also operated by Amtrak.

IN THE WASHINGTON FORESTS

By the time the train pulls out, the rain has abated somewhat. Rays of sunlight pierce the clouds, casting a watery glow onto Seattle's many tall buildings. The outskirts of Washington state's largest city eventually give way to towering forests. These are why Seattle is often known as the Emerald City, although on a day like today it feels more grey than green. From the observation car, open to all classes of passengers, you feel right in the thick of things. The sides of the train brush past huge trees, immovable forces of nature. A cheerful mood prevails in this part of the train. Families oohing and aahing at the sight of mist shrouding the forest canopy and merging seamlessly into the clouds. Lovebirds, hand-in-hand, barely tearing their eyes from each other except to rhapsodize at the beauty all around.

Just as we are enjoying another hearty meal in the dining car, the second on our journey so far, the scenery starts to alter. Now our views are of expansive plains, stretching out to a horizon marked by a mountain range. This is the image that remains with us as we close the door to our neat two-berth cabin, where the car attendant has kindly lowered the second bed from the ceiling. It even has its own window, so we can still keep an eye on those views. Despite the typical train noise and vibrations, we soon drift off to sleep, as if rocked by a comforting lullaby.

• *One of the many forests in Washington State.*

• *Portland, a small city growing in popularity.*

DESTINATION OREGON

As we sleep, we cross the border between the states of Washington and Oregon, arriving at Portland station shortly before two in the morning. Although not widely known elsewhere, this city, with a population of just over 600,000, is worthy of wider acclaim. Despite being compact, it boasts one of the country's largest urban forests and has become increasingly popular in recent years. Its tranquil vibe, thriving arts and culture scene and modest size combine with low-rise buildings, a younger-than-average population with a good level of education, and a permanent connection to the world of nature to explain why more and more students, backpackers and young couples are coming to view Portland as a healthier, gentler lifestyle choice.

296

SEATTLE → LOS ANGELES

25km	80km	5km	70km	100km	160km	50km	200km	60km	30km
⑪	⑫	⑬	⑭	⑮	⑯	⑰	⑱	⑲	⑳
DAVIS	EMERYVILLE	OAKLAND	SAN JOSE	SALINAS	PASO ROBLES	SAN LUIS OBISPO	SANTA BARBARA	VAN NUYS	LOS ANGELES

CALIFORNIA CONTRASTS

At six in the morning, we draw into Sacramento station and realize that we've made it to California. Despite often being overshadowed by other large cities in the Golden State – San Francisco, Los Angeles and San Diego – California's state capital is worth a visit on its own merits. All the more reason to take a stroll through its historic district, which feels rather like the set of a Western, and stop for breakfast in one of the many lively restaurants. Despite Sacramento's resolutely modern vibe, we still have that sneaking feeling that a sheriff, star emblazoned on his chest, might pop out in front of us at any moment. We make a point of visiting the Capitol, seat of the California state government, followed by the California State Railroad Museum, before finally returning to the train.

The stations that follow are a cautionary reminder that there's more to California than those big-name cities, so familiar from movie and TV screens: Oakland and its Jack London Square waterfront; San Jose, with its laid-back atmosphere and spooky Winchester Mystery House; Salinas, childhood home of author John Steinbeck (although the actual house is now a restaurant); and Santa Barbara, famous for its beaches and said to have the most affluent residents in the whole of the United States. All these cities combine to make up California's multifaceted soul, both incredibly urban, yet deeply rooted in its bountiful natural environment, astonishingly superficial in some respects, yet with a deep literary undercurrent.

• Sacramento, straight from the stills of a Western.

• Santa Barbara, with its miles of beaches and well-heeled residents.

🔊 TOMATOES, ALMONDS, FLOWERS AND TREES

Big Tomato, Almond Capital or Camellia City: the city of Sacramento has had many nicknames over the years. It's also known as the City of Trees, as, according to its residents, the city has more trees per capita than anywhere else in the world. These include elms, sycamores and oaks.

• Coast Starlight, approaching Los Angeles.

CALIFORNIA DREAMIN'

There's a whole range of different landscapes in the state. We seem to have seen the end of the luxuriant forests, and the tendency now is for a drier kind of habitat. Depending which side of the train we're sitting on at any given time, our views are either of coast or mountains. At times, the Pacific Ocean is barely metres away. Its immense blue expanse is defined only by a perfectly straight horizon. The occasional foam-crested wave crashes onto the dark-coloured rocks between the railroad and the sea. The noise of the train drowns out the familiar sounds of the surf, but it doesn't take much to conjure it up for ourselves. The astringent whiff of iodine still manages to infiltrate the air-conditioning system and tickle our nostrils nostalgically. It remains with us until Los Angeles, City of Dreams and source of so many disappointments, shining moments of glory interspersed with countless shattered hopes.

• Los Angeles, City of Angels and dream destination.

297

Seattle → Chicago
In the footsteps of a railroad tycoon

on board the
EMPIRE BUILDER

An Amtrak train retracing the steps of the empire builders.

Inspired by the epithet of industrialist James J Hill, a North-American railroad tycoon, this is probably one of the most iconic trains in the United States. It has now been carrying its passengers from Seattle (or Portland) to Chicago for just shy of a hundred years. A three-day adventure through some of the most glorious landscapes in the northern part of the country.

Opposite page: The famous Space Needle dominates Seattle's skyline.

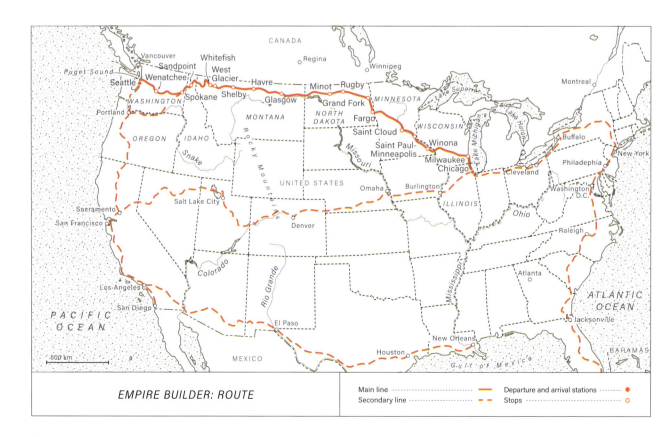

EMPIRE BUILDER: ROUTE

NORTH AMERICA

SEATTLE	EVERETT	WENATCHEE	SPOKANE	SANDPOINT	WHITEFISH	EAST GLACIER PARK	BROWNING	HAVRE	GLASGOW
30km	170km	80km	120km	140km	130km	80km	100km	150km	

Glacier National Park — East Glacier Park

OPERATING SINCE
1929

JOURNEY LENGTH
3 days, 2 nights

DISTANCE
3,550km

COUNTRIES VISITED
United States

▪ *King Street station, Seattle.*

TO THE EAST!

Chandeliers with softly glowing spheres of light are suspended from the ceiling, reflected on the intricate plaster mouldings of the vast white walls and the elegant tiled floor. In the centre of the room, dozens of people are patiently waiting for their trains, looking at newspapers, books or phones. We are at King Street station, right in the heart of Seattle. It's nearly 5pm and in just a few minutes we are due to board the Empire Builder.

Our train starts by heading north along Puget Sound. This arm of the Pacific Ocean extends deep into Washington state; we can clearly see its grey waters from our windows. The track is just a few metres from the water's edge, although sometimes the waves recede to reveal a typically northern beach where chunks of driftwood have been deposited by the tide. Just for a moment, a seabird seems to be trying to overtake us, but then it soars off into the distance. The fishing grounds here are so plentiful that there's certainly no need for any bird to go all the way to Chicago… Surely only a human could be so perverse (in the eyes of a bird, at any rate).

▪ *Three days on the tracks before Chicago.*

CLOUDS OVER THE CASCADES

Finally the train turns towards the east. The sky may be unremittingly grey, but the huge arable fields around us glow the brightest of greens. They surround large rectangular farmsteads, all with brand-new pick-up trucks parked out front. There's always something or other to transport in this vast country, be it sacks of grain, jerry cans of fuel for a generator, or a huge dog, far too muddy to sit on the passenger seat. Gradually we head away from human terrain to slip back into the world of the trees. These colossal masters of the woodlands stand tall along our route, competing with the Cascade Mountains in the background, their peaks shrouded in clouds. In the meantime, we've made our way to the observation car, where everyone is glued to the sights through the picture windows.

After a delicious three-course meal, which appears to be a tradition on Amtrak trains, we retire to our roomette, an extremely well-equipped two-berth cabin, for the night. But rather than drawing the curtains, we fall asleep watching the beautiful landscape of Washington state illuminated by the light of the moon. By the time we wake up, we've already passed Spokane, where the train from Portland merges with our own, and are now in Montana. There have even been subtle changes to the natural environment, but the basic elements are still the same: trees on an epic scale, far too huge to fell, thick clouds of mist concealing who knows what, and mountains with a different name – the Rockies, this time, no longer the Cascades.

▪ *Snow Lake in the Cascade mountain range.*

300

SEATTLE → CHICAGO

| 80km | 180km | 95km | 150km | 75km | 90km | 80km | 70km | 120km | 120km |

⑪ WOLF POINT   ⑫ RUGBY   ⑬ DEVILS LAKE   ⑭ FARGO   ⑮ DETROIT LAKES   ⑯ ST. PAUL-MINNEAPOLIS   ⑰ LA CROSSE   ⑱ COLOMBUS   ⑲ MILWAUKEE   ⑳ CHICAGO

• *Marias Pass in Glacier National Park.*

ENDURING BEAUTY

Miles go by and the spectacle refuses to let up. After Whitefish, a town set on a scintillating lake, we reach Glacier National Park, 4,101 square kilometres of wild nature, countless glaciers and thousands of different species of flora and fauna. This really is a jewel among jewels, in the perfect setting that is Montana.

Just as we start to make our way over Marias Pass, we have the strangest sensation that this beautiful journey will never come to an end. It is a metaphor for the enduring beauty of nature and its unerring ability to surprise us again and again. As we cross what the Americans call the Continental Divide, the ridge that determines whether rivers drain into the Atlantic and Arctic Oceans, or into the Pacific, Mother Nature strikes again. It's quite simple really: the view looks like a collection of all the best literary works ever written.

• *The varied scenery of Glacier National Park.*

📣 THE EMPIRE BUILDER

James Jerome Hill, after whom the Empire Builder was named, was the founder of the Great Northern Railway, a railroad linking Seattle with St. Paul and the most northerly of all the transcontinental routes in the USA. It was constructed in stages as a means of gradually developing profitable lines.

• *St. Paul, gateway to Minnesota.*

GHOSTLY PLAINS

Finally we leave the mountains behind. Ahead of us lie the plains, hundreds of miles of golden plains. So flat that they could almost have been compacted by an enormous steamroller to leave even more space for that boundless expanse of blue sky. With their rickety wooden houses and ghostly looking towns, some parts even have an eerie, desolate beauty that is strangely captivating. As we approach North Dakota, the overriding flatness is temporarily interrupted by a broken landscape known as the Badlands, with strange landforms not unlike ruined fortresses. We have almost reached the city of Minot by the time the sun sets during our second dinner on board.

On our third morning, we wake up in Minnesota. St. Paul, the capital, and Minneapolis, the largest city, together represent the largest urban settlements in the state. For much of this final stretch we travel over the wetlands surrounding the mighty Mississippi before eventually crossing this river to enter Wisconsin. The countryside outside has recovered its greener hues, but is also gradually becoming more urbanized. We scoot from one little town to another until we reach Milwaukee on the western shores of Lake Michigan. From here it's just one last push down to Chicago, also located on this vast body of water – all 58,030 square kilometres of it.

• *Chicago, on the shores of Lake Michigan.*

St. Paul, a relatively recent city built in 1854.

New Orleans → Los Angeles
Sunset over the south

on board the
SUNSET LIMITED

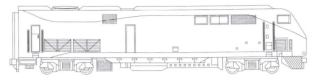

An Amtrak train through the southernmost United States.

From the lively party streets of New Orleans to the beaches and film sets of Los Angeles, the Sunset Limited covers an enormous swathe of the southern United States. Indeed, it pushes so far south that, as well as ticking off Texas and Arizona, it also skirts the Mexican border, famously marked by the Rio Grande.

Opposite page: Sunrise over Los Angeles.

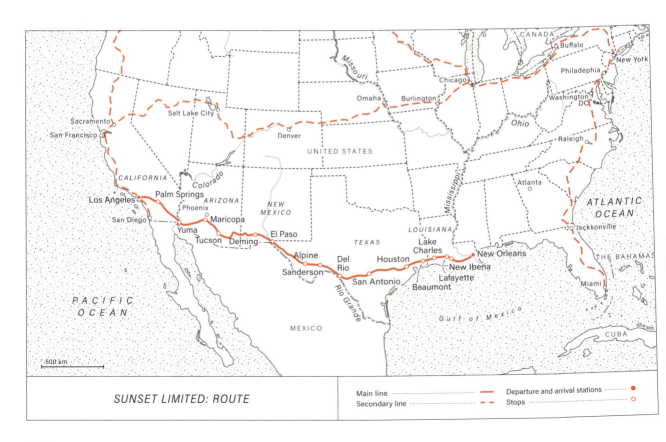

NORTH AMERICA

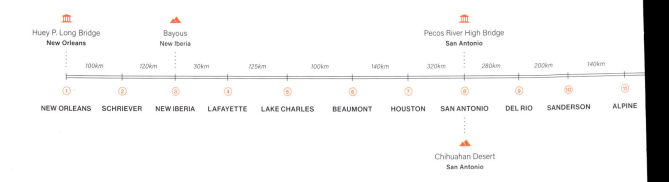

OPERATING SINCE
1894

JOURNEY LENGTH
46 hours

DISTANCE
3,211km

COUNTRIES VISITED
United States

LENGTH OF HUEY
P. LONG BRIDGE
7km

HEIGHT OF PECOS
RIVER HIGH BRIDGE
114m

• *Canal Street, New Orleans.*

• *Traditional Mississippi paddlewheeler.*

IN THE FRENCH QUARTER

Yesterday was an action-packed day. After wandering around the charming old buildings of New Orleans' French Quarter and taking a paddlewheeler cruise on the Mississippi, we stopped off at the Voodoo Museum to immerse ourselves in the mysteries of this culture, still practised today. Our feet then found their own way to Preservation Hall, the city's most famous jazz club. Its walls have resounded to the music of some of the most legendary names in the business over the years.

At 9am, when our train is due to depart, the sounds and tastes of Louisiana are still fresh in our mind. We take our seats in the lounge car to enjoy the views over the Mississippi as we cross the Huey P. Long Bridge, a 7-kilometre-long rail viaduct. From its highest point we are privileged to see another side to Louisiana: the immaculate suburbs with their large square houses and manicured lawns.

• *Huey P. Long Bridge on the Mississippi.*

FROM THE BAYOU TO THE DESERT

Des Allemands, New Iberia – so many names to remind us how much this area has been influenced by the Europeans who emigrated here long ago. Meanwhile, the landscape alternates between luminous rainforests and swampland, or bayous, which do not live up to their sinister reputation. You only have to look at them to imagine all the life thriving above and below the water. Beyond the Sabine River, which denotes the border between Louisiana and Texas, the scenery tends to stay much the same. It's perhaps a little drier, but not a lot, as the sun sets on the Lone Star State. Down here, we're a long way from the deserts for which the state is renowned. The train's name has never seemed so fitting as when the last red rays of the sunset cast a magical glow on the run-up to Houston. When we wake at 7 o'clock the following morning, we have already long since missed San Antonio. In fact, we're now crossing the Pecos River High Bridge. Then all of a sudden, we find ourselves amid the stark splendour of the Chihuahan Desert. Despite its arid appearance, the 501,896 square kilometres of this desert, spread over three American and six Mexican states, is teeming with life. Over 500 bird species can be spotted in the skies here, including golden eagles and roadrunners. On the ground you might see mule deer, black-tailed jackrabbits, prairie dogs, coyotes and Mexican pronghorns as they gambol, chase and roam across this dry landscape.

• *Traditional colonnaded mansion in Louisiana.*

• *Downtown San Antonio.*

NEW ORLEANS → LOS ANGELES

• *Ciudad Juárez, Mexico, opposite El Paso.*

TEXAS AT ITS FLAMBOYANT BEST

The afternoon may well be wearing on, but we're still in Texas. Every mile we travel is proof of the huge scale of this American state. Desert landscape – distant, steep-sided mountains, scrubby vegetation and soil in shades ranging from ochre to red – accompanies us until we reach El Paso, on the opposite side of the Rio Grande to the Mexican city of Ciudad Juárez. A few foodie travellers, no doubt familiar with the area and its traditions, take the opportunity to hop down and buy burritos from the local hawkers. There's no denying that Hispanic and South American influences are omnipresent at this juncture.

Yet again, the Sunset Limited starts to live up to its name. The whole horizon lights up with the most gloriously flamboyant colours – it's as if the sun and the sky are on fire, their flames diminishing in intensity as the sun slowly sets. The show peters out as we dine in the restaurant car, where passengers travelling in private cabins are entitled to three-course meals so delicious that many train operators across the world would be green with envy. This evening, we're treated to crispy coconut shrimps, flat iron steak (the company's signature dish), and chocolate mousse with caramel shards to finish. The ideal way to end a day, as we cross Arizona overnight, stopping in Tucson.

• *Downtown El Paso, on the Mexican border.*

📢 THE USA'S OLDEST NAMED TRAIN

Launched in 1894 by Southern Pacific Railroad, the Sunset Limited is the oldest continuously operating named train in America. In 1993, its route was extended to Florida, but onwards travel east of New Orleans was permanently halted in 2005 in the aftermath of Hurricane Katrina.

MORNING IN THE CITY OF ANGELS

It's just past five in the morning when we pull into Los Angeles, in California. Despite the fact that the sun is not yet up, the city is bathed in balmy temperatures, relieved only by the sea air blowing in from the Pacific Ocean. Beverly Hills, Santa Monica, Venice Beach, Hollywood... These names are familiar to us all. Surely every single person on the planet can summon up images based on these iconic words? Just as Arizona conjures up pictures of cacti and barren mountains. Unfortunately these rarely appear in the same films – with the honourable exception of a film featuring our epic voyage, perhaps?

• *Our terminus: Los Angeles, City of Angels.*

307

Creel → Los Mochis
Canyon country

on board the
CHEPE EXPRESS

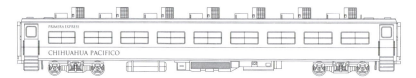

The railroad on which it runs is the only overland route in the region.

The Chihuahua-Pacific Railway is rarely given its full title. Known as El Chepe from the three-letter code (CHP) assigned to it by the Association of American Railroads, it connects Chihuahua, in the Mexican state of the same name, with Los Mochis in the state of Sinaloa. Its most spectacular section is the stretch between the latter and Creel, served by a remarkable train: the Chepe Express.

Opposite page: The Sierra Madre mountains, Creel territory.

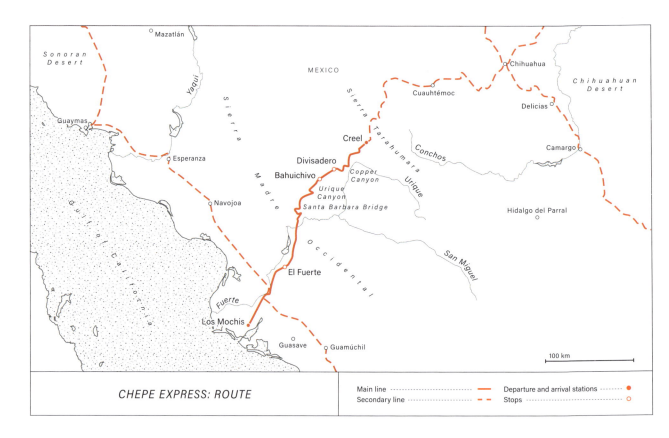

NORTH AMERICA

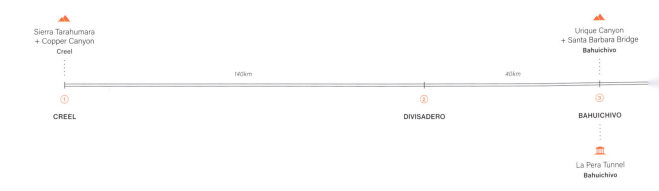

OPERATING SINCE	
1961	

JOURNEY LENGTH
9 hours, 40 mins

DISTANCE
350km

COUNTRIES VISITED
Mexico

LENGTH OF LA LERA TUNNEL
937m

LENGTH OF SANTA BARBARA BRIDGE
217m

• *Valley of the Mushrooms, near Creel.*

• *Rock formations in the Sierra Tarahumara.*

CREEL, A MAGICAL TOWN

Creel is a funny little place. Its main street bordered with wooden façades, this little town looks as though it's straight out of a Western film set. It has a population of a few thousand and is perched 2,340m above sea level. Originally built around a station on the Chihuahua-Pacific Railway back in 1907, it is currently one of the *pueblos mágicos* (magical towns), a tourist scheme dreamed up by the Mexican government to promote places of particular interest. It owes its membership of this exclusive club to its magnificent natural environment, not least the Barrancas del Cobre region, otherwise known as the Copper Canyon.

The Chepe Express departs very early in the morning and is a treasure in its own right, an elegant modern train in its dark blue livery with smart white stripes. It offers three classes – *turista*, *ejecutiva* and *primera* (or tourist, executive and first class for those who don't speak Spanish). It goes without saying that they all guarantee the same views but very different levels of service. At the most prestigious end of the spectrum, first-class passengers have access to a restaurant located in an observation car and to a comfortable bar carriage, which also has panoramic windows. This is where we take our places, all the better to admire the beauty of the forest-clad mountains all around. We are in the Sierra Tarahumara, another mountain range with craggy and dramatic peaks.

THE COPPER CANYON

This rugged terrain makes no concession whatsoever to human railway ambitions, forcing us to travel at a much reduced speed. It takes us two hours to cover the 30 or so kilometres separating Creel and Divisadero, our first stop. However, the jaw-dropping views are not the only reason to use this slowcoach of a train. The railroad on which it runs is the only overland route in the region. In other words, it's not just a railway line; it's an absolute lifeline. The train winds its way through the mountains with no sense of urgency, rebuffing all attempts by the landscape to thwart its progress. Eventually we reach an even more spectacular part of the journey: the Copper Canyon. If they were placed end-to-end, these six long gorges would be almost four times larger and twice as deep as the Grand Canyon in Arizona. On board our train, this rollercoaster journey feels like a voyage of discovery. Despite our comfortable seats, for a few minutes we genuinely feel like explorers setting out into uncharted territory. In the past, these brave souls believed they would be the first to see whatever discoveries lay ahead. Sadly, this was very rarely the case. In this part of the world, mountains have always provided shelter for the local people in their need to escape the worst excesses of the colonial invaders…

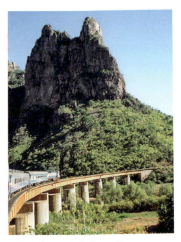

• *Chepe Express, in the Copper Canyon.*

CREEL → LOS MOCHIS

219km — ④ EL FUERTE — 90km — ⑤ LOS MOCHIS

- Bahuichivo station.

CO-EXISTENCE – A PROMISE COME TRUE?

The magnificent landscape of the Copper Canyon undergoes a subtle change as we reach Divisadero, a small village at an altitude of 2,250m, where there's also a cable car and zipwires should you feel inclined to soar over the canyons in a less conventional manner. Our train keeps firmly on its rails, however, navigating its descent with the aid of many bridges and tunnels, some of which are spine-tinglingly awe-inspiring. Shortly after Bahuichivo, a tiny town that has sprung up around the railway line, we reach Urique Canyon, even deeper than the Grand Canyon. Its beauty promises so much – can this be a world where people are able to co-exist with the wonders of nature, leaving no traces of human life behind them? From the bar on El Chepe, we truly believe that we're doing precisely that. We're not posing any threat to the natural world, the animals and plants that live here are well used to the train passing through and have come to terms with the engineering structures that allow the train to traverse this miracle of nature. These include Santa Barbara Bridge, a curved viaduct some 217m long, La Pera Tunnel, 937m long, and Chinipas Bridge, which spans the river of the same name. Silence reigns in the carriage as we cross these masterpieces of design. The view over the green waters down below, starting point for those mesmerizing mountains, takes on a dreamlike quality, a fantasy world conjured up by the vivid imagination of a thriller writer.

- Chepe Express, at El Fuerte station.

 AN UNUSUALLY COMPLICATED CONSTRUCTION PROJECT

It took nearly a hundred years to complete the construction of the Chihuahua-Pacific Railway line. Originally the brainchild of American engineer Albert Kinsey Owen back in 1880, the project was abandoned 20 years later before getting off the ground again with the backing of the Kansas City, Mexico and Orient Railway at the turn of the 20th century. It then stalled for the second time before the Mexican government awarded the contract to Enrique Creel and the project was finally completed in 1961.

THE BEAUTY OF SINALOA

Finally we arrive in the Mexican state of Sinaloa. Here, the land is so flat, so fertile and so well-utilized for agricultural purposes that the mountains and canyons are now but a distant memory. Slowly, we approach El Fuerte, a tranquil town where Mexican culture thrives in the unlikely setting of some extravagant colonial architecture. And then here we are at our final destination, Los Mochis. Could this be the start of a new adventure around Ohuira Bay or the Gulf of California?

- El Fuerte, a tranquil town with colonial-style architecture.

311

South America

8 TRAIN JOURNEYS
5 countries
Brave little trains tackling spectacular mountainscapes
FROM ALAUSI TO USHUAIA

① **Alausi → Sibambe**
NARIZ DEL DIABLO
p. 314

② **Cusco → Aguas Calientes**
HIRAM BINGHAM
p. 318

③ **Cusco → Arequipa**
ANDEAN EXPLORER
p. 322

④ **Villazón → Oruro**
WARA WARA DEL SUR
p. 326

⑤ **Morretes → Curitiba**
SERRA VERDE EXPRESS
p. 330

⑥ **Salta → La Polvorilla Viaduct**
TREN A LAS NUBES
p. 334

⑦ **Viedma → San Carlos de Bariloche**
TREN PATAGÓNICO
p. 338

⑧ **Ushuaia → Tierra del Fuego National Park**
TREN DEL FIN DEL MUNDO
p. 342

Alausi → Sibambe
A devil of a ride

on board the
NARIZ DEL DIABLO

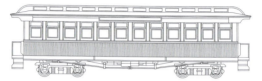

A tiny train regarded as one of the most dangerous in the world.

The Nariz del Diablo (or Devil's Nose) originally referred solely to a towering, steep-sided peak but has now been adopted by this sturdy little train that travels in its shadow. The line covers just 12km between the small Ecuadorian towns of Alausi and Sibambe. Nowadays, the train, often called 'the most dangerous train in the world', is purely a tourist attraction, travelling as it does on a fraction of the line that formerly linked Quito, Ecuador's capital, with Guayaquil, a city overlooking the Pacific Ocean.

Opposite page: The Devil's Nose, a small train tackling a giant mountain.

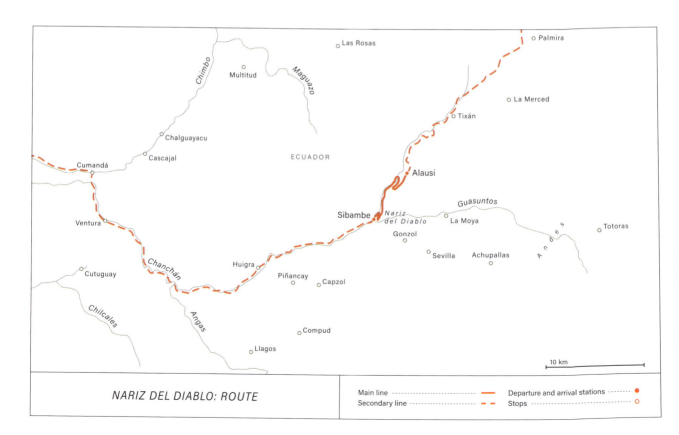

NARIZ DEL DIABLO: ROUTE

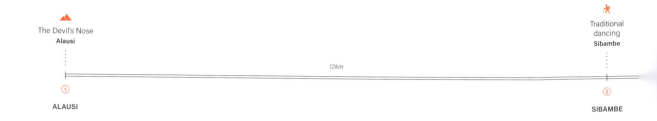

① ALAUSI

② SIBAMBE

CONSTRUCTED
1899–1908

JOURNEY LENGTH
2 hours, 30 mins

DISTANCE
12km

COUNTRIES VISITED
Ecuador

- *Alausi station.*

UNDER THE GAZE OF SAINT PETER

Perched on the hilltop viewpoint of Loma de Lluglli, an imposing statue of Saint Peter watches over Alausi, in the Ecuadorian province of Chimborazo.

This little town is home to some 6,000 people and stands at an altitude of 2,340m in the heart of the Andes. It is a jumble of modest, multicoloured houses, occasionally interspersed with elegant buildings with more than a hint of colonial architecture. Beautiful in its own right, Alausi is also the starting

- *Alausi, technicolour colonial architecture.*

point for a very special train ride on the Nariz del Diablo, or Devil's Nose.

We make our way to the attractive but understated town station, eager to set off on this trip of just over 12km through the peaks in the surrounding area. The first surprise is the train itself: with its handsome wood-panelled carriages and spacious, comfortable seats, it's nothing like the ageing boneshaker we were expecting in view of its route between two towns that are virtually unknown to the world at large.

ON THE BRINK

By the time the train departs, we're firmly ensconced in our seats, our noses pressed against the glass. It doesn't take long to understand why this little train is such a magnetic attraction for tourists, its only passengers nowadays. They flock to this hidden corner of South America specifically to experience this ride. The pretty colours of Alausi soon give way to monochrome green or brown as we plunge deep into the Andes. From this point on, the mountains are everywhere, our permanent companions on this trip. Like us, our train is but an insignificant insect on the substantial shoulders of these giants. This feeling is heightened as we contemplate the abyss, never far from sight. The Devil's Nose, which takes its name from the huge rocky peak ahead of us, skirts the rim of a hair-raising precipice. No barriers, no parapets, and certainly no retaining walls. Just the abyss, the antithesis of the vast mountains all around. At times, the topography of the terrain forms a small natural embankment, offering us a few seconds' respite. Although initially reassuring, these little interruptions to our perilous relationship with the void below start to niggle after a while. Strange that it only took us a matter of minutes to become accustomed to the yawning gulf just centimetres from our rails…

- *The Devil's Nose, just a handful of orange carriages teetering above the abyss.*

316

12km

③
ALAUSI

A STEEP LEARNING CURVE

After the initial shock, we start to appreciate the magnificent views all around us. The steepness, almost vertical in some cases, of the mountains at our side becomes a comforting presence, a protective buttress even. The peaks and ridges start to feel a little less jagged. The river seething at the bottom of the chasm suddenly sounds like a soothing lullaby. Even the famous Devil's Nose itself (the original, not the train!) now resembles a rather inoffensive hooter when we stop for the obligatory photo and selfie session. In fact, despite its reputation as the most dangerous train in the world, the Devil's Nose is perfectly safe these days, especially as passengers are no longer allowed to travel on the roof, as was once the case.

- Vertiginous route to the terminus.

- The Devil's Nose approaching Sibambe.

- Views of near-vertical mountainsides.

DANCING IN THE ANDES

We arrive in Sibambe, just a stone's throw from this diabolical appendage, where we are greeted by the sight of whirling dancers performing traditional dances. Under the platform canopy, men in red tunics and white trousers and women in white blouses and red skirts, all wearing traditional Andean headwear, run through their dance moves to the melodious sounds of the local classics. Then the tourists, ourselves included, are encouraged to join in and learn the right way to shake a leg high up in the cordillera.

As we down a well-earned beer, our train engages in a rather unusual manoeuvre: the locomotive is uncoupled, then moved to the other end of the carriages via a short stretch of parallel track so it can set off again in the opposite direction. This means it's ready to take us back to Alausi, where our journey ends. Time to retrace our route across this fascinating landscape, already engraved on our hearts. Once again, we are in awe of the ingenious ploys used by the engineers of yesteryear to conquer the steep slopes and often perpendicular rock faces. We are no longer surprised when the train goes into reverse and sets off in the opposite direction to ascend or descend – depending on the direction of travel – 500m over just 12km. These are the kind of tricks you need to tame the Andes…

- 12km of switchbacks and steep gradients.

📢 THE MOST DANGEROUS TRAIN IN THE WORLD

Although there have been accidents in the past that may account for the reputation of the Devil's Nose train, the fact is that this line was mainly dangerous for those who built it with their bare hands. A quick dip into the archives and historical records now suggests that nearly 3,000 workers, many of them prisoners, lost their lives while constructing this railway line. These are the cold, hard facts, but it doesn't make it any easier to take on board.

Cusco → Aguas Calientes
On the Inca trail

on board the
HIRAM BINGHAM

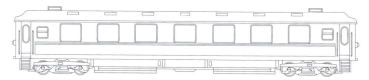

A luxury train in the land of the Incas.

Initially launched as the Machu Picchu Orient Express, the Hiram Bingham, operated by the renowned Belmond Group, offers luxury rail travel on a whole other level. It transports its well-heeled passengers from Cusco to the world-famous ruins of Machu Picchu, one of the highlights of the Inca empire.

Opposite page: Sacred Valley of the Incas, near Maras.

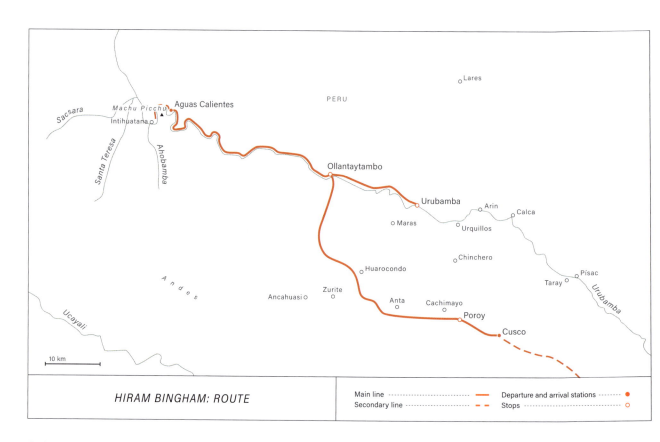

HIRAM BINGHAM: ROUTE

OPERATING SINCE
2003

JOURNEY LENGTH
3 to 4 hours

DISTANCE
112km

COUNTRIES VISITED
Peru

📢 *A CONTESTED DISCOVERY*

Constructed in the 15th century, the ancient Inca city of Machu Picchu has ruins covering an area of some 325.92km². Now a UNESCO World Heritage Site, it is often said to have been rediscovered in 1911 by Hiram Bingham, after whom our train is named. However, several academic sources indicate that local people were aware of the city's existence, as were a number of foreigners who probably didn't recognize its archaeological importance.

BUBBLES IN THE ANDES

Champagne bubbles fizz in our glasses to the rhythm of drums. Scarcely have we taken a mouthful than a uniformed stewardess is on hand to top us up. All around us, on the platform of the little station in Cusco, other passengers splurging their money on this trip of a lifetime savour their drinks as musicians and dancers in traditional garb put on a show to see us off. Just a few metres away, the Hiram Bingham, a distinguished dark blue train, awaits our arrival. This is how we are to travel to Machu Picchu.

After the short welcome ceremony, we climb aboard. The train is even more impressive viewed from the inside, its carriages featuring 1920s-style furniture, wood-panelled walls and fine fabrics. Through the picture windows we can see a vast landscape of reddish, rocky earth dotted with large and rather shaggy trees. The route drops down from Cusco, at 3,399m, with its Plaza de Armas and the Cathedral Basilica of the Virgin of the Assumption, as Machu Picchu is located much lower, at around 2,430m above sea level.

• *An elegant blue train.*

• *Fine dining in the restaurant car.*

ALONG THE SACRED VALLEY

As we lose height, the countryside becomes harsher and more rugged, in marked contrast to the festive atmosphere on board where a rock band in suits and ties play a lively number as we choose our poison from a lavish and varied drinks menu. The guitarist's fingers fly over his instrument's strings. The chords of an American classic are still reverberating around the carriage walls as we begin to follow the Urubamba River, which winds its way through the Sacred Valley of the Incas, also known as Willcamayu.

• *Urubamba River in the Sacred Valley of the Incas.*

It's lunchtime and all the passengers are seated at tables resplendent in white linen, finishing their glasses of pisco sour. Like magicians, the waiters conjure up dish after dish: salmon, lomo saltado, petits fours and many other delicacies besides. This is fine dining par excellence; it could hold its own on the menu of any classy restaurant on or off the rails. The sounds of glasses clinking, cutlery on plates and animated conversations fill the carriage. For a moment, we are struck by the paradox of our situation: this sumptuous train travelling merrily through this country where the GDP per capita is barely more than 7,500 dollars a year. In comparison, each passenger on the train seems to have struck lucky with the lost gold of the Incas.

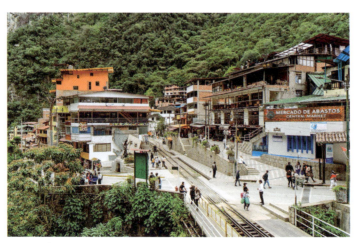

• *Aguas Calientes, starting point for the climb to Machu Picchu.*

EN ROUTE TO MACHU PICCHU

By this stage, the rugged appearance of the mountains has softened and they are now coated in a fuzzy layer of jungle green. We are in the heart of the Andes. This legendary mountain range exudes such a powerful vibe that every inch of our surroundings feels like sacred ground. The slightest undulation, the smallest peak and the merest wisp of a cloud concealing the horizon suggest the hand of an ancient god. This sensation lingers until we reach the station in Aguas Calientes, which is named after its hot springs and is the base camp for our climb to Machu Picchu, one of the most amazing structures ever created by mankind.

• Machu Picchu, world-famous Inca city.

Cusco → Arequipa
In the heart of the Andes

on board the
ANDEAN EXPLORER

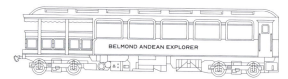

Palace on rails in the Andes.

Every Thursday, the opulent Andean Explorer departs the Peruvian city of Cusco on a three-day journey across the high Andean plains. This train conveys its passengers, cocooned in an embrace of constant luxury, through the wonders of the ancient Inca civilization and the breathtaking scenery of Lake Titicaca to the white city of Arequipa.

Opposite page: Andean Explorer, a smart blue and yellow train.

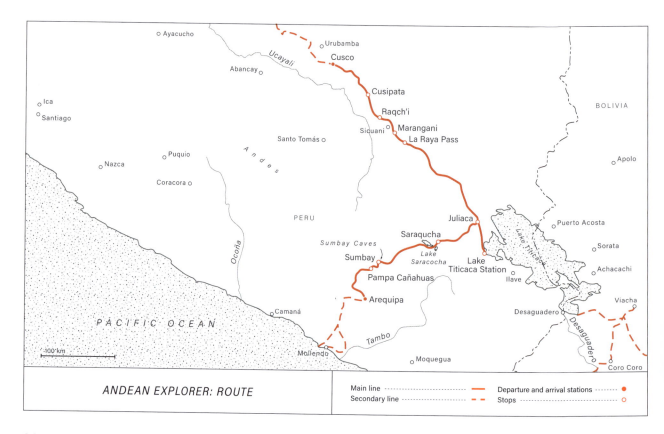

| ① CUSCO | 80km | ② CUSIPATA | 40km | ③ RAQCHI | 30km | ④ MARANGANI | 25km | ⑤ LA RAYA |

OPERATING SINCE
2017

JOURNEY LENGTH
3 days, 2 nights

DISTANCE
731km

COUNTRIES VISITED
Peru

IN THE LAP OF LUXURY AT CUSCO

It's 11 o'clock sharp as the Andean Explorer, a smart blue and yellow train, leaves Cusco station with 40 or so passengers on board. As we sip a glass of *chicha morada*, a Peruvian drink made from purple corn, we realize just how lucky we are to be making this journey. Much more modern than most other deluxe trains in the worldwide Belmond stable, this particular train is still an exhilarating spectacle.

Rather than the marquetry panelling inspired by Pullman, inventor of the first sleeper cars, the suites, cabins, lounge car, two dining cars, spa and observation car with its own open-sided platform are designed to reflect the crisp colours of alpaca wool against a backdrop of grey to emulate the slate of the Andes. The service on offer is nothing short of palatial and the food is fine dining at its best, inspired by Peruvian specialities. Each dish is the creation of the head chef at the prestigious Belmond Monasterio Hotel in Cusco. Our suite is a spacious 13.1m² and has a double bed and its own shower.

- *A luxury cabin measuring 13.1m².*

- *Sparse Andean vegetation, burnished golden by the sun.*

- *Craft stalls at La Raya.*

FROM HERE TO ETERNITY

If it weren't for the ever-changing scenery outside, we could almost forget we were on a train. Fortunately, the views from the open-air platform bordered by wrought-iron panels are absolutely staggering. Nothing but the Andes mountains as far as the eye can see, a vast and eternal presence. Below these giants of nature, small flat expanses glisten in the sunlight, while residual pockets of snow cling resolutely to the mountain tops. And suddenly we stop, seemingly in the middle of nowhere. We have reached La Raya, a tiny village with a population of just 200, where we soak up the views as we wander around the local craft stalls, then pop into the church.

We round off our day with a gourmet dinner: cream of pumpkin soup, tortellini with sun-dried tomatoes, sage, pine nuts and wood sorrel, fillet of beef, caramelized squash and Andean grains, cheese and chocolate mousse. A superb feast against such a beautiful, yet desolate backdrop, so stunning that you wouldn't believe it unless you saw it with your own eyes. When the meal finally draws to a close, the on-board team suggest we might like to turn in for the night as we have an early start ahead of us. Despite being gently roused at the unearthly hour of 5am, we have to admit that the spectacle outside is well worth sacrificing our beauty sleep for: sunrise over Lake Titicaca.

CUSCO → AREQUIPA

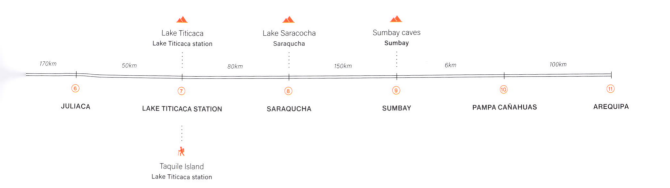

ISLANDS IN THE SUN

After breakfast and a shower on the train, we transfer onto boats to explore part of the lake, which covers an area of 8,372km². We begin with the man-made Uros Islands, made entirely from the totora reeds, which grow locally here. We then make for Taquile Island, home to just over 2,000 people who live and work according to age-old traditions; for them, tourism is a necessary evil – both a business and a disruption to their everyday lives. We end our outing with lunch on a beach accompanied by local artistes performing traditional dances for our entertainment.

Back on board the Andean Explorer, we continue to thrill at the magnificence of this mountain range, or cordillera: its very name is the epitome of grandeur, recognizable across the globe. As we follow this route among the most unforgiving peaks anywhere on Earth, we come to the conclusion that the reality is far greater than anything we could have imagined beforehand. From time to time, a few flimsy buildings or a herd of animals remind us that these isolated spots, no matter how remote they might seem, are not just random places on a map. They are lands that have been inhabited since time immemorial.

- One of the man-made Uros islands on Lake Titicaca.

- The Andean Explorer passing through the valleys of the Andes.

📢 ONWARDS TO COLCA CANYON

There is an optional excursion to Colca Canyon, to the north of Arequipa. Some 3,270m deep, this ravine has a number of natural hot springs and lodges to accommodate the many backpackers exploring the length of the canyon.

- Arequipa, at an altitude of 2,335m.

BREATHTAKING – IN EVERY SENSE

Another new day, another early wake-up call. This time we've arrived at the shores of Lake Saracocha, at an altitude of 4,278m. It's just after 5am as we alight from the train. We clamber a few dozen metres uphill to get a better view. The air is thin at this altitude, making climbing rather more strenuous than usual, but the unfolding spectacle is well worth the extra effort. Against the dawn colours of the sky, the sun rises behind the midnight blue of the train, contrasting with the greenish-yellow shades of the sparse vegetation and the metallic sheen of the lake itself.

Then it's onwards to the Sumbay caves, where, after nearly an hour's climb, we are rewarded by cave paintings dating back to between 6000 and 8000 BC. The train's medical team are always on hand to supply oxygen for those who need it, regardless of age. Finally, we head for Arequipa, our ultimate destination. Located 2,335m above sea level, the legal capital of Peru is the seat of the country's Constitutional Court and has a population of over 1 million. However, its main claim to fame is its stunning architecture, justifying its inclusion on the list of UNESCO World Heritage Sites in 2000.

- Cave paintings in the Sumbay caves (6000–8000 BC).

Villazón → Oruro
Starstruck

on board the
WARA WARA DEL SUR

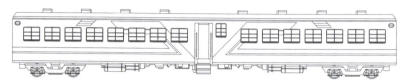

A train through the Bolivian Altiplano.

The railway line between the city of Oruro on the shores of Lake Uru Uru, and Villazón, on the Bolivian-Argentine border, was opened in stages between 1892 and 1925. A number of trains, including the Expreso del Sur and the Wara Wara del Sur, use this route several times a week to enable Bolivians and tourists alike to travel through this little-known part of South America.

Opposite page: 10-metre-tall cacti on the Uyuni Salt Flat.

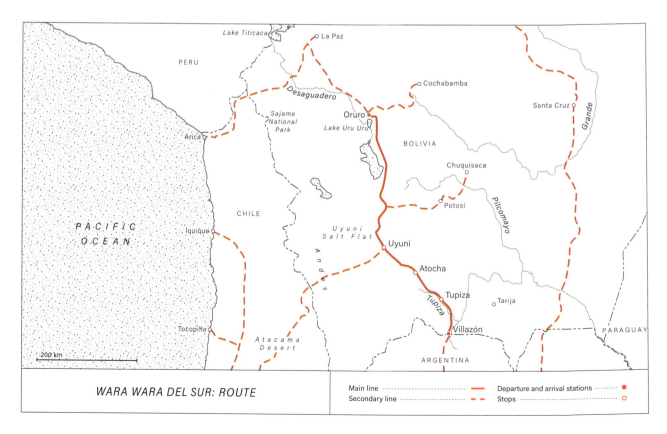

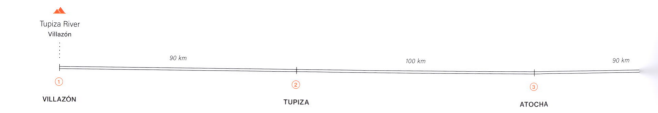

| VILLAZÓN | 90 km | TUPIZA | 100 km | ATOCHA | 90 km |

OPERATING SINCE
1925

JOURNEY LENGTH
16 hours

DISTANCE
approx. 620km

COUNTRIES VISITED
Bolivia

HIGH-LEVEL NEGOTIATIONS

On the streets of Villazón, the concept of *negocio* is all-important. Trade, or negotiations, in other words. Located at a height of 3,400m in the Altiplano region, this town is a renowned trading hub where large quantities of goods from the north change hands. Many of these transactions are entirely above board, whereas others are officially classed as smuggling. Prices are so low that Argentinians regularly cross the bridge spanning the La Quiaca River, the border between the two countries, to stock up on a wide range of products.

• *Abandoned church near Villazón.*

• *Wara Wara del Sur in its cream and blue livery.*

RIDING ON A STAR

Despite the heated exchanges between traders and their customers, it's almost always chilly at this altitude. All the more reason for us to leave the platform of the little white station building in Villazón and board our train, the delightfully named Wara Wara del Sur, Aymaran for 'Star of the South', with a smattering of Spanish just to confuse us. With its attractive cream and blue carriages, it looks more like a suburban train trundling through the English countryside than one about to embark on the descent from the world's second highest inhabited area.

• *Herd of llamas on the Bolivian Altiplano.*

AN ARID SCENE

Yet this is exactly what it prepares to do as soon as we are settled in its large and comfortable seats. For nearly three hours the Wara Wara del Sur dawdles across the Andean plateau, a landscape not unlike that of an unexplored planet. The cold that penetrates the carriage itself in no way lessens our appreciation of the arid wilderness outside, interspersed only by a few dense, yet sparse clumps of vegetation, eking out an existence from the limited resources in the soil.

As we descend from the highlands and approach the Tupiza River valley, our surroundings start to green up again, creeping across the rocks, gaining hold on the ground and assuming forms more suited to this battle of the elements. Shrubs or cacti here or there, or maybe a bush or even a large tree with drooping branches. The mountains themselves are never far away. They watch over us, holding up the sky, which otherwise looks as though it might come tumbling down and crush our train. Fortunately we reach Tupiza without having to deal with any celestial incidents...

• *Tupiza River valley.*

VILLAZÓN → ORURO

UYUNI   ORURO

- *The city of Uyuni.*

THE UYUNI SALT FLAT

The train stops for just 10 minutes – enough to buy bottles of water or snacks from the hawkers waiting hopefully at the station. Instead, we decide to visit the dining car to indulge in a huge plate of pique macho, an extremely popular Bolivian dish comprising chunks of beef and fries, topped with tomatoes, onions, hard-boiled eggs and even pieces of sausage and a variety of sauces.

After such a hearty meal, no wonder we nod off as night falls over the Bolivian landscape. Nevertheless, we can't allow ourselves to sink fully into the arms of Morpheus as the train is due to stop in Uyuni, where we alight to spend the night in a small hotel. We could have slept on the train, but that would have meant missing the Salar de Uyuni, huge salt flats, the following morning. This vast desert of salt covers an area of some 10,582km² and truly is a sight to behold: a great white expanse with many cracks on its surface. It almost acts like a mirror, reflecting mingled images of the earth, sky and clouds.

- *Incahuasi Island on the Uyuni Salt Flat.*

🔊 A HIGH-ALTITUDE CARNIVAL

Oruro Carnival was classified as one of UNESCO's Masterpieces of the Oral and Intangible Heritage of Humanity in 2008. Before the city was resettled by the Spanish in 1606, it was the site of many religious ceremonies held by the indigenous Uru people, including the large-scale Ito festival. This festival is notable for the *diablada*, a traditional folk dance portraying the battle between the forces of good and evil.

- *A flamboyance of rose-tinted flamingos on Lake Uru Uru.*

- *Wild llamas in Sajama National Park.*

IN THE HEART OF ORURO

After spending the day exclaiming over the wonders of this strange desert at over 3,600m, we get back on the train just before 2am, desperate for a good night's sleep. When we wake up, we have plenty of time for breakfast while enjoying the pleasant scenery on the way to our terminus, Oruro. Located at an altitude of 3,710m, about halfway between Bolivia's two capital cities, La Paz and Sucre, this city has a population of around 345,000.

From here we can explore Lake Uru Uru, a beautiful spot, which is now in grave danger due to pollution and its waters being diverted for other purposes. The charmingly named Lake Poopó and Sajama National Park are also within striking distance. Anyone with a yearning for more cultural or spiritual attractions need only turn their gaze to the towering statue of the Virgen del Socavón (Our Lady of the Mineshaft), which watches serenely over the city, or join in with the dancing

- *The compact city of Oruro, where the line terminates.*

at the renowned Oruro Carnival, held each year at Candlemas, in the first week of February.

Morretes → Curitiba
Brazil's forgotten forest

on board the
SERRA VERDE EXPRESS

A former freight train for a forest adventure.

Travelling through the vast and endangered Atlantic Forest, the Serra Verde Express introduces its passengers to a part of Brazil that is as spectacular as it is unknown. Originally constructed to carry goods from Curitiba to the coast, the line passes through magnificent mountain scenery clad in dense jungle, shrouded in mist.

Opposite page: *Mist over the Atlantic Forest.*

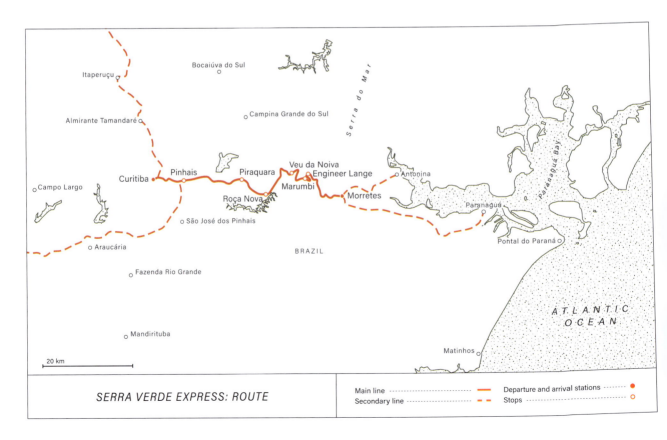

SERRA VERDE EXPRESS: ROUTE

SOUTH AMERICA

	10km	6km	5km	7km	
①		②	③	④	⑤
MORRETES		PORTO DE CIMA	ENGINEER LANGE	MARUMBI	VEU DA NOIVA

OPERATING SINCE
1885

JOURNEY LENGTH
4 hours

DISTANCE
72km

COUNTRIES VISITED
Brazil

• *Morretes, our starting point for this journey.*

BARREADO – A VERITABLE FEAST

If you're going to do the Serra Verde Express justice, you really have to start in one of the restaurants in the tiny city of Morretes where they serve barreado. Most of the travel agencies offering trips on this train also feature the opportunity to sample this traditional dish on their programmes. It's not hard to see why: the final stages of preparing barreado are a show in their own right. The waiter starts by sprinkling cassava flour on the plate before spooning on a hearty, but quite liquid stew, usually beef and bacon, which has been simmering away for a good few hours. He then mixes it all together until it forms a kind of paste and leaves it to each customer to add their own bananas. It sounds crazy but is one of the most amazing dishes you'll ever come across.

After performing this ritual, we stroll along the city's bustling streets, past brightly coloured houses, before making our way to Morretes station. It's a balmy day and there are many families out and about: children, parents and grandparents holding hands as they explore the city, or lingering on a shady terrace to cool off with a refreshing fruit juice or a fizzy drink. It feels a world away from the stifling sprawl of Rio de Janeiro. On the platform, this convivial atmosphere continues as we board the Serra Verde Express.

• *Morretes, compact city in the state of Paraná.*

• *A pale khaki-coloured train to blend in with the natural world.*

RIDING THROUGH THE ATLANTIC FOREST

With its unusual, pale khaki-coloured carriages, the Serra Verde Express seems ideally suited to this jungle expedition. Inside, there's plenty of space with an almost luxury vibe, round tables and banquette seating, rather like an upmarket café. There's a choice of drinks on offer, not least a selection of chilled beers. The windows are so huge, you almost feel you're in an open-sided carriage. However, this train's real USP only comes to light once it gets underway.

Within minutes of departing, we are right in the heart of the *mata atlântica*, or Atlantic Forest. Although it now only covers some 10 to 30 per cent of its original area, it is still home to 6,000 endemic species, including 1,500 vascular plants, 160 mammals and 263 amphibians. It goes without saying that we're unable to see them all from the train, but the panoramic view certainly doesn't disappoint. Quite the opposite: throughout the leisurely four-hour journey we are overwhelmed with sensational sights at every turn, with a mystic charm all of their own.

332

MORRETES → CURITIBA

MAJESTIC MOUNTAINS

Mile after mile, we plunge deeper into mountainous territory smothered with lush jungle. Stately trees stand proud on both sides of the track. Deep valleys open up all around us, leaving us guessing which side of the train we should be on to get the best possible views. Steamy clouds of tropical mist conceal the very bottom of these gorges, all the better to protect their secrets from prying eyes. Lost temples, secret lagoons or undiscovered animal species, perhaps? There's such an aura of mystery that who knows what might be hidden down there in the depths of the jungle. The only true limits are those set by our imagination...

The Sierra Verde Express traverses a whole range of engineering structures as it makes its way through this luxuriant paradise on earth. Viaducts, bridges, tunnels – the engineers certainly used every trick in the book when they built this line. Some are so ambitious that they have us clinging to our seats until we're safely on the other side. Was there really no other way to get around this mountain than via this ridiculously narrow, rickety wooden rail bridge? Maybe now there'd be other options, but certainly not back in the 19th century. And in any event, the views over the state of Paraná would definitely not have been as spectacular seen from a lesser vantage point.

• *Spacious carriages with an almost luxury vibe.*

• *Dense undergrowth in the Atlantic Forest.*

📢 BRAZIL'S OTHER ENDANGERED FOREST

Scientists reckon that the *mata atlântica* used to cover an area of over 1.29 million km². According to the WWF, it currently extends over the entire south-eastern coast of Brazil as far as eastern Paraguay and northern Argentina, yet the survival of this forest is at grave risk due to deforestation, both legal and illegal.

• *The end of the line in Curitiba, capital of Paraná.*

SECRETS IN THE MIST

After almost four hours on board, our verdant surroundings start to take on hints of yellow and brown. The terrain levels out and traces of human life appear. There are little houses dotted around, perimeter walls, power lines and vehicles. Our train has left the green confines of the Atlantic Forest. We continue our slow pace until we reach our terminus, Curitiba. A large conurbation with a population of 3.4 million, Paraná's capital grew up here mainly due to its trading links with the coastal regions. It also has some must-see treasures of its own, including the impressive Ópera de Arame (or Wire Opera House), elegant botanical gardens and the fascinating Oscar Niemeyer Museum. Remember we said that the mist hides a multitude of secrets?

• *Oscar Niemeyer Museum, Curitiba.*

333

Salta → La Polvorilla Viaduct
On cloud nine

on board the
TREN A LAS NUBES

A former mineral ore train for a journey to the top of the world.

Originally constructed in the 1920s to carry borax – a mineral extracted from mines in this area and used in a variety of household products – to the nearby coast of Chile, Section C14 of the former General Manuel Belgrano railway has now changed not only its name but also its purpose. Since 1990 it has played host to a little train known as the Tren a las Nubes, or Train to the Clouds; its name is more than just a metaphor.

Opposite page: 214 kilometres of track all the way to La Polvorilla Viaduct.

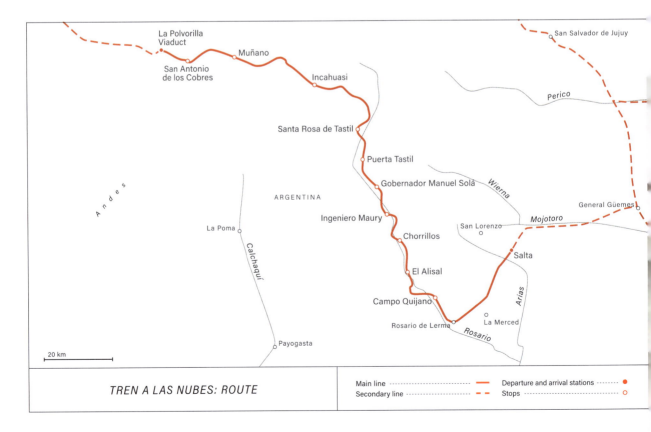

TREN A LAS NUBES: ROUTE

① SALTA	② CAMPO QUIJANO	③ EL ALISAL	④ CHORRILLOS	⑤ INGENIERO MAURY	⑥ GOBERNADOR MANUEL SOLÁ
	35 km	10 km	15 km	10 km	17 km

OPERATING SINCE
1972

JOURNEY LENGTH
2 hours, 45 mins

DISTANCE
217km
(line as a whole)

COUNTRIES VISITED
Argentina

ALTITUDE OF LA POLVORILLA VIADUCT
4,200m

NUMBER OF TUNNELS
21

NUMBER OF BRIDGES
29

▪ *Church of Saint Francis, Salta.*

SUNNY SALTA

Unusually for us, this journey begins with a bus ride. We board this road-based vehicle in Salta, in north-west Argentina, at seven in the morning. The sun is already high in the sky, but its rays aren't quite strong enough to take the chill off the air in this city a lofty 1,187m above sea level with a population of over half a million. Yesterday we made time to visit the unmissable Museum of High Mountain Archaeology and admired the Church of Saint Francis and the Cabildo de Salta, former seat of the colonial administration. Perhaps more importantly, we gorged on local specialities, starting with *locro*, a meat stew with corn, beans and pumpkin.

Until 2017, Salta was the starting point for the Train to the Clouds, but the track was so antiquated that part of the line has since been closed. Hence why the first part of our journey entails a bus replacement service – at least until the popularity of this little train conjures up funding for the necessary repairs. In the meantime, we are resigned to travelling by road for four hours through the rugged, barren splendour of the Andes, so remote it almost feels like an alien planet. It's a long haul up to San Antonio de los Cobres, 3,775m above sea level, but at last we meet up with our train.

▪ *San Antonio de los Cobres.*

A VAST BLUE EXPANSE OF SKY

At this altitude, the air is a little thin. But the sky more than makes up for it. It's so vast, it dwarfs everything, almost as if it has decided to renege on its peaceful co-existence with our planet and instead is determined to swallow us whole, engulfing us in its infinite blue depths. The Earth won't give up without a fight though. With all its might, it lines up the peaks of this colossal mountain range to hold off this relentless celestial vault, like an indefatigable modern-day Atlas.

Caught in the crossfire of this battle of the immortals, San Antonio de los Cobres station, a rectangular, white building, feels like the last outpost of a space colony abandoned by the human race. The Train to the Clouds itself, the blue of its carriages shimmering in this extraterrestrial landscape, looks like the last vessel to take us back to the safe haven of Planet Earth... It has already opened its doors as if to lure us to its cosy seats. Once we're all aboard, the diesel locomotive powers up, ready to haul us to the mountain tops. Who would have thought this modest machine could take us to such lofty heights?

▪ *At San Antonio de los Cobres station.*

SALTA → LA POLVORILLA VIADUCT

- Sign for La Polvorilla Viaduct.

- La Polvorilla Viaduct, 4,200m above sea level.

CLOUD CUCKOO LAND

As we climb higher and higher, the impression that we're travelling through space to land on another planet grows ever stronger. We're fascinated, disorientated even, by the strange shapes of these peaks with their rocky outcrops soaring skywards. The scrubby vegetation that barely manages to survive in this high-altitude desert landscape makes us doubt our own eyes. Is this real? Have we somehow stepped onto the set of a 1980s science fiction film without realizing? The doubts remain right up to the moment when our locomotive is uncoupled from the front of the train and reconnected to the back so it can push, rather than pull us. No film director, no matter how creative, could have come up with this idea. Only an engineer inured to taming steep mountain slopes would be ingenious enough to dream up this kind of solution.

Crazy or not, this is how we reach the highest point on our journey, La Polvorilla Viaduct, at an altitude of 4,200m. From time to time, clouds nestle beneath this gigantic metallic structure, some 224m long. At last the reason for our train's name becomes clear. Sometimes there's just the odd one, bashfully drifting beneath the supports, yet at other times they appear in large numbers, almost covering up the ground below, filling the gaze of passengers and the valley floor itself. Today, these huge fluffy clouds are so dense that they resemble an ocean of cotton wool, the perfect place for a relaxing snooze.

📢 FROM SECTION C14 TO THE TRAIN TO THE CLOUDS

Before it became a tourist route, this stretch of the General Manuel Belgrano Railway, named in honour of one of the architects of Argentina's independence, continued on to Chile. From here, the borax extracted from the ground could be exported from the ports in this narrowest of South American countries. As mining activities gradually declined and Argentina ran into economic difficulties, the freight wagons were eventually replaced by passenger carriages.

- A bright blue train shimmering in this desert landscape.

HIGH UP IN THE CLOUDS

Once on the other side of this bridge leading nowhere, the Train to the Clouds stops for about half an hour.

It deposits us on a promontory with a superb view of these craggy mountains, their wispy companions and the viaduct itself. From here, we can finally appreciate the full scale of this project, with its 21 tunnels, 29 bridges and 12 viaducts on the line down to Salta and understand what it must have meant for those involved in its construction. All these feats of engineering, including two spiral loops, were needed to build a railway covering the 3,000 metres of ascent to the home of the clouds.

- 12 viaducts, 29 bridges and 21 tunnels over a 217-km stretch of line.

337

Viedma → San Carlos de Bariloche
Patagonia – from east to west

on board the
TREN PATAGÓNICO

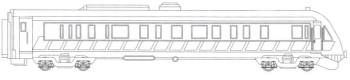

A unique train, the saviour of a region.

After privatization and the collapse of the Argentine rail network in the 1990s, the province of Río Negro stepped in to save the line between Viedma and San Carlos de Bariloche. The Tren Patagónico, which runs from the Atlantic coast to the foothills of the Andes, is almost the last train operating in this vast and magnificent region.

Opposite page: Nahuel Huapí Lake covers an area of 530km^2 at an altitude of 768m.

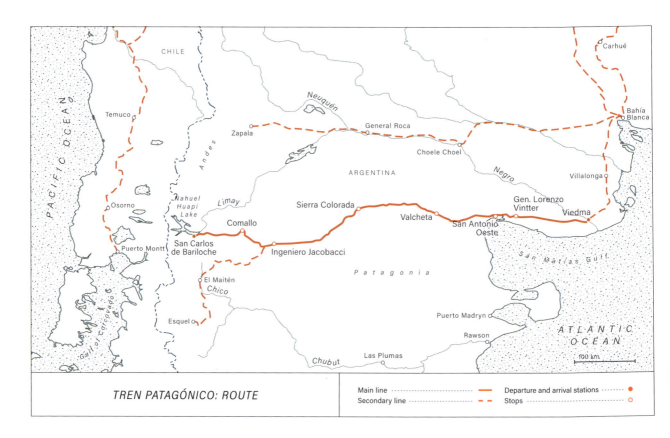

TREN PATAGÓNICO: ROUTE

①	②	③	④
VIEDMA	GENERAL LORENZO VINTTER	SAN ANTONIO OESTE	VALCHETA

Patagonian Steppe
Viedma

140km · 60km · 120km

OPERATING SINCE
1993

JOURNEY LENGTH
19 hours

DISTANCE
856km

COUNTRIES VISITED
Argentina

- *Viedma, Río Negro's capital.*

SUNSHINE IN RÍO NEGRO

It's late afternoon and the sun is shining on the little station with its mint-green and white walls. We're in Viedma, the capital of the province of Río Negro, on the right bank of the river of the same name. On the opposite side we can see Carmen de Patagones, the southernmost city in the province of Buenos Aires. All is calm inside the station. There are a couple of tourists weighed down by massive rucksacks leafing through their guidebooks as the locals chat among themselves while waiting for the locomotive to be coupled to its carriages. These bear the train's name in prominent letters, just in case we were in any danger of forgetting.

There's no doubt that this train, with its comfortable, brightly coloured seats and sun blinds, is an immensely important link to the most remote corners of Patagonia. It doesn't merely carry passengers; it also transports goods, even vehicles, to make sure that far-flung populations can enjoy a relatively modern standard of living despite their isolation. For these remote areas, this represents as much a lifeline as a railway line. In fact, when the train departs, it is watched by a small group of bystanders as if it were a special event. As these spectators vanish from view, their place is taken by disused or dilapidated trains, some of them rusting into oblivion.

- *A yellow and blue train, its stocky carriages equipped with sun blinds.*

- *Patagonian coastline.*

STEPPE BY STEPPE TO INFINITY

We soon encounter the fabulous vista of the vast Patagonian Steppes. These steppe-like plains extend on and on to infinity, devastatingly flat as far as the eye can see. There are no trees to punctuate the horizon, which is a perfect straight line. Just clusters of ghostly buildings every now and again as we push ever onwards. What's even more surprising is that some of these are inhabited. We get the impression that the train tends to stop here to deliver vital supplies rather than dropping off passengers. In this part of the world, civilization feels a long way away.

The setting sun takes forever to disappear in this resolutely desert-like landscape. Inch by inch, the entire sky becomes suffused with a reddish glow, as if on fire. And so it remains until our appointed dinner time, as agreed earlier with the stewardess when she passed through to take orders. We enter the dining car to find tables draped with green linen, lively conversations echoing through the carriage and the cheerful sound of cutlery clinking against the tableware. The menu may only be two short sentences in Spanish, but the grilled vegetables, meat and salad disappear all too quickly.

HERE COME THE ANDES

At around 11pm, we return to our seats and the carriage lights dim. Conversations gradually wind down and our eyes start to close. The next time we open them, it's to see the lights of a station blazing in the pitch black of Patagonia. At 7.30am, we stop at Ingeniero Jacobacci, named after the man responsible for building the line from San Antonio Oeste (which we passed while we were sleeping) to San Carlos de Bariloche.

Outside, the scenery changes as we eat our breakfast in the bar carriage. Then, as we approach the Andes, the horizon suddenly takes on a very different shape: unprepossessing barren hills, undulating before our eyes, suggest that we are about to begin climbing. After the tiny village of Clemente Onelli, which looks like a collection of buildings cobbled together from wood and tin, the mountains really start to make their presence felt. We are already at an altitude of over 1,000m and the rocky terrain is becoming increasingly rugged. The peaks come ever closer, more menacing as we inch nearer. They contrast with the laid-back atmosphere inside the carriage, where the Argentinians seem remarkably blasé about the length of this trip. I suppose familiarity with wide open spaces breeds contempt for time...

• *San Carlos de Bariloche.*

📢 ON BOARD LA TROCHITA

The province of Río Negro, which owns and operates the rail network and its rolling stock, also runs a very old steam train known as La Trochita. This tourist attraction is widely known across Argentina and travels on a 43-km stretch of track between Ingeniero Jacobacci station and Ojos de Agua in just over two hours. A fine way to enjoy the stunning Patagonian landscape.

• *Nahuel Huapí Lake, which means 'Jaguar Island' in the Mapuche language.*

JAGUAR ISLAND

Just before we cross the Pichí Leufu river, trees suddenly reappear, multiplying to give a more forested feel to parts of the landscape. In the distance, magnificent mountain tops can be seen quite clearly. At irregular intervals, micro-communities start to proliferate again. Then, on our right, we catch our first glimpse of Nahuel Huapí Lake, its name translating from the Mapuche language to mean 'Jaguar Island'. Originally created by glacial activity, it now covers 530km^2 at an altitude of 768m. Finally, after 19 hours on board, we arrive in San Carlos de Bariloche, nestled on the shores of the lake. We have crossed virtually the whole of Argentina, and indeed South America, from east to west. Just the narrow strip that is Chile separates us from the Pacific Ocean.

• *Nahuel Huapí Lake, originally formed by glacial activity.*

341

Ushuaia → Tierra del Fuego National Park
The end of the world in the Land of Fire

on board the
TREN DEL FIN DEL MUNDO

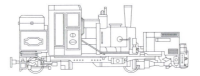

An old prison train to the end of the world.

The Southern Fuegian Railway is barely 25km long and originally served to transport building materials to a prison located in the Argentine province of Tierra del Fuego (literally 'Land of Fire'). Since 1994, the eight-kilometre stretch of track between Ushuaia and the heart of the Tierra del Fuego National Park has been used by a train with a very fitting name: Tren del Fin del Mundo, or the End of the World Train.

Opposite page: The 240-kilometre long Beagle Channel.

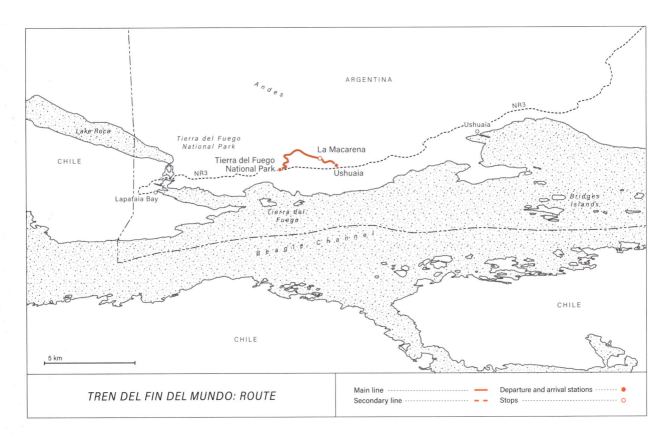

TREN DEL FIN DEL MUNDO: ROUTE

OPERATING SINCE
1994

JOURNEY LENGTH
2 hours, 15 mins

DISTANCE
8km

COUNTRIES VISITED
Argentina

📢 **A FORMER PENAL COLONY**

Before it became known as the Tren de la Fin del Mundo, this little workhorse was called the Prisoners' Train (Tren de los Presos). Built back in 1902, it was used to carry rocks, sand and firewood to the Ushuaia penal colony, which opened in 1884. No wonder that, for many of these prisoners, the world really did end in the heart of Tierra del Fuego.

THE END OF THE WORLD AS WE KNOW IT?

Ushuaia. Tierra del Fuego. These names are bound to resonate with any keen traveller, evoking images of the ultimate adventure. One that takes us to the ends of the Earth, way beyond traditional human terrain. In the olden days, people genuinely believed the world had an edge and you could fall off it – precisely the kind of image these words conjure up. Nowadays, although we do understand that the planet is round, we are still drawn to the extraordinary image conveyed by the End of the World Train. With its pretty little green carriages, beautifully wood-panelled on the inside, our train sets off from Ushuaia, the world's southernmost city.

Despite its remoteness, the station in this community of some 82,600 people is surprisingly large and well equipped. There are an astonishing number of tourists waiting for the train, taking the opportunity to snap pictures of the mesmerizing sights all around them. The old-fashioned steam engine, the sign emblazoned with the words Estación del Fin del Mundo (End of the World Station), the breathtaking mountain panorama in the background – all camera fodder extraordinaire. Once everyone has squeezed on board, great clouds of steam fill the air. The train slowly pulls out of the station.

• Ushuaia, the world's southernmost city.

• A red locomotive and old-fashioned green carriages.

HEY MACARENA...

We hardly have time to admire the spectacularly verdant scenery of Tierra del Fuego before we make our first stop at La Macarena station. Once again, we're amazed by what we see. Despite the wild splendour all around us, there are benches and litter bins almost everywhere. A perfectly waymarked trail edged with painted wooden fences leads us up to a pretty waterfall surging over moss-encrusted rocks, its gentle burbling echoing the sounds of visitors' feet.

After this delightful interlude, we continue our journey. With snow-capped mountains as a backdrop, Patagonia reveals itself in its true natural glory. This is no longer typically highland terrain; there are now tall, leafy trees surrounded by lush, cropped grassland. Large chunks of driftwood dry out on the banks of a small river, a herd of wild horses grazing serenely on a bend. There's certainly no sign of any owner. Hard to imagine a more fitting symbol of freedom before we arrive at our destination: the station for the Tierra del Fuego National Park.

• Tierra del Fuego National Park.

• Colony of cormorants in the Beagle Channel.

THE END OF THE WORLD – OR IS IT?

It takes us just over half an hour to walk through this fabulous national park, the whole thing covering 63,000 hectares, until we reach a small bay overlooking the Beagle Channel. We have yet more surprises in store for us here. On the other side of this vast strait in the Tierra del Fuego Archipelago, steep-sided islands rear out of the water under the admiring gaze of tourists picnicking on the shore after leaving their pick-up trucks in the small car park provided for this very purpose. There's even a post office and a little jetty. Who would have thought the end of the world would be so busy? Certainly not us. Fortunately, this in no way detracts from its rugged beauty.

• *Lighthouse in the Beagle Channel.*

Oceania

3 TRAIN JOURNEYS
2 countries
Long-distance trains Down Under
FROM SYDNEY TO CHRISTCHURCH

① **Sydney → Perth**
🇦🇺 *INDIAN PACIFIC RAILWAY*
p. 348

② **Adelaide → Darwin**
🇦🇺 *GHAN*
p. 352

③ **Picton → Christchurch**
🇳🇿 *COASTAL PACIFIC*
p. 356

Sydney → Perth
An Australian outback adventure

on board the
INDIAN PACIFIC RAILWAY

Cruising through the Australian outback by train.

Linking Sydney, on the shores of the Tasman Sea, with Perth, on the Indian Ocean, the Indian Pacific Railway crosses Australia from east to west – and vice versa. Most importantly, it introduces its passengers to the hypnotic, desert-like landscape of this nation, particularly the formidable expanse of Nullarbor Plain.

Opposite page: Fisherman's shack in Perth.

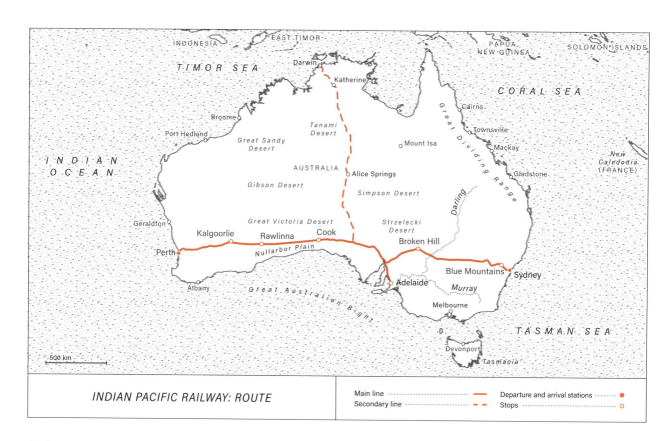

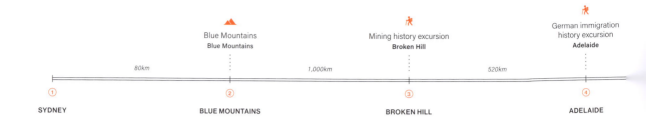

① SYDNEY	② BLUE MOUNTAINS	③ BROKEN HILL	④ ADELAIDE

OPERATING SINCE
1970

JOURNEY LENGTH
4 days, 3 nights

DISTANCE
4,352km

COUNTRIES VISITED
Australia

AN IMPRESSIVE TRAIN FOR AN IMPRESSIVE JOURNEY

Some say it resembles a shell, others see the distinctive lines of a yacht. Under this morning's bright blue skies, Sydney Opera House looks more like a colossal alien being with scaly body armour, huddled in the very heart of the city. Its world-renowned silhouette contrasts with the 19th-century architecture of the Queen Victoria Building and the spires of Sydney's St Mary's Cathedral. At this time of day and in this weather, par for the course in this part of the world, the beaches must already be thronged with sunseekers and surfers, all oblivious to the fact that we are about to depart their fine city. But leave we must, making our way to Sydney's Central Station, visible for miles around thanks to its splendid clock tower.

At the station, our train awaits us, so long that two different platforms have to be used for boarding. Its impressive blue and gold locomotive hauls substantial, yet unexceptional grey carriages that give the impression of being built to withstand whatever the journey might throw at them. The passengers who arrived before us are sitting around small tables dotted about, enjoying refreshments and canapés handed out by the train's serving staff as a band plays local favourites in the background. In case we haven't made it clear, this is a luxury train, with two levels of service: Platinum, if money is no object, and the more affordable Gold for lesser mortals. We are travelling Gold Class, so are taken to a small but comfortable cabin with faux wood panelling.

- *Queen Victoria Building (19th century), Sydney.*

- *The Blue Mountains, 100km from Sydney.*

A FEAST IN THE BLUE MOUNTAINS

Despite its size, this modest cabin, our home for the next four days and three nights, boasts a number of features, not least its own bathroom with a selection of toiletries and fresh towels on a daily basis. No wonder we feel like guests in a hotel on rails as we feast our eyes on the landscape of New South Wales, the first of the three Australian states our train is set to cross. Contrary to our expectations, this area turns out to be incredibly green, with tall trees and little towns made up of ultra-modern buildings. As the day draws to a close, we reach the Blue Mountains, which extend for around 3,000 kilometres and are a UNESCO World Heritage Site in their own right.

Time for us to check out the elegant dining car in our section of the train, where the attentive stewards twirl up and down the aisle taking orders as fast as they can. Just like their athletic antics, the menu is rather impressive: chicken galantine, hazelnut, broccoli and cauliflower tart, a substantial steak served with Brussels sprouts, kangaroo loin and Tarte Tatin. As we drift off to sleep later that evening, a stray thought comes to mind: we certainly won't die of starvation in this desert…

- *Sturdy, undistinguished-looking carriages in a subtle shade of grey.*

- *Silverton Hotel, famed throughout the outback.*

- *The outback, an arid land with a hot, dry climate.*

- *Eyre Highway, on the Nullarbor Plain.*

A GERMAN OASIS

As we wake from our slumbers the next morning, we are approaching Broken Hill, where an off-train experience awaits those keen to learn about this city's mining past and rich trade union history. We are still in New South Wales, but the surrounding scenery is already the stereotypical Australia we recognize from our movie screens and travel magazines. The earth is reddish, brown or yellow depending where we are, with very few trees, scrubby vegetation and a vastness that goes on and on until the faraway mountains. Our journey to Adelaide is like dipping into the history of Australia. Huge lorries thunder past on the roads running parallel to our track. Dilapidated buildings remind us that even the swankiest places turn to dust in the end, especially in such a hostile environment.

On arriving in Adelaide, there's another bus to take us to Hahndorf, in the Adelaide Hills. Established by German settlers, this little town has made quite a name for itself promoting its heritage and becoming a major tourist attraction. Waitresses in *dirndls*, musicians in *lederhosen*, enormous tankards of beer and German food galore – they haven't missed a trick in the many and varied establishments lining the main street. We return to the train for our second night on board to the poignant sound of the accordion, our bellies rather fuller than when we left.

THE MAGNIFICENT HELLSCAPE OF THE NULLARBOR PLAIN

Next morning, our little German oasis seems a million miles away. The Australian outback has reasserted its authority. Once again, we're back in the world of dry, rust-coloured earth and scarce vegetation, cowering under the sun's rays. We've reached the immense Nullarbor Plain, its name allegedly taken from the Latin *nulla* (no) and *arbor* (tree). Aboriginal Australians call it Oondiri, which means 'without water'. In other words, an incredibly desolate tract of land, one so hostile that even the tiniest of shrubs would struggle to survive here. Humans stand no chance whatsoever. The town of Cook, our sole stop in this barren area, was abandoned in 1997 in any event. These days, there are just a few ghostly buildings, including a dusty railway station with a few derelict shacks.

At Rawlinna station, as the light starts to fade, the on-board team set up large wooden tables for our final meal. After a tour of the locomotive, we are invited to sit down and enjoy a veritable banquet of barbecued meat and vegetables, salads and desserts, with wine and beer flowing generously while a guitar gently strums in the background. It's pretty dark when we finally stagger back to our cabin. On day four, normal service is resumed and Mother Nature is back in all her glory. And then, after one last hearty breakfast, we arrive in the fair city of Perth, on the shores of the other Australian ocean.

- *Perth, in the south-west corner of this vast island.*

📢 DESERT RECORD-BREAKER

Right in the middle of the Nullarbor Plain, there's something rather special, definitely worthy of a mention. It's the world's longest stretch of straight railway track, extending 478 kilometres across the desert with not a curve in sight. As impressive as this sounds, it really does need to be put into perspective. There are very few places in the world with such a vast, flat area of desert-like terrain. And if these conditions aren't fulfilled, perfect straight lines just aren't an option.

351

Adelaide → Darwin
On the trail of the Afghan camel drivers

on board the
GHAN

A rail journey through Australia's heartland.

Stretching a full 900 metres long, the Ghan connects Adelaide, in South Australia, with Darwin, the most populous city in the Northern Territory. Along the route, passengers can enjoy breathtaking panoramic views of the centre and northern parts of this huge country in considerably more comfort than the Afghan camel drivers after whom this train is named.

Opposite page: The MacDonnell Ranges in Australia's Red Centre.

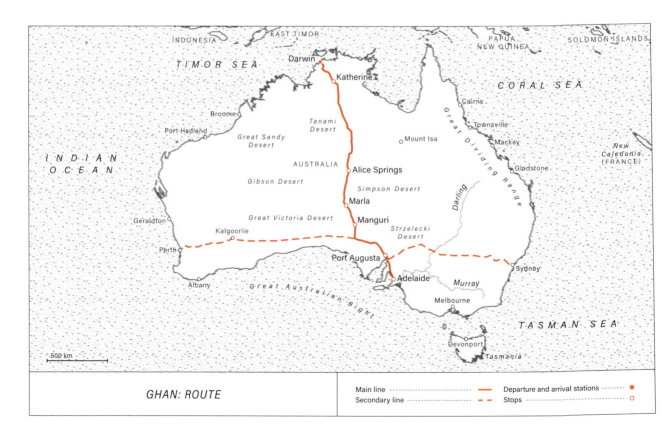

GHAN: ROUTE

OCEANIA

OPERATING SINCE
1929

JOURNEY LENGTH
4 days, 3 nights

DISTANCE
2,979km

COUNTRIES VISITED
Australia

NUMBER OF CARRIAGES
36

TRAIN LENGTH
902m

LENGTH OF ELIZABETH RIVER BRIDGE
500m

RIDING ACROSS THE DESERT

We only have to glance at the train alongside Platform 1 at Adelaide's Parklands Terminal to be sure that we're in the right place. Both the powerful red locomotive pulling the Ghan and its long silver carriages bear the silhouette of a man riding a camel (specifically a dromedary – one hump, not two!) in pride of place between the bold letters spelling out the train's name. It refers to the Afghan camel drivers, often called cameleers for short, brought over by the British settlers in the 1840s to explore the Australian outback. Message received and understood: the landscape ahead of us is harsh, hostile and arid. Our giant silver steed resembles a gargantuan 902-m-long serpent made up of 36 carriages, dating back to the 1970s or '80s.

Yet in the inner reaches of this monster of the rails, the atmosphere has nothing in common with an explorers' base camp. The train staff show us to a bar carriage not unlike an old-fashioned speakeasy, then on to a dining car with elegant white linen, before eventually welcoming us to our Gold Access cabin. Modern, comfortable, spacious and lined with varnished wood panelling, it contains two easy chairs that convert to beds at night, a mobile table and a large bathroom specially adapted for the mobility-impaired. Fully reassured that we won't have to sacrifice any material comforts to cross the Australian desert, we head back to the lounge where our fellow passengers have already started on the cocktails.

• Adelaide, capital of South Australia.

• The outback, promised land of blue skies and scorching heat.

FINE DINING IN THE OUTBACK

As the outskirts of Adelaide disappear from view, we are summoned to sample our first dinner on board this epic train. Chargrilled pork tenderloin, chicken ballotine, oven-roasted cauliflower, chocolate and mandarin delice and a ricotta, honey and fig ice cream – the ample menu is in sharp contrast to the barren fields of yellowing crops we can see through the windows. Enclosed by dark, low-lying hills dotted with gigantic wind turbines, their blades lazily rotating, this landscape looks as though it would be more suited to cowboys tucking into baked beans than tourists enjoying the very best of fine dining. After our meal, the Flinders Range appears in the distance.

LIVING UP TO ITS PROMISE

After Port Pirie, we encounter our first glimpse of the outback on this trip, looking just as we'd imagined it from all those Hollywood movies. Blue sky and searing heat, sandy soil broken up only by sparse vegetation and the occasional enormous electricity pylon. Once we've made it past Port Augusta, the landscape takes on a more orange hue. The cinema certainly didn't lie… In Australia, sundown seems to come around earlier than it does in America, and the night is altogether darker; in our case, the daylight vanishes as we're enjoying yet another substantial meal in the restaurant car.

ADELAÏDE → DARWIN

SUNRISE OVER MARLA

It's the crack of dawn, around 6:15am, and there's a sudden change of mood. The train has stopped near Marla, some 1,070km north of Adelaide and 450km before Alice Springs. The train crew have laid out breakfast tables and braziers for a very special breakfast in the middle of this vast expanse of desert. Passengers with early-bird tendencies are already dressed for the day ahead, whereas others have clearly thrown on whatever they can lay their hands on for this unaccustomed dawn start. Nobody cares. It's all about the spectacle as the sun slowly rises over the central Australian landscape, gradually filling the skies with a veritable rainbow of colours.

• Ghan, a 900-metre-long train.

NOT-SO-NEWCOMERS

Introduced by the British in the 1840s as a means of exploring Central Australia more easily, the dromedary camels have never left the island. They are very much at home in this hostile environment and their numbers had grown to over a million by 2021. Capable of roaming a wide area, they have now populated a huge part of the outback and cause major damage to vegetation and certain natural sites. So much so that a large-scale national culling campaign was launched, reducing their population to approximately 300,000 two years later.

THE DESERT'S TRUE COLOURS

Back in our cabin, we press our noses to the glass, all the better to take in the incredible sights we are seeing. Bushes in a flaming red, trees clad in sultry orange or palest yellow, all encircled by low-lying shrubs – it's as though nature couldn't make its mind up how best to welcome us. Eventually, as we approach Alice Springs, the geographical heart of Australia, it makes its decision. At this point, we are surrounded by an immense and fiery red everywhere we look. Hardly surprising, as the town lies in the shadow of the MacDonnell Ranges in the fittingly named Red Centre. Also known as Central Australia, this area is more of a notion than a region with strict geographical boundaries. Now for another off-train experience, this time to explore Alice Springs Desert Park, the town itself and Simpsons Gap, where we walk between the local red cliffs under the curious gaze of black-footed rock wallabies.

FROM RED TO GREEN...

When we wake up on the train for the third time on this epic voyage of discovery, Alice Springs, that incongruous juxtaposition of a town with 31,000 inhabitants in the middle of a desert, is behind us. The sun rises over a scene where, for the first time in a while, green is more dominant than red. We have arrived in the Top End. Much greener and certainly less well-known than its red predecessor, this eco-region feels like a tropical oasis. It's as though we've crossed the dividing line between the realms of life and survival. The track passes alongside tall trees as we arrive in Katherine, where there are yet more excursions on offer to explore the spectacular network of gorges in Nitmiluk National Park and the indigenous rock art in this area, some dating back over 40,000 years.

This final outing sets us thinking as we continue on to Darwin. We are briefly distracted as we cross the awe-inspiring Elizabeth River Bridge, 500m long, but that doesn't quite stop us pondering on the paradox of our monumental rail journey. We've enjoyed every possible comfort, luxury even, in a land that is so challenging for the few species that can survive there, where humans have made very few inroads. As Darwin station draws ever nearer, a final thought comes to mind. If we have to make this journey, let it be by train.

• Darwin, the end of a 2,979-kilometre-long journey.

355

Picton → Christchurch
In the shade of Kaikōura

on board the
COASTAL PACIFIC

A scenic train to make the most of the New Zealand coastline.

Operating since 1988, the Coastal Pacific runs along the New Zealand coast between Picton, a sea port on South Island, and Christchurch, the country's second-largest city. As well as exploring the stunning seaboard, it also passes through the Marlborough wine-growing region, skirts the Kaikōura mountain range and traverses the Canterbury Plains. An extraordinary experience in one of the remotest spots on Earth.

Opposite page: Queen Charlotte Sound.

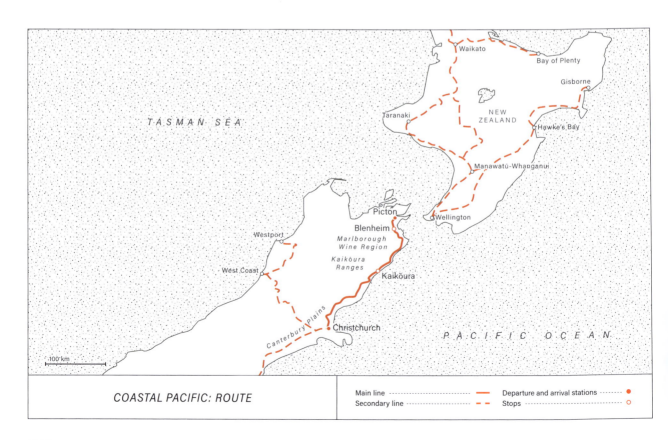

COASTAL PACIFIC: ROUTE

OCEANIA

① PICTON

② BLENHEIM — Marlborough Winery

25km · 130km

OPERATING SINCE
1988

JOURNEY LENGTH
5–6 hours

DISTANCE
348km

COUNTRIES VISITED
New Zealand

NUMBER OF TUNNELS
22

AT THE NORTH END OF SOUTH ISLAND

A white ferry cruises serenely between the impressive forested hills of Queen Charlotte Sound. It has come from Wellington, New Zealand's capital, on North Island, on the other side of Cook Strait. Its destination is none other than our departure point, the little town of Picton. This modest place with a population of around 4,000, wedged between the mountains and the sea, is where the Coastal Pacific takes to the rails, heading for Christchurch, some 348km further south.

The station is a pretty Edwardian building clad in white clapboard with slender columns and old-fashioned canopies. As a bonus, it's only a few hundred metres from the port where the hulking ferries dock. In some cases, containers are disgorged straight from their cavernous holds onto the freight wagons of this very train. However, the passenger area of the train is made up of large white carriages with comfy seats equipped with power sockets, next to which are pockets containing menus. Huge picture windows line each side of the carriages, teasing us with the delightful prospect of spectacular scenery along the way.

Within the first few minutes, the Coastal Pacific is as good as its word. As it sets off between colourful houses, the sight of caravans and boats balanced on trailers bears witness to New Zealanders' love of travel, adventure and the great outdoors. The green summits all around us contribute to make this a magical scene. So much so that we almost feel we've stepped onto the pages of one of JRR Tolkien's fantasy novels – or at least one of his many imitators. Peter Jackson's decision to shoot the film adaptation of *The Lord of the Rings* here feels increasingly justified every minute we spend on this train.

- *Picton, a small town with 4,000 inhabitants.*

- *Enchanting views.*

- *A 348-kilometre-long railway line.*

BEFORE HUMANS WALKED THE EARTH...

It's early afternoon, lunchtime on the Coastal Pacific. On the menu there's a choice of lamb shank, beef cheek, roast chicken, sausage and mash or vegetarian lasagne – all perfect to whet our growing appetite from seeing the beautiful sights. The food arrives promptly. We collect our freshly cooked meal, albeit pre-prepared, and a miniature bottle of white wine before taking our seats again to make the most of that superb scenery. A timeless green palette, not too far removed from what this planet must have looked like before humans came on the scene. New Zealand has that sort of feel about it, more so than any other place on Earth.

358

PICTON → CHRISTCHURCH

Kaikōura Range
+ Canterbury Plains
Kaikōura

180km

③
KAIKŌURA

④
CHRISTCHURCH

PRETTY AS A PICTURE

This seemingly endless vista of emerald green is interrupted by the sudden appearance of the Wairau River, which looks rather like a tropical lagoon at the point where we cross it. Some 170km long, this waterway plays an all-important role in the success of the great vineyards in the Marlborough wine region. Rows of vines stretch out on all sides, filling every available space granted by the encroaching mountains. Silence reigns in the carriage. Our gaze lingers on their ranks as we think of the bottles of Sauvignon they will one day become.

Then we start to climb gently, giving us a tantalizing glimpse of North Island, especially on such a clear day. Outside, the vineyards have given way to more mountainous terrain, almost alpine in appearance. The view is short-lived as before long we are passing through the salt flats of Lake Grassmere. But before we know it, nature's show resumes, this time with snowy peaks in the distance, despite the time of year. Eventually we drop down again to the area that inspired this train's name: New Zealand's magnificent Pacific coast. A huge blue canvas, with the occasional fleck of foam and perhaps a few dabs of green to convey that maritime vegetation. Such a beautiful picture that we feel compelled to visit the train's open-air viewing carriage to take full advantage – with the added bonus of a whiff of iodine.

- *Wairau River, 170km long.*

- *Marlborough vineyard.*

📢 EARTHQUAKES ON REPEAT

In 2011, the Coastal Pacific service was suspended as a result of damage caused by an earthquake measuring 6.3 on the Richter scale. In 2016, a second earthquake, with a magnitude of 7.8, destroyed some of the track in the Kaikōura region. The third and latest one occurred in 2022, but since then the train has been able to operate as normal, much to the delight of locals and tourists alike.

- *Lake Grassmere, near Canterbury.*

HARMONIOUS IRREGULARITY

Even before this spellbinding spectacle comes to an end, the next one is upon us. This time it's the Kaikōura mountain range, its peaks almost nudging the clouds. Such a strange juxtaposition of the picture-perfect coast on one side, renowned for sightings of sperm whales and dolphins, just a stone's throw from those snow-capped mountains basking in the sunshine. Out of the blue, our view is snatched away by a series of 14 tunnels (there are 22 on the route overall) over a short section of just 19 kilometres. When we emerge, the Kaikōura mountains have disappeared. It's just us and the Pacific Ocean.

Now on the gentle approach to Christchurch, we renew our acquaintance with New Zealand's more agricultural side. The Canterbury Plains, where cattle and sheep, so many sheep, safely graze. Yet, on this island at the edge of the world, nothing is ever truly flat. Right to the end of our journey, there's always another summit, a rocky outcrop, a peak, a headland or a peninsula breaking up the horizon and drawing our gaze. Nature's irregular patterns have never felt as harmonious as they do here.

- *Train running along the Pacific coast.*

359

• Pacific coast at Kaikōura.

Index of place names

A

Abisko 13
   Abisko National Park 13
Adana 176, 178
   Sabancı Central Mosque 178
Adderly 204
Adelaide 351, 354
Adrano 74, 75
Adriatic Sea 111
Africa 112–149
South Africa 144, 148
Aguas Calientes 318, 320
Ahvaz 183
Aihole 193
Ajaccio 50, 52
Ajigasawa 244
Akita 242, 245
Alaska, State of 264, 266, 267
Alausi 314, 316
   Loma de Lluglli, viewpoint 316
Alberta, Province of 271
Alborz Range 182
Alcantara valley 75
Alcoletge 98
Alexandria 118, 120
   Library of Alexandria 120
   Citadel of Qaitbay 120
   Ras El Tin Palace 120
Alice Springs 355
Alice Springs Desert Park 355
   MacDonnell Ranges 355
   Red Centre 355
Des Allemands 306
Allier Gorges..................... 38, 40
Alp Grüm 86
Alpnachstad 88, 90
Altamira Cave 94
Altiplano 328
North America 262–307
South America 308–345
Amherst 278
Anatolia 174, 178
Anchorage...................... 264, 266
Andes, mountain range 316, 324, 341
Andimeshk 183
Angola 138
Anhui, Province of 220, 222
Ankara 172, 174
   Kocatepe Mosque 174
Aoike, Lake 245
Aomori 242, 244
Arak 183
Arbatax 76, 78
Arc-et-Senans 36

Saline Royale 36
Arequipa 322
Argentina.......... 336, 340, 341, 344
Arisaig 16, 20, 21
   Skye, Isle of 21
Arizona 304, 307
Asia.......................... 188–261
Aswan 114, 116
Atar 129
Athi River 136
Atocha 328
Aumont-Aubrac 46
Australia....................... 350, 354
   Adelaide Hills 351
   Central Australia 355
   Flinders Range................. 354
   New South Wales 350
   Outback.................... 351, 354
Austria 32, 33
Auvergne....................... 40, 44
Ayutthaya 252

B

Badami 193
Badulla 208, 210
Banhado 333
Bahuichivo 311
   Urique Canyon................. 311
   Santa Barbara Bridge........... 311
Baikal, Lake....................... 156
Balaguer 98
Sant Llorenç de Montgai 99
Ballymena 28
Ballymoney....................... 28
Baltimore......................... 286
Bandar-e Emam Khomeyni 180, 183
Bandar-e Torkaman............. 180, 182
Bandipur 192
Bandung 258, 260
Banff 268, 271, 274
Bengalaru 190, 192
   Cubbon Park.................. 192
   Iskcon Temple 192
Bangkok.......... 246, 248, 250, 252
Bar 108, 111
Barents Sea....................... 164
Batasia Loop...................... 197
Bathurst.......................... 278
Beagle Channel 344
Bédarieux 45
   Salagou Lake 45
Beitbridge 148
Bela-Bela......................... 148

Belfast 26, 28
   Lanyon Place station 28
   Samson and Goliath 28
Belgrade 108, 110
Bellarena 29
Belogorsk 156
Ben Aïsha 129
Ben Amera 129
West Bengal, State of 196
Benin 132
Berwick-upon-Tweed 25
   Royal Border Bridge 25
Besac 111
Beverly Hills 307
Béziers 42, 44, 45
Biguglia 52
Bilbao 94
Blenheim 359
Blue Mountains 350
Bocognano 52
   Voile de la mariée waterfall 52
Boden............................ 13
Bolivia 328
Book Cliffs....................... 293
Borobudur 261
Bosco Seleni 78
Bosnia and Herzegovina 110
Brazil 330, 332
Brioude 40
Broken Hill........................ 351
Bronte 75
Brusio............................ 86
Buenos Aires, Province of 40
Bulawayo 148

C

Cairo 114, 116, 118, 120
California 297, 306, 307
   Gulf of California 311
Calvi 52, 54, 56, 57
Campbellton....................... 278
Campo Quijano 336
Canada.................. 282, 278, 293
Cantal........................ 42, 44, 45
   Monts du Cantal 44
   Garabit Viaduct 44
   Truyère Gorge 44
Cape Town 142, 144
Cappadocia 174
Carmen de Patagones 340
Casablanca..........122, 124, 125
   Hassan-II Mosque 125
Casamozza 52

Cascade Range 300
Caspian Sea 180, 182
Castlerock........................ 29
Catania..................... 71, 72, 74
Cellers, Lake....................... 99
Cévennes 38, 40, 41
Chamborigaud 40, 41
Chanteuges....................... 40
Chao, Lake 222
Charleston 284
Chassezac 41
Chelmos-Vouraikos National Park 106
Chelmos Mountains 106
Chennai 198, 200
Chicago 290, 292, 298, 300, 301
   Art Institute 292
   Doughnut Vault 292
   John Hancock Center 292
   Millennium Park 292
   Willis Tower 292
   Windy City 92
Chihuahua Desert 306
Chile 341
China 212, 216, 220, 222, 226
Chinguetti 129
Chita 156
Chisimba Falls 141
Chorrillos......................... 336
Choum 126, 128, 129
Choir 215
Christchurch....................... 359
Cilacap........................... 260
Cinque Terre 52, 64
   Corniglia 64, 66
   Manarola 64
   Monterosso al Mare 62, 64
   Riomaggiore................. 62, 64
   Vernazza 62, 64
Ciudad Juárez 307
Clemente Onelli 341
Clermont-Ferrand 38, 40
   Cathedral..................... 40
   Puy de Dôme 40
Cluj-Napoca 33
   Peles Castle 33
Cochrane 280, 282
Chur....................... 84, 86
Coleraine......................... 28
British Columbia, Province of 270
Colombo 208, 210
Colorado 290, 292, 293
   State of Colorado 290, 292, 293
La Concha Bay 94
Continental Divide 301

362

Cook . . . 351
Coonoor . . . 205
Corsica . . . 50, 52, 54
Corte . . . 50, 52
Cotonou . . . 130, 132
Craigendoran . . . 20, 21
Falls of Falloch . . . 21
Loch nan Ceall . . . 21
Spean Bridge . . . 21
Creel . . . 308, 310
Barrancas del Cobre . . . 310
Sierra Tarahumara . . . 310
Cullybackey . . . 28
Curitiba . . . 330, 333
Opera de Arame . . . 333
Oscar Niemeyer Museum . . . 333
Cusipata . . . 324
Cusco . . . 318, 320, 322, 324
Belmond Monasterio Hotel . . . 324
Plaza de Armas . . . 320

D

Da Nang . . . 257
Dakota, State of . . . 301
Dar es-Salaam . . . 138, 140
Darjeeling . . . 194, 197
Darlington . . . 25
Darwin . . . 355
Dassa . . . 133
Datong . . . 214
Damavand, Mount . . . 182
Democratic Republic of the Congo . . . 138
Denali . . . 267
Denver . . . 293
Derry-Londonderry . . . 26, 28, 29
Bogside . . . 29
Foyle . . . 29
Waterside . . . 29
Dete . . . 148
Dez Valley . . . 183
Diakopto . . . 104, 106
Jeddah . . . 186
Dole . . . 34, 36
Clauge . . . 36
Rhône-Rhine Canal . . . 36
Đông Ha . . . 257
Dubrovnik . . . 61
Durham . . . 25

E

Scotland . . . 21, 24, 25
Loch Lomond . . . 21, 24
Edinburgh . . . 18, 20, 22, 25
Edmonton . . . 274
Egypt . . . 116, 120
Yekaterinburg . . . 156
Church of All Saints . . . 156
Sevastyanov House . . . 156
El Alisal . . . 336
Divisadero . . . 310, 311
El Fuerte . . . 311
El Paso . . . 307
Emali . . . 136
Emeryville . . . 290, 293, 297
Engineer Lange . . . 332
Ecuador . . . 316
Erzincan . . . 175
Eskişehir . . . 176, 178
Spain . . . 94, 98
L'Estaque . . . 46, 48, 49
Estonia . . . 170, 171
Etna . . . 70, 71, 72, 74, 75
Europe . . . 8-111
Everest . . . 197

F

Fairbanks . . . 264, 267
Ferrol . . . 94
Fisherman's Cove . . . 278
Florida, State of . . . 284, 287
Fort William . . . 14, 21
Inverlochy Castle Hotel . . . 21
Fos-sur-Mer . . . 48, 49
Fraser Canyon . . . 270
Fuji-San (Fuji-Yama) . . . 238
Fujian, Province of . . . 220
Fukushima . . . 234
Furiani . . . 52
Fuzhou . . . 220, 223

G

Gairo . . . 76, 78
Galle . . . 210
Gansu, Province of . . . 226
Gardon valley . . . 41
Grotta del Gelo cave . . . 75
General Lorenzo Vintter . . . 40
Ghum . . . 197
Gijón . . . 94
Glacier National Park . . . 301
Goa . . . 190, 193
Basilica of Bom Jesus . . . 193
Se Cathedral . . . 193
Church of Our Lady of the Immaculate Conception . . . 193
Gobi Desert . . . 212, 214, 215, 227
Great Rift Valley . . . 141
Greece . . . 106
Guayaquil . . . 314
Gurrida, Lake . . . 75
Gwaai . . . 148

H

Hahndorf . . . 351
Hakodate . . . 232, 234
Halebidu . . . 193
Shiva and Parvati Temple . . . 193
Halifax . . . 276, 278
Halong Bay . . . 256
Hanoi . . . 254, 256, 257
Hoan Kiem Lake . . . 256
Hejaz . . . 186
Hefei . . . 220, 222
Hermida Gorge . . . 94
Hex River Valley . . . 144
Highlands . . . 16, 21, 24, 25
Ben Nevis . . . 16
Hillgrove . . . 204
Himalaya . . . 197, 218
Hiroshima . . . 238
Ho Chi Minh City . . . 254, 257
Hoi An . . . 257
Hokkaido . . . 234
Hollywood . . . 307
Hungary . . . 32, 33
Houston . . . 306
Huangshan . . . 222
Hudson Bay . . . 282
Hue . . . 257
Hwange National Park . . . 148

I

Yaroslavl . . . 156, 160, 162, 163
St Elijah the Prophet's Church . . . 163
St Michael the Archangel Church . 163
Bute, Isle of . . . 18, 20
Île-Rousse . . . 54, 56
Île de la Pietra . . . 54, 56
Illinois, State of . . . 290, 292
India . . . 192, 196, 200, 205
Indonesia . . . 260
Ingeniero Jacobacci . . . 341
Ingeniero Maury . . . 336
Iowa, State of . . . 290, 292
Iran . . . 180, 182
Istanbul . . . 30, 32, 61
Bosphorus Strait . . . 61
Cihangir . . . 61
Grand Bazaar . . . 61
Sultanahmet Mosque . . . 61
Topkapi Palace . . . 61
Istres . . . 48
Étang de Lavalduc . . . 48
Italy . . . 60, 62, 64, 70, 71, 74, 75, 76, 78, 86
Ivangorod . . . 171

J

Japan . . . 230, 234, 238, 242, 244
Jasper . . . 272, 274
Yellow Mountains . . . 220
Java . . . 258, 261
Juliaca . . . 324
Juniko Lakes . . . 245
Jura . . . 34, 36, 37
Arbois vineyards . . . 36
Bienne valley . . . 37
Crottes Viaduct . . . 37
Col de la Savine . . . 37
Syam . . . 36
Tunnel des Frasses . . . 36, 37

K

Kagoshima . . . 236, 238
Kaikōura . . . 359
Kaikōura Range . . . 359
Marlborough wine region . . . 359
Kakopa . . . 141
Kalavrita . . . 104, 106
Kalgoorlie . . . 351
Kamloops . . . 268, 271
Kanchanaburi . . . 248
Kandy . . . 208, 210
Kanetsuri . . . 230
Kangchenjunga . . . 197
Karnataka, State of . . . 190, 192
Kars . . . 172, 175
Katherine . . . 355
Nitmiluk National Park . . . 355
Kayseri . . . 174
Kenitra . . . 124, 125
Kenya . . . 136
Keyakidaira . . . 228
Khabarovsk . . . 156
Kibwezi . . . 136
Kimberley . . . 144
Big Hole . . . 144
Kiruna . . . 13
Ice Hotel . . . 13
Jukkasjärvi . . . 13
Nutti Sámi Siida . . . 13
Kizukuri . . . 244
Kolašin . . . 111
Kolwezi . . . 141
Konya . . . 176, 178
Kostroma . . . 160, 162
Church of the Resurrection . . . 163
Krasnoyarsk . . . 156
Kroya . . . 261
Kuala Kangsar . . . 249
Sultan Azlan Shah Gallery . . . 249
Ubudiah Mosque . . . 249
Kuala Lumpur . . . 249
Cuito . . . 141
Kurobe Gorge . . . 228, 230
Kurseong . . . 197
Kutoarjo . . . 261
Kyoto . . . 238
Gion district . . . 238
Kyushu . . . 238
Nishiki Market . . . 238

L

La Macarena . . . 344
La Malautière . . . 41
Mecca . . . 184, 186
La Paz . . . 329
La Pobla de Segur . . . 96, 99
La Polvorilla Viaduct . . . 334, 337
La Raya . . . 324
Langeac . . . 40
Langogne . . . 40
Lanusei . . . 78
Lanzhou . . . 224, 226
Le Monastier-Pin-Moriès . . . 45
Lleida . . . 96, 98
Lhasa . . . 216, 218
Potala Palace . . . 218

Ljubljana 60
   Central Market 60
   Dragon Bridge 60
Lobito 138, 141
Lochailort 16
London 22, 25
   Alexandra Palace 25
   Welwyn Viaduct 25
Lopburi, Province of 250
Los Angeles 294, 297, 304, 307
Los Mochis 308
Louisiana 306
Luxor 114, 116
Lozère 40, 42, 45
   Chanteperdrix Viaduct 45
   Crueize Gorge 45
South Luangwa National Park 141
Lubumbashi 141
Luena 141
Lwishia 141

M

North Macedonia 61
Machu Picchu 318, 320
Madras 200
Malaysia 248, 249
Maletto plateau 75
Mallaig 14
   Loch Morar 16
Malonga 141
Manguri 354
Marangani. 324
Marla 355
Morocco 122, 124
Marseille 40, 41, 48
Marumbi 332
Marvejols. 44, 45
Massif Central 40
Mata atlântica 332
Matapédia 278
Matobo. 148
   Matobo Hills 148
   Matobo National Park 148
Mauritania 128
Medina 184, 186
Mehdia 125
Messina 68, 70
Mettupalayam 202, 204
Mexico 310
Mezzana 52
Miami. 284, 286, 287
Michigan, Lake. 292, 301
Millau. 45
   Millau Viaduct 45
Milwaukee 301
Minneapolis 301
Minnesota, State of 301
Minot 301
Miramas. 46, 48, 49
Miramichi 278
Mishima 238
Modimolle 148
Mombasa. 134, 136

Moncton 278
Mongolia 212, 215
Inner Mongolia 214
Mont-Joli 278
Montana, State of. 300, 301
Montenegro 110, 111
Montreal 276, 278
Montsec mountain range 99
Moosonee 280, 282
Morar 16
Morbier 37
Morez 37
   Musée de la Lunette 37
Morioka 234
Morretes 330, 332
Moscow 152, 156, 160, 168, 170
   Gorky Park 156
   Kremlin 156
   Red Square 156
   St Basil's Cathedral 156
Mostar 60
Mosteirô. 102
Mouchard 36
Murmansk 164, 166
Mtito Andei 136
Muñano 337
Munich 32
Mutshatsha 141
Mysore 192
   Amba Vilas Palace 192

N

Nagoya 238
   Atsuta-jingu shrine 238
   Nagoya Castle 238
Nairobi 134, 136
Nanjangud 192
Nanping 223
Nariz del diablo 316
Narva 171
Narvik 10, 13
Nebraska, State of 290, 292
Neussargues-en-Pinatelle 42, 44, 45
Nevada 290
   State of Nevada 290
   Sierra Nevada. 290
New Iberia 306
New Orleans 304
   French Quarter 306
   Preservation Hall 306
   Voodoo Museum 306
New York 284, 286, 287
   The Bronx 286
   Brooklyn 286
   Central Park 286
   Greenwich Village 286
   Manhattan 286
   Moynihan Train Hall 286
   One World Trade Center 286
   Penn Station 286
   Williamsburg 286
Newcastle upon Tyne 25
   Millennium Bridge. 25

Nilgiri Mountains (Blue Mountains)
. . . . 202, 204, 205
Nîmes 38, 40, 41
   Gardens 41
   Maison carrée 41
   Tour Magne 41
Ninh Binh 256
New Brunswick, Province of 278
Nova Scotia, Province of 278
New Zealand 358
   Canterbury Plains 359
   Lake Grassmere. 359
   North Island 358
Novosibirsk 156
Nullarbor 351
Nuwara Eliya 210
Nyingchi 216, 218

O

Oakland 297
   Jack London Square 297
Oceania 346-361
Ohuira Bay 311
Omaha 292
Omsk 156
Ontario, Province of 274, 282
Ooty 202, 205
Orlando 284
Ortigia Island 71
Oruro 326, 329
   Lake Poopó. 329
   Lake Uru Uru 329
   Sajama National Park 329
Osaka 238
Ospizio Bernina 86
Ottawa 282
Oviedo 94

P

Pa Sak Jolasid Dam 250, 252
Palermo. 68, 71
Pamban Island 200
Parakou. 130, 133
Paraná, State of 333
Paris. 30, 32
Patagonia 340, 341, 344
Paternò 74
Pattadakal 193
Peggy's Cove 278
Beijing 212, 214
   Forbidden City 214
Peru 320, 322, 324
Persian Gulf. 180, 183
Perth. 351
Peso da Régua. 103
Philadelphia 286
Picton. 358
Pilatus-Kulm 88, 90
Pinhais 333
Piraquara 333
Pocinho 100, 103
Podgorica 111

Ponte-Leccia. 52, 54, 56, 57
Pontresina 86
Port Augusta 354
Port Pirie 354
Port-de-Bouc 48
Portland 296
Porto. 100, 102
Porto de Cima 332
Portugal 102
Postojna, Caves of 60
Potes 94
Potpec Lake 110
Prades-Saint-Julien 41
Prambanan 261
Pretoria 142, 144, 146, 148
Puerta Tastil 337
Puget Sound. 300

Q

Qom 183
   Grand Bazaar 183
   Jamkaran Mosque 183
   Lake Namak 183
   Shrine of Fatima-Masoumeh 183
Quito 314

R

Rabat 125
   Kasbah of the Udayas 125
Rameswaram 198, 200
Randazzo. 75
Raqchi 324
Rawlinna 351
Ribadeo 94
Richmond 284
Rimouski 278
Rio de Janeiro 332
Río Negro, Province of 340
Riposto. 72, 75
Rivière-du-Loup 278
Roça Nova. 333
Rocky Mountains. 271, 274, 293, 300
   Rocky Mountains National Park. . . 274
Rome 68, 70
Rostov 160, 163
   Church of St John the Evangelist . . 163
   Dormition Cathedral 163
   Rostov Kremlin 163
Red Sea 186
Russia 154, 162, 164, 170, 212

S

Sacramento 293, 297
Sacred Valley of the Incas 320
State Railroad Museum 297
St. Paul. 301
Saint-Chély-d'Apcher 45
Saint-Claude. 34, 37
Saint-Flour 44
Santiago de Compostela 92, 94
Saint-Moritz 80, 82

St Petersburg 164, 166, 168, 170
  Church of the Saviour on the
    Spilled Blood 170
  Hermitage Museum 170
  Nevsky Prospect 170
  St Isaac's Cathedral 170
San Sebastián 92, 94
Sainte-Foy 278
Salinas 297
Salt Lake City 293
Salta 334, 336
San Antonio 306
San Antonio de los Cobres 336
San Antonio Oeste 341
San Carlos de Bariloche 338, 341
San Diego 297
San Francisco 290, 297
  San Francisco Bay 293
San Jose 297
  Winchester House 297
Sanqingshan, Mount 220, 223
Sant Antoni reservoir 99
Sant Llorenç de Montgai 99
Santa Barbara 297
Santa Monica 307
Santa Rosa de Tastil 337
Santillana del Mar 94
Saracocha, Lake 324
Sarajevo 60
Saraqucha 324
Sardinia 76, 78
Saskatchewan, Province of 274
Saskatoon 274
Saudi Arabia 186
Savannah 284
Seattle 294, 296, 298, 300
  Needle Tower 296
  Public Market Center 296
Sendai 234
Senjojiki 244
Serbia 110
Seriev Possad 160, 162
  Trinity Lavra of St Sergius 162
Shangrao 223
Shirakami-Sanchi 245
Shirakami mountain range 245
Shkodër, Lake 111
Sibambe 314, 316
Sicily 68, 70, 71
Sierra Colorada 341
Siliguri 194, 196
Sinaloa, State of 308, 311
Singapore 246, 248, 249
  Gardens by the Bay 249
  Kampong Glam 249
Sivaganga 200
  Vettangudi Bird Sanctuary 200
Skopje 61
Skovorodino 156
Sofia 61
  Alexander Nevsky Cathedral 61
  St George's Church 61
  Soviet Army Monument 61
Spokane 300

Sri Lanka 210
Srirangam 200
  Sri Ranganathaswamy Temple 200
Stockholm 10, 12
Sucre 329
Switzerland 82, 86, 90
Sumbay caves 324
Sundsvall 13
Sydney 350
  Queen Victoria Building 350
  St Mary's Cathedral 350
Syracuse 71

T

Tallinn 168, 171
Tamil Nadu, State of 198, 200
Tangier 122, 124
Tanzania 138
Tasikmalaya 260
Taurus Mountains 178
Tehran 182, 183
  Azadi Tower 182
  Golestan Palace 182
  Mausoleum of Imamzadeh Saleh . . 182
  Museum of Contemporary Art 182
  Shahr Theatre 182
Térmens 98
Terradets reservoir 99
Tierra del Fuego 342, 344
Texas 304, 306, 307
Thailand 246, 249, 252
Thanh Hoa 257
Tibet, Autonomous region of 218
Tierra del Fuego National Park 344
Tiger Hill 197
Tindharia 196
Tyumen 156
Tirano 84, 86
Titicaca, Lake 322, 324
  Lake Titicaca station 324
  Taquile Island 324
Tohoku region 242
Tokyo 232, 236, 238
  Akihabara 236
  Shibuya 236
  Shinjuku 236
Toronto 272, 274
Tortoli 78
Toyama, prefecture 230
Trieste 60
  Castello di Miramare 60
  Piazza Unità d'Italia 60
  San Giusto Hill 60
Truro 278
Tsavo National Park 136
Tupiza 328
  Tupiza valley 328
Turkey 172, 174, 178

U

Udzungwa National Park 140
Ulaanbaatar 212, 215

Narantuul Market 215
Sukhbaatar Square 215
Winter Palace 215
Ulan-Ude 156
Ulster 26, 28
Urals 156
Umeå 13
Unazuki 228, 230
United Kingdom 25
United States 266, 284, 286, 289, 292, 293,
    294, 296, 297, 298, 300, 304, 306
Uppsala 12
Urumqi 224, 227
  Shaanxi Mosque 227
Ushuaia 342, 344
Ussuriisk 156
Uyuni 329
  Uyuni Salt Flat 329

V

Val-d'Acormie 45
Valcheta 340
Valjevo 110
Vallfogona de Balaguer 98
Vancouver 268, 272, 274
Varna 33
Venaco 52
Venice Beach 307
Venice 58, 60, 61
  Doge's Palace 60
  Grand Canal 60
  Rialto Market 60
  St Mark's Square 60
Veu da Noiva 332
Victoria Falls 146, 148
Viedma 338, 340
Vienna 32
Vietnam 256, 257
Vilanova de la Barca 98
Villa San Giovanni 70
Villazón 326, 328
Villefort 41
Vinh, Dong Hoi 257
Vivario 52
Viveiro 94
Vizzavona 52
  Grand Hôtel de la Forêt 52
  Vizzavona National Park 52
  Vizzavona Tunnel 52
Vladivostok 152, 156
Voi 136
Vouraikos Gorge 106

W

Washington 286, 296, 300
  Lake Washington 296
  Washington Forest 296
  Washington State 300
Washington D.C. 286
  Capitol Building 286
  White House 286
Wassila 266

Wellington 358
  Queen Charlotte Sound 358
Whitefish 301
Winnipeg 274
Wisconsin, State of 301
Wuyi, Mount 220, 223
Wuyuan 222

X Y Z

Xi'an 224, 226
  Terracotta army 226

Yogyakarta 258, 261
  Kraton Palace 261
York 25
  York Minster 25

Zachlorou 106
Zagros Mountains 183
Zambia 138, 141
Zermatt 80, 82
Zimbabwe 148
Zouérat 126, 128

365

Photo Credits

© 79Photography/Alamy: 191; © A Belmond Train: 20 B., 324 T., 325 C.; © A-plus image bank/Alamy: 359 B. R.; © Adam Stoltman/Alamy: 286 C.; © Additive stock creatives/Alamy: 98 B.; © Adli Wahid/Unsplash: 20 T. L.; © Adwo/Alamy: 344 C. L.; © Aflo Co., Ltd./Alamy: 237, 243.; © AGB Photo Library/Alamy: 333 B. R.; © Agefotostock/Alamy: 123., 133 B., 140 C., 141 C. T., 149.; © Ajeng Larasati/Unsplash: 229.; © Alberto Bianchini/Unsplash: 85.; © Alberto Maisto/Alamy: 78 T. .; © Alberto Rigamonti/Alamy: 221.; © Aleksey Suvorov/Alamy: 154 B.; © Alexander Kaufmann/Unsplash: 290.; © Alexandr Savchuk/Alamy: 111 C. © Alexander Smagin/Unsplash: 162 T.; © Alexander Spatari/Getty Images: 248 C., 252 T. B.; © Alexis Rodriguez/Unsplash: 64 C.; © Alice McBroom/Alamy: 361.; © Alice/Unsplash: 252 C. R.; © Alice Yamamura/Unsplash: 332 C. © Alimdi.net/Alamy: 49 C.; © Amanda Klamrowski/Unsplash: 349.; © Ampersand Studios/Unsplash: 268.; © Amtrak Train Ventura California: 297 B. L.; © Anastasia Rozumna/Unsplash: 75 T. L.; © Andrea Leopardi/Unsplash: 299.; © Andrei Bortnikau/Alamy: 61 T.; © Andrew Catta/Alamy: 166 B.; © Andrey Khrobostov/Alamy: 215 C. B.; © Andrey Moisseyev/Alamy: 354 T.; © Andrew Bain/Alamy: 353.; © Andrian Rubinskiy/Unsplash: 154 B. L.; © Andriy Blokhin/Alamy: 307 T.; © Andy Kuo/Unsplash: 244 C.; © Anna Berdnik/Unsplash: 33 B.; © Anna Hunko/Unsplash: 12 T., 33 T.; © Ananya Anand/Unsplash: 193 C. © Anton Petrus/Getty Images: 94 B. L.; © Antonio Batinić/Alamy: 120 T.; © Arda savaşcıoğulları/Alamy: 175 T., 175 C. T.; © Armando Oliveira/Getty Images: 102 B.; © Art Kowalsky/Alamy: 49 T.; © Arthur Lookyanov/Alamy: 162 B.; © Arunabh Bhattacharjee/Alamy: 204 T.; © AsiaDreamPhoto/Alamy: 82 B.; © Aurélien Romain/Unsplash: 161.; © Aurora Kreativ/Unsplash: 287 B.; © Axp photography/Unsplash: 117.; © Ayadi Ghaith/Unsplash: 12 b; © Belikart/Alamy: 163 C. B.; © Benjamin Jopen/Unsplash: 63, 66; © Bernhard Schmid/Alamy: 223 B.; © Best View Stock/Alamy: 227 B.; © Bianca/Unsplash: 82 C. B.; © Bibars-h Bara/Unsplash: 169.; © Blake LisK/Unsplash: 360.; © Blickwinkel/Alamy: 144 C. B., 148 C.; © Boaz Rottem/Alamy: 214 C.; © Bobby Stevenson/Unsplash: 296 C.; © Bogdan Lazar/Alamy: 60 B.; © Bonnie Fink/Alamy: 278.; © Bosiljka Zutich/Alamy: 204 B.; © Brandy Willetts/Unsplash: 24 T.; © Brian Hartshorn/Alamy: 41 C.; © Bryan Goff/Unsplash: 267 T.; © Brian Overcast/Alamy: 311 B.; © Bunditinay/Getty Images: 252 B.; © Cannon Photography LLC/Alamy: 35, 197 T.; © Carmen Hauser/Alamy: 125 C.; © Carol Thomas/Alamy: 359 T.; © Cavan Images/Alamy: 341 C.; © Cavan Images/Getty Images: 267 B. L.; © Charles O. Cecil/Alamy: 186 C. R.; © Chloe Frost-Smith/Unsplash: 23.; © Chris Craggs/Alamy: 99 C.; © Chris Hellier/Alamy: 47, 48 C.; © Chris Henry/Unsplash: 288, 289.; © Chris Howarth/Australia/Alamy: 355 T.; © Chris Murray/Unsplash: 286 B.; © Chris Pratt/Alamy: 205 B.; © Christian Chen/Unsplash: 234 T.; © Christian Mesina/Unsplash: 270 T.; © Christopher He/Alamy: 274 C. B.; © Ciscardi Gabriel/Alamy: 48 B.; © Claude Da Costa/Alamy: 43.; © Claude Thibault/Alamy: 36 T.; © Claudio Schwarz: 90 C.; © Clem Onojeghuo/Unsplash: 25 C.; © Clement McCarthy/Alamy: 332 B.; © CPA Media Pte Ltd/Alamy: 226 B.; © Colin Lloyd/Unsplash: 293 T.; © Colin Meg: 267 C.; © CoinUp/Alamy: 106 C. R., B.; © Cultura Creative RF/Alamy: 350 T.; © Dalibor Brlek/Alamy: 90 T.; © Damien Calmal/Alamy: 45 T.; © Dan Breckwoldt/Alamy: 116 C. B.; © Daniel Burka/Unsplash: 61 B. L.; © Daniel Valla FRPS/Alamy: 317 B.; © Danita Delimont/Alamy: 135, 301 T. L., 306 B. T., 311 C.; © Darjeeling Alamy: 196 B.; © Darly Figuero/Unsplash: 187.; © Dave Cameron/Alamy: 56 C. B.; © David Foster/Alamy: 354 B.; © David Kilpatrick/Alamy: 98 T.; © David South/Alamy: 340 T.; © David Tadmor/Unsplash: 67.; © Delphotos/Alamy: 52 T.; © Demian Tejeda Benitez/Unsplash: 305.; © De pictz/Alamy: 192 T.; © Derek Trask/Alamy: 277 B. R.; © Design Pics Inc/Alamy: 266 C.; © Dietrich Burgmair/Alamy: 186 C. L. B.; © Dewpixs Photography/Getty Images: 251.; © Dillon Shook/Unsplash: 297 B. R.; © Dimitar Donovski/Unsplash: 271 b R.; © Dinodia Photos/Alamy: 192 C. B., 196 T., 196 C., 200 T. R., 203.; © Dpa picture alliance/Alamy: 329 C.; © Douglas Lander/Alamy: 41 B.; © Duncan Sharrocks/Alamy: 350 C.; © Duy Phuong Nguyen/Alamy: 231.; © Ekaterina Brycheva: 165; © Ekaterina Sazonova/Unsplash: 156 T.; © Elk Animal/Alamy: 279.; © Emma Claire/Unsplash: 296 T.; © Enrico Della Pietra/Alamy: 306 T.; © Éric Lafforgue/Alamy: 186 T. R.; © Éric Laudonien/Alamy: 49 B.; © Erik AJV/Alamy: 83.; © Erik Peterson/Alamy: 215 B.; © Eugène/Unsplash: 102 C. T.; © Eugene Ga/Alamy: 205 T.; © Eugenio Pingo/Alamy: 71 C.; © Evan Krause/Unsplash: 248 T., 252 C. L.; © Evgeny Haritonov/Alamy: 166 T.; © Eyesite/Alamy: 52 B.; © Fabideciria/Alamy: 337 B. R.; © Fady Fouad/Unsplash: 121.; © Fakhri Labib/Unsplash: 261 B.; © Falaq Lazuardi/Unsplash: 260 T.; © Fernando Quevedo de Oliveira/Alamy: 335 B. L., 337 B. L.; © Filiz/Unsplash: 238.; © Florian Blümm/Alamy: 214 B.; © Frédéric Reglain/Alamy: 132 C.; © Fsreeartist/Alamy: 56 B.; © Gabbro/Alamy: 178 B., 320 B.; © Gable/Alamy: 131.; © Gaetan Spinhayer/Unsplash: 44 T.; © Gala Images/Alamy: 44 B.; © Gareth McCormack/Alamy: 29 B.; © Gavin A. Fernandes/Alamy: 257 B. R.; © Gavin Hellier/Alamy: 301 B. R. © Gary Cook/Alamy: 21 T. R., 206-207.; © Geoffwiggins.com/Alamy: 205 C. B.; © George Clerk/Getty Images: 238 B.; © George Youssef/Unsplash: 119.; © G.I. Dobner/Alamy: 70 B.; © Gigi/Unsplash: 249 B.; © Giulio Ercolani/Alamy: 75 T. R.; © Giuseppe Spartà/Alamy: 75 B.; © Glenn Waters in Japan/Getty Images: 244 B. L. and R.; © Gnomeandi/Alamy: 197 B.; © Gower Brown/Unsplash: 271 B. L.; © Grace Nandy/Unsplash: 136 C. T.; © Grant Rooney Premium/Alamy: 320 T., 320 C. L.; © Greatstock/Alamy: 144 B.; © Greg Balfour Evans/Alamy: 98 C. T.; © Hakan Tanak/Alamy: 179.; © Handmade Pictures/Alamy: 144 C. T.; © Hang Kaiyv/Unsplash: 214 T.; © Hata Life/Unsplash: 248 B. R.; © HelloWorld Images/Alamy: 277.; © Henrique Ferreira/Unsplash: 71 B.; © Hercules Milas/Alamy: 106 T.; © Historic Collection/Alamy: 282 T.; © Hossein Javadi: 181, 182 T.; © Hugh Mitton/Alamy: 307 C.; © Iakov Filimonov/Alamy: 171 T.; © Ian Collins, Osaka/Getty Images: 234 C. T.; © Ian Dewar/Alamy: 300 T.; © Ian Lai/Unsplash: 235.; © Ianni Dimitrov Pictures/Alamy: 61 C.; © Ida Baranyai/Alamy: 183 B. R.; © ImageBroker.com GmbH & Co. KG/Alamy: 53 T., 79, 103 T., 111 T., 274 C. T., 310 B., 329 T. L., 336 T., 335 B. R., 344 T., 344 C. L.; © Image Professionals GmbH/Alamy: 109, 132 B.; © Incamerastock/Alamy: 310 C.; © Imaginechina Limited/Alamy: 222 C., 222 B. R., 223 T.; © IndiaPicture/Alamy: 193 T.; © IndustryAndTravel/Alamy: 136 C. B. and 136 T.; © Ingo Oeland/Alamy: 351 B. L. and 351 T.; © Ira Budanova/Alamy: 105.; © Irina Iriser/Unsplash: 215 C. T.; © Irina Kononova/Alamy: 156 C. L.; © Isaac Matthew/Unsplash: 247.; © Ishanseefromthesky: 185.; © Iurii Buriak/Alamy: 325 B. L.; © iStock/Getty Images/9parusnikov: 94 C. T.; © iStock/Getty Images/Anna Dudek: 77, 78 C.; © iStock/Getty Image/Apostolos Giontzis: 64 T.; © J. Enrique Molina/Alamy: 329 B. R.; © Jack Krier/Unsplash: 116 T.; © Jan Fritz/Alamy: 39.; © Jan Wlodarczyk/Alamy: 52 C. L.; © Janice and Nolan Braud/Alamy: 292 T. L.; © Jan Weber/Unsplash: 274 T.; © Jason Carr/Alamy: 230 C. T.; © Jay EE/Unsplash: 256 T.; © Jaubert French Collection/Alamy: 37 B., 41 T.; © Jbdodane/Alamy: 141 B.; © Jeffrey Isaac Greenberg 16+/Alamy: 287 T.; © Jeremy Horner/Alamy: 249 C.; © Jet de la Cruz/Unsplash: 257 B. L.; © Jixiang liu/Alamy: 230 C. B.; © Joachim Lesne/Unsplash: 21 T. L.; © Joana Kruse/Alamy: 60 C.; © Joel Protasio/Unsplash: 293 B.; © John Cameron/Alamy: 16 C.; © John Crux/Alamy: 222 B. L.; © John Henshall/Alamy: 217 B.; © John Keates/Alamy: 271 T.; © John Lander/Alamy: 170 T.; © John Peter Photography/Alamy: 16 B.; © John Warburton-Lee Photography/Alamy: 136 B., 140 B.; © John Zada/Alamy: 282 B.; © Johannes Hofmann/Unsplash: 87.; © Johanser Martine/Unsplash: 293 C.; © Jon Bilous/Alamy: 292 B. R.; © Jon Mikel Duralde/Alamy: 98 C. B.; © Jorg Angeli/Unsplash: 285.; © Juan Nino Unsplash: 121.; © Juan Tapias/VWPics/Alamy: 327.; © Juanma Aparicio/Alamy: 94 C. B.; © Juergen Ritterbach/Alamy: 328 B. L.; © Julio Etchart/Alamy: 340 C.; © K. Mitch Hodge/Unsplash: 27, 28 B. L.; © Kal K/500px/Getty Images: 265.; © KalypsoWorldPhotography/Alamy: 315,: 316 B.; © Karina Azaretzky/Alamy: 343.; © Karine Avetisyan/Unsplash: 86 T.; © Karl Werner/Unsplash: 86 C. T.; © Kathleen Smith/Alamy: 12 B. R.; © Kenan Talas/Alamy: 173, 174 C.; © Kentaro Toma/Unsplash: 234 C. B.; © Kess16/Alamy: 56 T.; © Kilarov Zaneit/Unsplash: 260 B. L.; © Kim Gordon-Bates/Alamy: 183 B. L.; © Kim Karpeles/Alamy: 306 C. L.; © Kir Shu/Unsplash: 155 T.; © Kjetil Kolbjørnsrud/Alamy: 351 B. R.; © Klaus Oskar Bromberg/Alamy: 48 T.; © Konrad Zelazowski/Alamy: 183 T. 183 C.; © Konseki1/Unsplash: 230 B. T.; © Kyle Philip Coulson: 145 T.; © Kyle Thacker/Unsplash: 275.; © Laura Lanckriet/Unsplash: 261 T.; © Lemonade/Alamy: 358 T.; © Leonid Andronov/Alamy: 12 T., 45 B.; © Léopold Stenger/Unsplash: 93.; © Liam Riby/Unsplash: 15.; © Lil Lang/Alamy: 324 B.; © Lilyana Vinogradova/Alamy: 163 B.; © Ljubomir Zarkovic/Unsplash: 110 C.; © Loch Fad: 21 B.; © Lory/Unsplash: 51.; © Lucja Ros/Unsplash: 20 T. R.; © Luckat/Alamy: 170 B.; © LuisPortugal/Getty Images: 102 c/B.; © Luke Porter/Unsplash: 25.; © Luoxi/Alamy: 227 T.; © Madebynoval/Unsplash: 261 C.; © Makasana photo/Alamy: 94 B. R.; © Manfred Gottschalk/Alamy: 340 B.; © Marc Poveda/Alamy: 40 B. T.; © Marco Sieber/Alamy: 333 C.; © Mario Effendy/Unsplash: 233.; © Mário Sergio Andrioli/Alamy: 333 B. L.; © Marion Kaplan/Alamy: 36 C.and B., 37 T., 141 C. T.; © Martha Barreno/VWPics/Alamy: 316 T.; © Martin Katler/Unsplash: 64 T.; © Martin Lindsay/Alamy: 317 C.; © Mateusz Butkiewicz: 73.; © Matt Barton/Unsplash: 302.; © Matt Crossick/Alamy: 323.; © Matt Rosko/Unsplash: 102 T.; © Matthew Williams-Ellis Travel Photography/Alamy: 341 B.; © Mauritius images GmbH/Alamy: 11, 12 C., 29 T., 82 C. T., 128 C., 154 C. T., 192 C. T., 226 T., 226 C. T.; © Maxim Toporskiy/Alamy: 166 C.; © Max Van Den Oetelaar/Unsplash: 213.; © Mediacolor's/Alamy: 311 T.; © Meelis Kalev/Alamy: 171 B.; © Megan O. Hanlon/Unsplash: 297 T.; © Mhmd Sedky/Unsplash: 116 B.© Max McClure/Alamy: 120 B.; © Michele Falzone/Alamy: 345.; © Mike Benna/Unsplash: 274 B.; © Misael Glauss/NortePhoto.com/Alamy: 309 © Mlorenzphotography/Getty Images: 282 C.; © Mohammad Nouri/Alamy: 182 C.; © Moarave/Getty Images: 245 C. T.; © Mon Hermans/Unsplash: 52 B. R.; © Mueed Ahmed/Unsplash: 125 B.; © Mykhailo Karlov/Unsplash: 61 B. R.; © Naeblys/Alamy: 145 B. L.; © Nakaharu/Unsplash: 235 C. T.; © Nasarudheen Markmedia/Alamy: 186 T. L.; © Nathalia Segato/Unsplash: 277 B. L.; © Newscom/Alamy: 230 T.; © Niccolo Bertoldi/Alamy: 167.; © Niels van Kampenhout/Alamy: 56 C. T.; © Nika Lerman/Alamy: 320 C. R.; © Nikola Johnny Mirkovic/Unsplash: 12 B. L.; © Nikolai Ignatiev/Alamy: 215 T.; © Nikolay Vinokurov/Alamy: 163 T.; © Nitish Waila/Alamy: 205 C. T.; © Nkeskin/Alamy: 178 T.; © Nomadic Julien/Unsplash: 239.; © Nova Poigo/Unsplash: 74 T.; © Nqobile Vundla/Unsplash: 148 B.; © Olaf Protze/Alamy: 81, 90 B. L.; © Oleksandr Korzhenko/Alamy: 55.; © Oleg Znamenskiy/Alamy: 141 T.; © Oleh Slobodeniuk/Getty Images: 260 B. R.; © Olga Gajewska/Alamy: 124 T.; © Oliver Förstner/Alamy: 328 C.; © Ollirg/Alamy: 75 C.; © Omar Elsharawy/Alamy: 115.; © Orada Jusatayanond - Thailand/Alamy: 252 T.; © Padi Prints/Troy TV Stock/Alamy: 154 T.; © Pamban Bridge/Alamy: 199.; © Panther Media GmbH/Alamy: 332 T., 337 T.; © Paul Bill/Unsplash: 59.; © Paul Caruso/Unsplash: 91.; © Paul Rushton/Alamy: 155 B. R.; © Paul Shawcross/Alamy: 40 T. L.; © Paul Springett 06/Alami: 200 B. L.; © Pedro Marroquin/Unsplash: 295.; © Performance Image/Alamy: 273.; © Peacock-Pictures/Alamy: 210 B.; © Peter Forsberg/EU/Alamy: 60 T.; © Peter Horree/Alamy: 94 h ,120 C. T.; © Peter Lopeman/Alamy: 192 b; © Peter Titmuss/Alamy: 145 C.; © Peter Wormstetter/Unsplash: 86 C. B.; © Philipp Trubchenko/Unsplash: 153.; © Photogilio/Alamy: 316 C.; © PhotoStock-Israel/Alamy: 178 C. B.; © Pierre Brye/Alamy: 40 T. R.; © Piggyfoto/Getty Images: 222 T.; © PixHound/Getty Images: 234 B. R.; © Premium Stock Photography GmbH/Alamy: 52 C. L., 53 C.; © Prisma by Dukas Presseagentur GmbH/Alamy: 144 T.; © Pulsar Imagens/Alamy: 331, 333 T.; © Punchim/Getty Images: 248 B. L.; © Qui Nguyen/Unsplash: 255.; © Quynh Anh Nguyen/Getty Images: 257 T.; © Rafal Cichawa/Alamy: 193 B, 325 T., 328 B. R.; © Realy Easy Star/Alamy: 74 B.; © Reda & Co. srl/Alamy: 306 C. R.; © Regis Martin/Alamy: 355 B.; © Reinhard Dirscherl/Alamy: 116 C. T.; © Reisegraf.ch/Alamy: 337 C.; © Remo Savisaar/Alamy: 171 C.; © Richard Bradley/Alamy: 310 T.; © Ricardo Gomez/Unsplash: 89.; © Rob Crandall/Alamy: 267 B. R.; © Rob Whitworth 2012/Alamy: 257 C.; © Robert Harding/Alamy: 12 C., 120 C. B., 125 T., 200 B. L., 219, 278 T., 339, 357.; © Robert Ruidl/Alamy: 200 C. B.; © Robert Smith/Alamy: 110 T.; © Robert Wyatt/Alamy: 201, 317 T.; © Roberto Cornacchia/Alamy: 127, 128 T., 128 C. T.; © Rocky Grimes/Alamy: 266 T.; © Roger Bradley/Alamy: 28 T.; © Rolf_52/Alamy: 307 B.; © Roman BayAndin/Unsplash: 158.; © Romeo/Unsplash: 241.; © Ron Yue/Alamy: 271 C.; © Ryan Booth/Unsplash: 24 B.; © RZAF_Images/Alamy: 137, 140 T.; © Sabyasachi Ghosh/Alamy: 195.; © Şafak Oğuz/Alamy: 178 C. T.; © Samir Kharrat/Unsplash: 74 C.; © Santi Rodriguez/Alamy: 99 T.; © Scott Hortop Travel/Alamy: 40 B. B.; © Scott Kemper/Alamy: 318.; © Sebastian Jakimczuk/Alamy: 328 T.; © Sébastien Staines/Unsplash: 259.; © Sergi Reboredo/Alamy: 148 T., 324 C.; © Sergio Nogueira/Alamy: 204 C.; © Serkant Hekimci/Alamy: 155 B. L.; © S. Forster/Alamy: 277 C.; © Shawn Williams/Alamy: 29 C., 245 T.; © Shawn ccf/Alamy: 244 T.; © Shawnn Tan/Unsplash: 240.; © Sherzod/Unsplash: 286 T.; © Shino/Unsplash: 230 B.; © Shoults/Alamy: 210 T.; © Simon Reddy/Alamy: 200 T. L.; © Simon Hermans/Unsplash: 53 B. R.; © Simone Polattini/Alamy: 86 B. R.; © Sopa Images Limited/Alamy: 292 T. R.; © Sourcenext/Alamy: 245 C. B. and B.; © Spacetoco/Unsplash: 358 C.; © Spencer Davis/Unsplash: 70 T.; © Stanislav Khokholkov/Alamy: 156 B.; © Stanislav Moroz/Alamy: 11 B.; © Steven Cordes/Unsplash: 301 T. R.; © StoryLife/Alamy: 197 C. T.; © StudioPB/Alamy: 211.; © Sun Studio Creative/Unsplash: 303; © Suranga Weeratuna/Alamy: 209.; © Susanne Neumann/iStock/Getty Images Plus 28 B. R.; © Suzuki Kaku/Alamy: 147.; © Statikmotion/Alamy: 341 T.; © Stuart Black/Alamy: 359 C.; © Sylvain Oliveira/Alamy: 57.; © Szymon Bartosz/Alamy: 177.; © Tam DV/Unsplash: 256 B.; © Tao Images Limited/Alamy: 217 C. B.; © Tasfoto/Alamy: 103 B.; © Tatiana Kashko/Alamy: 225.; © Taylor Murphy/Unsplash: 266 B.; © Teo Zac/Unsplash: 235 C. B.; © Theo Moye/Alamy: 270 C.; © Tevin Trinh/Unsplash: 270 B.; © Tim E. White/Alamy: 133 T., 133 C.; © Tim Johnson: 142; © Timsimages/Alamy: 350 B.; © Tim Oun/Unsplash: 52 B. L.; © Tim Wolliscroft/Unsplash: 16 h, 19.; © Tinimage/Alamy: 217.; © Tjetjep Rustandi/Alamy: 182 B.; © TMI/Alamy: 300 B.; © Tmyusof/Alamy: 358 B.; © Tobias Rademacher/Unsplash: 17.; © Tobias Reich/Unsplash: 145 B. R.; © Tony Eveling/Alamy: 110 B.; © Tran Nguyen/Unsplash: 297 C.; © Travelib india/Alamy: 200 C. T.; © Travellinglight/Alamy: 45 C., 359 B. L.; © Travelstock44/Alamy: 82 T.; © Tribune Content Agency LLC Alamy: 325 B. R.; © Universal Images Group North America LLC/Alamy: 90 R., 129 T.; © UrbanImages/Alamy: 300 C.; © Uwe Michael Neumann/Alamy: 129 C. B.; © Vadim Nefedov/Alamy: 186 C. L. T.; © Valeria Venezia/Alamy: 344 B.; © Veronika Jorjobert/Unsplash: 101.; © Victoria Alexandrova/Unsplash: 159.; © View Stock/Alamy: 223 C.; © Viktor Karasev/Alamy: 163 C. T. © Viktor Posnov/Alamy: 106 C. L., 107.; © VCG/Getty Images: 217 C. T.; © VSOE: 32 B. and T.; © Wei Zeng/Unsplash: 292 B. L.; © Westend61 GmbH/Alamy: 97.; © Weston M. Jox/Unsplash: 301 B. L.; © Wirestock, Inc./Alamy: 124 B, 157, 174 B., 335.; © Witold Skrypczak/Alamy: 306 B. B.; © Woldt/Getty Images: 78 B.; © Wolfgang Kaehler/Alamy: 132 T., 226 C. B.; © Xavier Fores - Joana Roncero/Alamy: 99 B.; © Xiyan/Unsplash: 321.; © Yana Marudova/Unsplash: 69.; © YokoAziz 2/Alamy: 129 B.; © Yulia BabWkina/Alamy: 170 C.; © Yuga Kurita/Getty Images: 234 B. L.; © Yury Zap/Alamy: 329 T. L.; © Yvette Cardozo/Alamy: 279.; © Zack Spear/Unsplash: 296 B.; © Zoonar GmbH/Alamy: 31, 71 T., 86 B. L., 197 C. B., 317 B.; © Zuma Press, Inc./Alamy: 175 C. B., 218 T.

Key: B = bottom, T = top, C = centre, L = left, R = right

ACKNOWLEDGEMENTS

Many thanks to my father who will sadly never see my name on a book cover. He gave me not only his unconditional love and support but also the two greatest privileges you can imagine: security – without which it is much harder to believe in the future – and confidence – without which it's a struggle to make dreams come true.

Thanks too to my mother for her unfailing support and her very Mediterranean brand of love, for giving me a passion for art and the finer things in life, and for teaching me to think outside the box and look at the world through a different lens.

Also to my sister, who helped me grow up, for making me see that I was the elder sibling even though she taught me so much about life in general, and for making me believe that I was the author and artist in the family, even though she has so many talents of her own.

I'm also grateful to Alice Gauvin, Ibrahim Kadiri, Jean de Lussac, Anaïs Bisson, Franck Eusebio, Marie Morel, Tristan Bonnet, Louise Verley, the Mitches, the Aveng'Ours and everyone else for their continued support.

Thanks too to Anna Topaloff, Adrien Aumont, Romain Payet and my editors, Emmanuel Le Vallois and Faris Issad.

First published in Great Britain in 2025 by

Greenfinch
An imprint of Quercus Editions Limited
Carmelite House
50 Victoria Embankment
London EC4Y 0DZ

An Hachette UK company
The authorised representative in the EEA is Hachette Ireland, 8 Castlecourt Centre, Dublin 15, D15 XTP3, Ireland (email: info@hbgi.ie)

All rights reserved. Published by arrangement with éditions du Chêne
(58, rue Jean Bleuzen, 92178 Vanves Cedex, France)
© 2023, éditions du Chêne - Hachette Livre
www.editionsduchene.fr

English translation by Claire Cox

No part of this publication may be reproduced or transmitted in any form or by any means, electronic or mechanical, including photocopy, recording, or any information storage and retrieval system, without permission in writing from the publisher.

A CIP catalogue record for this book is available from the British Library

ISBN 978-1-52944-232-8

Front cover image: photomontage by Marie Abeille.
© Leon Neal/Getty Images Europe (compartment);
© Dave Collier (landscape).
Back cover image: © Nicholas Swanson/Unsplash.
Inside front cover image:© Derek Story/Unsplash.
Inside back cover image:© Anton Stasiuk/Unsplash.

Lead editor: Emmanuel Le Vallois
Editor: Faris Issad, assisted by Lucas Lescure
Art Direction: Sabine Houplain
Artistic creation and layout: Bureau Berger
Proofreading: Franck Friès
Second proofreading: Mireille Touret
Iconographic research: Marie Abeille and Maud Simon
Maps: Cyrille Suss, Blanche Lambert, Élise Poulain
Production: Marc Chalmin
Reproduction: Hyphen-Group
Press relations: Valentine Baud
(presse-chene@hachette-livre.fr)
Printed in Spain by Grafica

10 9 8 7 6 5 4 3 2 1